GLOOSKAP'S CHILDREN

Glooskap—Klose-kur-beh—"The Man From Nothing," was claimed by all the children of the Red Man to be the first person who came upon the earth. And he was their teacher! He taught them how they must live, and told them about the spiritual power, how it was in every living thing, and it was the same power that had sent him to prepare the way on earth for the generations to come; and to subdue all obstacles which are against the nature of mankind; and to reduce the earth to such a state as to become a happy land for the people.

Joseph Nicolar, *The Life and Traditions of the Red Man*, 1893

GLOOSKAP'S CHILDREN

Encounters with the Penobscot
Indians of Maine

PETER ANASTAS

Photographs by Mark Power

BEACON PRESS   BOSTON

Beacon Press books are published under the auspices of the Unitarian Universalist Association
Simultaneous publication in Canada by Saunders of Toronto, Ltd.

9 8 7 6 5 4 3 2 1

Library of Congress Cataloging in Publication Data

Anastas, Peter, 1937–
  Glooskap's children.
  1. Penobscot Indians. I. Title.
E99.P5A5   970.3'09741   72–75534
ISBN 0–8070–0518–5   .

Grateful acknowledgment is made to the following for use of their material in this book: Horace P. Beck and Suzy Dana for "Anebees" and Horace P. Beck for "Glooskap and the Frog," both copyright © 1966 by Cumberland Press, Inc., reprinted with permission from *Gluskap the Liar and Other Indian Tales,* Bond Wheelwright Co., Freeport, Maine; Theodore Enslin for his poem "A View Towards Indian Island," copyright © 1971 by Theodore Enslin and published in *The Aroostook Indian,* May 1971.

To the memory of Charles Olson, 1910–1970

We also knew Olson as a secret spy of
all the Gods in disguise. Walking around
Gloucester as a big man in sloppy pants:
hanging around the bars; talking to the
fishermen; shuffling around in the registry
of deeds; looking at old court records
to find out who first stole the land
from the Indians; how much they got when
they resold the land; and how the new
owners abused the land, subdivided it,
killed the Indians and the animals; and
how their descendents continued exploiting
their stolen property, and turned it into
inhuman plastic to the present day; with
special attention to all the heroic
examples of beautiful persons who
resisted the money wheel and used the
land and sea for genuine human nourish-
ment and beauty.

Allen Ginsberg
Gloucester: January 13, 1970
Gloucester Daily Times

Deepest acknowledgments and warmest thanks:

To Governor Francis J. "Bunny" Ranco for his toleration of my presence among the people he represents; to Ken and Jean (Sipsis) Thompson of the *Maine Indian Newsletter*, Jim Sappier of Mainstream, and Mike Ranco, who offered me their friendship and opened their homes and their hearts to me; to Wayne and Terri Mitchell for their hospitality, patience, and goodwill; to Martin Neptune and Tim Love for theirs; to all the Penobscot Indians of Indian Island, those whose names appear and those who are not named, for allowing me the freedom to pass among them and talk with them about their lives;

To *Akwesasne Notes* for keeping me in touch with the Indian Movement in America, and to the *Maine Indian Newsletter* for local news;

To Stillman P. Hilton, Librarian of the Sawyer Free Library, Gloucester, and to Margot Williams and the staff for all the help librarians give writers and are never thanked enough for; to the Robert Peabody Foundation Library of Andover, Massachusetts, the Boston Public Library, and the libraries of Harvard University for sending me hard-to-find books on interlibrary loan; and to the staff of the Salem Public Library, where I have also worked pleasantly;

To Peter Smith, publisher, of Gloucester, Massachusetts, who one morning disappeared into his stock room to reappear with an armload of indispensable Indian books for me;

To Ray Bentley, my editor at Beacon Press and longtime friend, who first suggested I do this book and who gave me, along with an absolutely free hand, the kind of support and advice a writer dreams of from his editor and publisher; to Beacon Press, where book publishing is an act of moral and political responsibility, for making it possible for me to write the kind of book I wanted to write and allowing me to associate in print with some of the men I most admire in our time;

To Debra Maguire, who helped me with research under the Neighborhood Youth Corps of Gloucester and to Director Ron Kimball and counselor Peter Parsons who made that possible;

To George Gabin, who gave me a place to live and work in the crucial moments of the writing; to Vincent Ferrini, Jonathan Bayliss, Jay McLauchlan, and Gerrit Lansing, men who care to talk and to listen—men who *care*;

To Christina Wiener for moral support; to Jennifer Rochow for moral support as well as typing help; to my parents for their faith in me; and finally to Jeane Wiener Anastas, who gave me the idea for the book's form, for everything I am today and hope to be tomorrow.

Peter Anastas

GLOOSKAP'S CHILDREN

PRE/VIEW

[Letter to Mark Power, March 1, 1971]

Dear Mark,

You ask for some background material on the Penobscots, and I refer you to two books which the Library of Congress should be able to furnish, Frank G. Speck's *Penobscot Man* (1941) and Fannie Hardy Eckstorm's *Old John Neptune and Other Maine Indian Shamans* (1945). Speck's is anthropology—probably more like "ethnology"—a study of material and social life based on field work done in the first quarter of the century, with a brief return trip in 1936, added as an appendix. It's packed with information; observations; lots of illustrations on making canoes, baskets; song and dance; language. Really fine. Speck's from Gloucester [Massachusetts] originally, and his major work was done among the Montagnais-Naskapi of Labrador, so his *Naskapi* (1935) is really his masterwork. He's thought highly of by such diverse men as Loren Eiseley and Edmund Carpenter, both of whom I trust. The Naskapi named him "old rag and bone man," which I love. But so far no one has surpassed *Penobscot Man*, though apparently there's a long overdue Penobscot dictionary or glossary—lexicon, I don't know—which Speck's colleague Frank Seibert has been laboring over for years. There are some earlier monographs like Sullivan's *History of the Penobscots* (1804) and Fr. Vetromile's *The Abenakis and Their History* (1866), but they're ill-informed and essentially racist. Sullivan still called Indians "savages," etc. And Fannie *savages* Sullivan and Vetromile herself, wow!

Her book is inside dope—and I wish to hell someone would reprint it. One family from the life of its shaman-leader who was also governor and lt. governor of the tribe from time to time in the 19th century, a great magician, sexually prodigal—epical stuff, done in the most beautiful, careful, laconic, Yankee prose. Fannie treats the period before Speck—the transitional acculturation just beginning, when Thoreau went down on his three trips, 1846, '53, and '57. (*The Maine Woods* is a gorgeous thing itself;

and I guess I would toss that in as both early ethnology and the report of the first white man who really understood what Indians are all about.) Fannie, who incidentally didn't like Thoreau (she wrote a devastating review of *The Maine Woods* in *Atlantic Monthly* in 1908), thought he thought he "knew it all" from three trips down, while she was born on the site of Penobscot camps and lived near and among Indians all her life. She does give much of the flavor of 19th-century life among Indians and whites in Maine in her unhurried and most lovingly accurate way. She worked on *Old John Neptune* for about 25 years, and you ought to read it for the pure delight of a labor (hers) and a telling accuracy. She was a tireless bird and people watcher, widowed early and lived in Brewer—across river from Bangor—until she died in the late 1940s.

The Penobscots are Eastern Woodlands Indians of the Algonquin, or Algonquian, language stock, some of whom occupied Canada from Labrador to Hudson's Bay. They came south in two groups, one traveling down the Mississippi Valley and the other along the Eastern seaboard. Some "authorities" say they came late, around 1000 A.D., but most think (Willey's *Introduction to American Archaeology*, Vol. 1, 1966, is superb on all this) they were in Maine as long ago as nine or ten thousand years. If you consider (as I do) the so-called Red Paint People of Maine, whose relics, buried in red ocher dye (hence their name) dating back at least nine thousand years, have been found on Indian Island in Old Town—right on the Reservation, in other words—as the *first* Algonquins, you have an unbroken line of habitation and a single location. And men do tend to inhabit the same place for as long as they can, and if run off, they come back eventually to where their ancestors' bones lie, and where their gods dwell and protect them.

The Penobscots are part of the *Abenaki,* or "People of the Dawn," "Children of Light," or "Eastern Sunrise," branch which also includes the Micmacs and Malacites, now living in New Brunswick and Nova Scotia, and the Passamaquoddies, living near Eastport, way Down East in Maine, about whom there is a new picture book called *Land of the Four Directions,* 1970.

They were called *Panawampskewiak,* which means "people of the white rock country," or even "people of the place where the river (*Panawapskik*) broadens out," tribal name and habitat being synonymous, like *Passamaquoddy,* which means "plenty-pollock-place-people." This was not their name for themselves, but a sort of "locative" or nickname, given them by other Indians, as was the custom, sometimes very derogatorally.

Each tribe had its own private name for itself, just as each Indian had his own name related to his clan, which no one else knew as well as his tribal or family name, which was public. In the case of the tribe's own name for itself, it usually meant something like "Men" or "Human Beings." The Penobscots call themselves *Alnambak*, which is the plural of *arenabe*, "a man," and the Passamaquoddies' real name is *Skijim*, "Indian." (Fannie is great on all this; see her chapter on the Maine tribes.)

By the time the first white men arrived, the Penobscots were more an agricultural than the hunting and gathering people they had been anciently. They followed a seasonal pattern of movement which incorporated the earlier modes of life. Fannie describes it in a letter to Speck (*Penobscot Man*, p. 36):

In spring our Penobscots stayed by the rivers to take the alewives, shad, salmon and sturgeon when they ran up the streams to spawn. Then they planted their corn and beans and a few potatoes. About the first of June the black-flies and mosquitoes drove them out of the woods, and they went to the seashore for seal and porpoise, to get the oil and the skins; also, in earlier years, to get the eggs and nestlings of sea birds. They also dried quantities of clams and lobsters which they stored for winter use. In September they went up river to harvest their crops. In October they moved on into the big woods and prepared their lines of traps for the fall fur-hunt. Before Christmas they came back to their villages and feasted for not less than two weeks. Then they went into the woods again, moose-hunting in the deep snow and trapping. Before the ice broke up, in March or April, they made their spring catch of otter and beaver, and when the rivers were clear, they came down in bark or skin canoes to the villages again, ready for the spring catch of muskrat and the fisheries and planting. The seasonal migrations of the tribes as a whole depended upon the climatic conditions which governed the fish and game they lived upon.

Speck adds, "What a picture of abundance to regale the senses of the primitivist!" And the ecologist in me can only mourn the loss, not only of that way of life with its deep respect for the earth, but of the very land it was lived upon and *in*.

If you're at all interested in going back a bit, there is a legendary early Indian-White confrontation with the Vikings on Mt. Desert Island, c. 1004 A.D., in which I believe implicitly, since it figures in an epic. Maine, for me anyway, is Vinland, and I think it will be proven soon. [Addition, as of January, 1972: if the three "runic stones" found at Popham Beach in June, 1971, by Walter Elliott prove to be authentic, they record that a Bishop Henrikus arrived in "Vinland" in 1123 A.D. See the *Maine Times*, beginning December 3, 1971, for complete and continuing account of the find, and its attendant "controversy."]

Other contacts—and their accounts—begin in the late 1400s and continue for two hundred years with rather sound remarks on the Maine Indians by Champlain, who came in 1605 for the French monarchy, and Weymouth, who sailed up the Penobscot River—to Old Town site?—for the English the same year. Then the settling began around 1615 with English fishing stages on islands off the Maine coast and spin-off colonies from Massachusetts Bay beginning around 1620. You know: fish, fur, hunting—Puritanism (Olson: "Was it Puritanism or was it fish?")—the beginnings of exploitation and genocide, call it what you will; the debacle of white economic and cultural imperialism in New England.

Before 1617 there were 40,000 Indians in Maine alone, the Penobscots being the largest tribe. A war between the Penobscots and tribes west of them, plus a devastating smallpox epidemic which swept down the entire Atlantic coast among the native Americans, cut their population down by two-thirds. The Penobscots then came much under the influence of the French through our dear friends the missionaries, who replaced Glooskap with God, the good life with *sin* and *guilt*; and though something can be said for a certain "protective" quality in these influences, they precipitated the cultural schizophrenia which has plagued the Red Man to this day and which I think—and as I hope to show in the book—he's finally beginning to deal with, break out of, especially.

The Penobscots, actually a very peaceful people, fought again with the Mohawk from 1662–69. Territorial wars, ancient hostilities. By 1669 the chief village was in Old Town on the present Indian Island. With the land so overrun by warring white men and fleeing Indians, life perforce was becoming more centralized.

In 1722 Lovewell's War, a miniature French and Indian War, broke out with the Penobscots still dominated by French interests and hostile to the English. They were, of course, pawns: so many little dark people (like the natives of Southeast Asia) to be pushed around in the expansionist chess of superpowers—and what were France and England of those days if not "superpowers"? In 1723 Col. Westbrook of Portland destroyed the fort on Indian Island in the name of the English. The inhabitants had escaped, and the stockade was apparently 14 feet high and held 23 wigwams. (It's been recently excavated.) In 1746, largely due to English aggression, the Penobscots, who, according to Speck, had largely refrained from committing themselves directly in the French and English hostilities, leaped into battle. So in 1755 and 1756 the General Court of Massachusetts declared them "enemies," and offered bounties for Penobscot scalps, including those of women and children.

Fortunately the Penobscots stayed clear of most of the French and Indian War, in full flower by 1755. This caused the tribes west of them, the Aroosaguntacook and the Norridgewock, to break with them ultimately. And by the time of the fall of Quebec and the end of the war itself those tribes retired into Canada, leaving the Penobscots sole resident in central and southeastern Maine, with the Passamaquoddies Down East.

The Penobscots signed a peace treaty with Massachusetts—remember, Maine was part of Massachusetts until 1820—in April, 1760. During the Revolutionary War (one blanches with shame to think on't today! with Nixon in the White House you'd think it never happened—well, it really didn't, did it?) the Penobscots "served the Colonial cause" (in the jargon, or obscurantism, of historians) for which they were rewarded, in 1786, by having the honor of ceding to Massachusetts all their tribal lands in the Penobscot valley from tidewater to the mouth of the Piscataquis, i.e., central and southern Maine! In 1818 and 1833 they "quitted" a good deal more inland territory (just in time for the big Maine land and lumber boom, during which era an acre of land sold for fourteen and a half cents) "retaining" for their own use around 146 or 147 islands in the Penobscot River, about 4,500 acres in all. (Currently Maine Indian activists are re-examining all the treaties and deeds of the period.) When Maine became a state in 1820 it supposedly took all the treaty "obligations" over from Massachusetts. Maine Indians then came under state jurisdiction, unlike any other U.S. group, all of which were to come under federal control.

This was no blessing, for it wasn't until 1965 that a true Bureau or Department of Indian Affairs was created by the legislature for the Penobscots and Passamaquoddies. Until then they were under Health and Welfare (and didn't have much of either) and had no commissioner of their own. They didn't become U.S. citizens until 1924 (many have refused citizenship over the years), and, dig this, they weren't enfranchised until 1955! However, they can only vote in state and national elections, and the two tribes send one *nonvoting* Representative to the legislature of Maine.

By the end of the 19th century the life of hunting, fishing, and living off the land was over. The mills and sweatshops of the textile and lumber

PROCLAMATION

GIVEN at the Council Chamber of the Great and General Court of the Province of Massachusetts in Boston this third day of November 1755.

Whereas the tribe of Penobscot Indians have repeatedly in a perfidious manner acted contrary to their solemn submission unto his Majesty long since made and frequently renewed,

I have, therefore, at the desire of the House of Representatives, thought fit to issue this Proclamation and to declare the Penobscot Tribe of Indians to be enemies, rebels and traitors to his Majesty. And I do hereby require his Majesty's subjects of the Province to embrace all opportunities of pursuing, captivating, killing and destroying all and every of the aforesaid Indians.

And whereas the General Court of this Province have voted that a bounty be granted and allowed to be paid out of the Province Treasury, the premiums of bounty following, viz.:

> For every scalp of a male Indian brought in as evidence of their being killed as aforesaid, forty pounds.

> For every scalp of such female Indian or male Indian under the age of twelve years that shall be killed and brought in as evidence of their being killed as aforesaid, twenty pounds.

By his Honour's command

J. Willard, Secry.

God Save the King

by-products companies came to Old Town, and later, the shoe and leather industries, and like all the immigrants of my father's generation—the Greeks and Italians and Poles and the earlier Irish—many of these internal immigrants went to work in them and, often, died in them. Interestingly enough, however, the Penobscots have been steadily on the increase. In 1900 the census lists 387; 410 in 1910; 580 in 1939, and well over 800 last year.

Basta! Let's go down ourselves. I know you aren't free until this summer. So I look forward to then.

Love,

Peter

LEGENDS 1

THE COMING OF GLOOSKAP

Glooskap, The Man From Nothing, first called
the minds of his Red Children to his coming into the world
when the world contained no other man, in flesh, but himself.
When he opened his eyes lying on his back in the dust,
his head toward the rising of the sun,
and his feet toward the setting of the sun;
the right hand pointing to the north
and his left hand to the south.
Having no strength to move any part of his body,
yet the brightness of the day revealed to him
all the glories of the whole world:
the sun was at its highest standing still,
and beside it was the moon without motion
and the stars were in their fixed places
while the firmament was in its beautiful blue.
While yet his eyes were held fast in their sockets
he saw all that the world contained.
Beside what the region of the air revealed to him,
he saw the land, the sea:
mountains, lakes, rivers, and the motion of the waters;
and in it he saw the fishes.
On the land were the animals and beasts,
and in the air the birds.
In the direction of the rising sun
he saw the night approaching.

While the body clung to the dust
he was without mind,
and the flesh without feeling.

[Freely adapted from *The Life and Traditions of the Red Man* by Joseph
Nicolar, Old Town, Maine, 1893, privately printed.]

At that moment the heavens were lit up,
with all kinds of bright colors most beautiful,
each color stood by itself,
and in another moment
every color shot a streak into the other,
and soon all the colors intermingled,
forming a beautiful brightness in the center of the heavens
over the front of his face.
Nearer and nearer came the brightness toward his body
until it got almost to a touching distance,
and a feeling came into his flesh,
he felt the warmth of the approaching brightness,
and he fell into a deep sleep.

The wind of the heavens fanned his brow,
and the sense of seeing returned to him,
but he saw not the brightness he beheld before,
but instead of the brightness
a person like unto himself,
standing at his right hand,
and the person's face was toward the rising of the sun.
In silence he raised his right hand
in the direction of the rising sun,
passed it from thence to the setting of the sun,
and immediately a streak of lightning
followed the motion of his hand
from one side of the earth to the other.
Again he raised his right hand to the south,
passing it to the north,
and immediately another streak of lightning
followed the motion of his hand.
Immediately after the passing of the lightning over his body
a sense of thought came into him,
and the Great Spirit answered his thought
saying these words:

"Arise from thy bed of dust
and stand on thy feet,
let the dust be under thy feet,

and as thou believest,
thou shall have strength to walk."

Immediately strength came into him,
and he arose to his feet,
and stood beside the Great Spirit.

After this the Great Spirit moved
and turned half around
toward his right hand,
facing the sun.
Lifting both hands and looking up he said:

"Go thy way!"
and immediately the whole heavens obeyed.
The sun, moon, and all the stars
moved toward the setting of the sun.
The night coming slowly toward their standing,
when the Great Spirit sending up his voice, saying:

"Let us make man in our own image,"
and immediately dropped his two hands
and cast his eyes upon the land
and moved halfway around again toward his right hand
facing the setting of the sun
and passed his right hand from the north to the south.
The lightning followed the motion of his hand
from the north to the south,
and again passing his hand
from the setting of the sun
to the rising of the sun,
and when the lightning came upon the night which was
        approaching
it disappeared. . . .

HOW GLOOSKAP MADE THE ELVES AND THEN MAN

Glooskap came first of all into this country, into Nova Scotia, Maine, Canada, into the land of the Wabanaki, or children of light. There were no Indians here then, only wild Indians very far to the West.

First born were the Mikumwess, small Elves or little men, dwellers in rocks.

And in this way he made Man: He took his bow and arrows and shot at trees. Then Indians came out of the bark of the Ash trees. And then the Mikumwess said, "Let us call him tree-man."

Glooskap made all the animals. He made them at first very large. Then he said to the great Moose who was as tall as a giant,

"What would you do should you see an Indian coming?" The Moose replied, "I would tear down the trees on him." Then Glooskap saw that the Moose was too strong and made him smaller so that Indians could hunt him.

Then he said to the Squirrel, who was of the size of a Wolf, "What would you do if you should meet an Indian?" And the Squirrel answered, "I would scratch down trees on him." Then Glooskap said, "You also are too strong." And he took the Squirrel in his hands and smoothed him down, and he made him little.

Then he asked the great White Bear what he would do if he met an Indian; and the Bear said, "Eat him." And the Master sent him to live among rocks and ice, where he would see no Indians.

So he questioned all the beasts, changing their size or allotting their lives according to their answers.

He took the Loon for his dog; but the Loon absented himself so much that Glooskap chose for this service two wolves, one black and one white.

Many years ago a man very far to the North wished to cross a bay, a great distance from one point to another. As he was stepping into his canoe, he saw a man with two dogs, one black and one white, who asked to be set across. The Indian said, "You may go, but what will become of your dogs?" Then the stranger replied, "Let them go round by land." "Nay," replied the Indian, "that is much too far." But the stranger saying nothing, he took him across. And as they reached the landing place there stood the dogs. But when the Indian turned his head to address the man, he was gone. So he said to himself, "I have seen Glooskap."

GLOOSKAP AND THE FIRST MOTHER

Of old times, when Glooskap, the great teacher, lived in the land, there came to him one day at noon a youth. And the youth stood before Glooskap and called him "mother's brother," and said: "I was born of the foam of the waters; for the wind blew, and the waves quickened into foam, and the sun shone on the foam and warmed it, and the warmth made life, and that life is I. See, I am young and swift, and I have come to abide with you and be your help in all things."

Again on the day at noon there came a maiden and stood before the two and called them "my children," and the maiden said: "I have come to abide with you, and I have brought with me love. I will give it to you, and if you will love me and grant my wish, all the world will love me well, even the very beasts. Strength is mine, and I give it to whosoever may get me; comforts also, for though I am young my strength shall be felt all over the earth. I was born of the beautiful plant of the earth; for the dew fell on the leaf, and the sun warmed the dew, and the warmth was life, and that life is I."

Then Glooskap lifted up his hands towards the sun and praised the Great Spirit, and afterwards the young man and the maid were man and wife, and she became the first mother. Glooskap taught their children and did great works for them. But the people increased until they were very many and there came a famine and the first mother grew more and more sorrowful.

The husband reached out his hand and wiped away her tears and said, "My wife, what can I do to make you happy?" And she answered, "Take my life."

"I cannot take your life," said the man. "Will nothing else make you happy?"

"Nothing else," she answered. "Nothing else will make me happy."

Then the husband went away to take counsel with Glooskap and with the rising of the seventh sun he came again and said, "O wife, Glooskap has told me to do the thing you wish." Then the woman was glad and said, "When you have slain me, let two men lay hold of my hair and draw my body all around a field, and when they have come to the middle of the field, there let them bury my bones. Then they must come away, but when seven moons have passed let them go again into the field and gather all that they find and eat it. It is my flesh, but you must save a part of it to put into the ground again. My bones you cannot eat, but you may burn them, and the smoke will bring peace to you and to your children."

On the morrow when the sun was rising the man slew his wife, and, as she had bidden, men drew her body all about an open field, until the flesh was worn away, and in the middle of the field they buried her bones. But when seven moons had gone by, and the husband came again to that place, he saw it all filled with beautiful tall plants, and he tasted the fruit of the plants and found it sweet and called it Skarmunal, corn. And on the place where her bones were buried, he saw a plant with broad leaves, bitter to the taste, and he called it, Uter-mu-wa-yeh, tobacco.

Then the people were glad in their hearts, and they came to his harvest; but when it was all gathered in, the man did not know how he should divide it and he sent to Glooskap for counsel. When Glooskap came and saw the great harvest, he gave thanks to the Great Spirit and said:

"Now have the first words of the first mother come to pass, for she said she was born of the leaf of the beautiful plant, and that her power should be felt over the whole world, and that all men should love her. And now that she is gone into this substance, take care that this, the second seed of the first mother, be always with you, for it is her flesh. Her bones also have been given for your good. Burn them and the smoke will bring freshness to the mind. And since these things came from the goodness of a woman's heart, see that you hold her always in memory. Remember her when you eat, remember her when the smoke of bones rises before you. And because you are all brothers, divide among you her flesh and her bones—let all shares be alike—for so will the love of the first mother have been fulfilled."

GLOOSKAP AND THE BABY

Now it came to pass when Glooskap had conquered all his enemies, even the Kewahqu', who were giants and sorcerers, and the m'teoulin, who were magicians, and the Pamola, who is the evil spirit of the night air, and all manner of ghosts, witches, devils, cannibals, and goblins, that he thought upon what he had done, and wondered if his work was at an end.

And he said this to a certain woman. But she replied, "Not so fast, Master, for there yet remains one whom no one has ever conquered or got the better of in any way, and who will remain unconquered to the end of time."

"And who is he?" inquired Glooskap.

"It is the mighty Wasis," she replied, "and there he sits; and I warn you that if you meddle with him you will be sorry."

Now Wasis was a baby. And he sat on the floor sucking a piece of maple-sugar, greatly contented and troubling no one.

As Glooskap had never married or had a child, he knew little of the way of managing children. But he was quite certain, as such people are, that he knew all about it. So he turned to the baby with a bewitching smile and bade him come to him.

The baby smiled again, but did not budge. And the Master spoke sweetly and made his voice like that of the summer bird, but it was of no avail, for Wasis sat still and sucked his maple-sugar.

Then the Master frowned and spoke terribly, and ordered Wasis to come crawling to him immediately. The baby burst out crying and yelling, but did not move for all that.

Then, since he could do but one thing more, the Master turned to magic. He used his most awful spells, and sang the songs which raise the dead and scare the devils. And Wasis sat and looked on admiringly, and seemed to find it very interesting, but all the same he never moved an inch.

So Glooskap gave up in despair, and Wasis, sitting on the floor in the sunshine, went "Goo! Goo!" and crowed.

And to this day when you see a baby well contented, going "Goo! Goo!" and crowing, and no one can tell why, you will know it is because he remembers the time when he overcame the Master who had conquered all the world. For of all the beings that have ever been since the beginning, the baby is alone the only invincible one.

JOURNAL 1

To go to the Indians. . . .

To go to the Indians you must go north, and you can drive north of Boston on Route 1, which becomes Route 95 to Portsmouth, the Maine Turnpike to Augusta—it's practically a straight line, green of the evergreens gradually deepening and thickening as you travel farther north where trees still proliferate—and Route 95 again to Bangor. An Old Town exit will drop you right down the long bumpy hill of Stillwater Avenue onto the Main Street of Old Town, just beyond a couple of green and white Indian-head signs reading: OLD TOWN BUSINESS DISTRICT on the way in. It's a three and a half hour drive at the speed limit. A right hand turn and two lefts take you, after a minute, to the foot of the bridge to the Island. Go on over.

I chose to approach Indian Island along the Penobscot River, cheatingly by car, of course. I would take the Bangor turnoff on Route 95, and, keeping the river on my right, idle my way into Old Town through the City, which I came gradually to admire for what remains in it of older times, specifically a 19th century Main Street of solid red-brick shops— THE BOSTON STORE—overlooked by Gilded Age civic buildings, considered ugly and vulgar enough, and monstrously eclectic by some, but which are, like it or not, part of what little architectural heritage we possess in America, and which are being pulled down at a great rate all over the country to be replaced by concrete blocks fashioned out of smaller concrete blocks and either painted over or left to stain or take the graffiti which record the small history, if not the aggressions and yearnings, of each neighborhood: JACKIE SUCKS COCK . . . GOD IS ALIVE AND WELL IN ARGENTINA.

Bangor looks to be a larger city than its population of 33,000 might seem to indicate. Thoreau arrived here directly by Bangor Packet out of Boston in 1846, by which time the waterways were already seasonally swollen by the logs endlessly ripped out of the earth and bled down along the river amid a great traffic of trading barges. By then the streets, some of them, were paved with cobblestones, and merchants and lumber-

men competed in the grandeur of their Greek Revivals. Old Town's road-
ways were still dirt—and of course just yellow mud in spring. And in the
19th century it was all sawmill noise and pulp flack.

Continuing to keep the river to your right, when you can see it, you
drive north to Veazie, named after General Samuel Veazie, who owned the
first railroad in the area, and then to Orono, practically indistinguishable
from Veazie as to boundaries and faces, though Orono is the seat or main
campus of the state university, which you know anyway, and which I mention to prove that you don't know why it's called Orono (he was a Penobscot Sagamore who died in 1900 at the age of 113); but you know what's
there: a college town surrounded by the usual cheapie pizza and non-ice-
cream froth palaces which go to seed six months after their plastic facades
are glued up.

It gets a bit desperate between Orono and Old Town. There's a stretch
of flat, "undeveloped" land to your left between you and the rather envi-
able if not splendid isolation of the university—no great shakes academically, though Norbert Wiener once taught here on his first appointment,
and, like most state universities, in the stranglehold of conservative trustees,
who use it, its funds, appointments, and building expansion contracts as
political pawns in their shoddy chess of educational and legislative preten-
sions and self-serving. We all know who owns Maine (and America) and it
ain't the Indians.

Here were once somebody's farms and you just know it's going to be
WHOPPER-BLOPPER hamburg and used-car city any year now. Next,
Greatworks and the hill down into Old Town, again river, now slight and
full of white foam. What used to be a view of remarkable prospect—river
and the woods of Milford—is now Diamond International, paper and pulp
products, chimneys spouting gray gas death and a stink as of septic tanks
suddenly down and hot on you, and in your lungs and at the back of your
throat. Think of the folks who suffer it daily, year in, year out.

It is often useful, if exasperating, to see how others see themselves,
or want themselves seen. On my first excursion I purchased a copy of
State O' Maine Facts, published annually by the Rockland Courier-Gazette
and subtitled, A Handbook of Maine. This is what I read while standing
above the river at Greatworks on the way into town:

PENOBSCOT COUNTY
Penobscot County, the last county to be incorporated before Maine became
a state, occupies the entire valley of the Penobscot River. The county,

incorporated in 1816, takes its name from the river which is the longest in the state. It is the fourth largest county in Maine and is a great diversified lumbering, farming, manufacturing and recreational area in East Central Maine, containing 3,408 square miles.

The Penobscot River which bisects the county was a principal highway used by travelers, both Indians and white men, on their way to and from Canada. In 1604 in his search for fabulous Norumbega, city of gold, de Champlain sailed up this river which has a rich and colorful history.

Pulp, paper and lumber are the major industries in the county. The largest newsprint mill in the United States, The Great Northern Paper Co., is located at Millinocket. New industries are moving into the county at a steady rate.

Bangor is the hub of the county as well as for Northern and Eastern Maine. The county seat is located at the southern end of the county and at the head of tidewater on the Penobscot, 60 miles from the Atlantic Ocean. It is an urban, commercial, financial, shipping, cultural and transportation center (an international airport is located here). Throughout its history, Bangor has been a meeting place for lumbermen, hunters, fishermen, trappers, settlers, traders and mariners. A century ago it was a leading lumber port in the world. During the boom years beginning in 1830, Bangor attracted national attention as land speculation reached its height and gamblers and adventurers were attracted to this city. During the spring through fall months, the river harbor was jammed with schooners and full-riggers, loading up lumber cargoes bound for the far corners of the globe. Today the city has its civic sights aimed at economic expansion and cultural growth. The Bangor Public Library has one of the best libraries in the state and ranks among outstanding libraries in larger cities throughout the country.

Opposite Bangor on the eastern side of the Penobscot River is Brewer, a residential, industrial and commercial city which is included in the port of Bangor.

Old Town is 12 miles north of Bangor on the west bank of the Penobscot River. Although the city has numerous industries, it is a commercial and farming area as well. The famous Old Town canoe, known to canoeists, is manufactured here. The town is also the site of the largest Indian reservation in New England, that of the Penobscot Tribe of the Abenaki Indians.

Miles northeast of Bangor, also on the west bank of the Penobscot, is Orono, famed as the center of the University of Maine. As the center of

*higher education in the state, Orono with its beautiful campus and
attractive homes provides a beautiful setting for a university town. The
town takes its name from a distinguished chief of the Tarratine Tribe of
Indians.*

*The county's forests, lakes and streams are increasing its popularity as
a place for tourists. Sebasticook Lake is an area famous for its bass fishing.*

DEVELOPMENT
*Bangor-Brewer Area—shoes, warehousing, transportation and commercial
center of central Maine.*

*Millinocket and East Millinocket—sites of plants of largest newsprint
manufacturers in the United States.*

The prose is predictable, bustling still with the latent optimism of
19th-century expansionism: "business exalts." Yet today the superlative
somehow minimizes: longest river, oldest house, fourth largest county . . .
who cares? You don't come for that, and I suspect few even heed such
rhetoric today. The college girls who work in the state information booths
are into—barely—their brightly flowered microskirts and leather hot pants
rather than the content of the sleek pamphlets they fan out nonchalantly
on coffee-stained Formica counter tops before the ogling eyes of the
middle-aged tourist from Des Moines in his baggy madras jacket, wilted
white handkerchief drooping from the breast pocket while his wife attends
in their air-conditioned vehicle.

No, you don't come here for "one of the best libraries in the state,"
or "the largest Indian reservation in New England." In Maine, still—though
this is changing, and that prose which is beginning to flower all over is a
harbinger of disaster—things speak for themselves, and people, too, mostly
because there are still things and people: individual and authentic places
and objects which arrest and force remark: *attention.*

For this reason alone Old Town is not without interest to aficionados
of the phenomenology of American small-town life and folkways, which
I'll touch upon later. The fact book tells you its population is 9,057, but it
doesn't mention that in a couple of square miles there are two shoe factories, two lumber mills, a pulp mill, a pulp products factory, a foundry,
a woolen mill, two canoe companies, and a large engineering firm, or that
instead of "new industries moving into the county at a steady rate," the
shoe factories are closing down and unemployment here is heavy, money
scarce as hen's teeth, food prices much higher—before the freeze—than

in Massachusetts, and people are grim. They look and feel it. In May of 1971, while having coffee at Jack's Restaurant on the main drag in Old Town, I overheard a man lamenting to his friend that his snowmobile had been repossessed that day.

"Tough titty," his buddy snapped back. "Norm's gonna lose his house!"

It is here the Indians live—about 400 on the Island near the end of town, several hundred in and around the town itself or spread out between Bangor and Mattawamkeag where the river arches first eastward and then doubles back to the west to Millinocket and Katahdin: the Great High Place, from which Glooskap looked down upon his children.

It's all there in Senabeh's painting, which is the first thing you see on your right after you cross the green-painted steel one-way bridge from Main Street to Indian Island and the causeway dips down to Center Street. Five by ten feet: you might call it an outdoor mural. It stands on slender green-tinted saplings, a beautifully vivid view of the clear river, the Island itself on the right—teepees, cornfields, hides drying, campfires—just about where Senabeh, woodworker, painter, craftsman, and sometime hermit, has his shack now, the ash logs whose bark is used for basketry piled alongside it. In the left foreground of the painting a man and woman return home in a canoe on untroubled water. The upper left is all Island, and high above everything else, in a yellow and rose sky, Katahdin rises. It is a careful, accurate painting in lacquers and oils, all the visible flora just as you find them, or did. Senabeh's ecology is flawless: his is an ideal view of things as they were to counterpose to things as they are now.

On your left is Chief Poolaw's Teepee and Trading Post, where you can buy Indian baskets, moccasins, and souvenirs, and where they advertise "Rest Rooms." The teepee is a white-shingled wooden affair with a red top, orange "tent poles" sticking out of it, and a sign, INDIAN MOC-CASINS, with a small American flag at either end of the sign. Poolaw is a Kiowa Indian from Oklahoma who survives his Penobscot wife, Princess Watawaso—"her stage name"—who lies under the most imposing stone in the new cemetery.

To the right, again, beyond Senabeh's painting is St. Anne's Church, the rectory and convent, a newly weather-shingled two-story square house, the largest on the Island. In an angle formed by the functional, white-spired church and the Rectory-Parish House is a hot-topped parking lot with spaces marked off for a couple dozen cars. It is used during the week by tourists, as is a vacant lot across the street beyond Skee-jim's moccasin and souvenir shop, owned by the Loring family, to the rear of which is a newly constructed asphalt-lined swimming pool and the old Tribal Hall, a large barnlike structure, perhaps more accurately described as looking like an old-time schoolhouse, with a bell tower on top, except that it is essentially windowless. Neither the Tribal Hall nor the former Council House, directly across Center Street from the far boundary of the Parish House, is in use today. In Frank Speck's *Penobscot Man*, there is a photograph of the Council House, taken about forty years ago, and sitting snugly, tightly in the middle of an immense snowdrift, picket-fenced, shingled, smoke pouring from its slim brick chimney: the picture of stability. Now it's derelict, boarded up, sagging.

The people's dwellings begin at the entrance to the Island and continue to the right and left all the way up Center Street. Eight small houses are clustered behind Skee-jim's, some recent, others much older and done up in white clapboards. A couple, even, have miniature mansard roofs. Each has its kitchen garden; and oil drums stand on metal or wooden supports outside the back doors, the owners' cars parked in backyards or common driveways.

Center Street dips again. Houses on the right, small, two-stories with green or tan asphalt shingles; on the left the Mainstream office, which is really a green wooden shack, then the Indian Agent's office, the same green and not much more elaborate, except that Raymond Ellis has two rooms to Mainstream's one. Over Ellis's desk a big crane-type fluorescent lamp, like an architect's, burns day and night, though Ellis leaves the office between five and six P.M.

West Street branches off Center on the left and leads up a low hill with larger and more elaborate dwellings on either side; here are willow trees, again the careful gardens of squash, pumpkins, corn, beans, tomatoes, peas, and potatoes. Here and there are rosebushes at front doorways and gates, and wild flowers and weeds run rampant in the vacant patches of land between houses and between road and houses. As you go up West Street you pass Nelson's basket works with the wares in the window, more a workshop than a store. I always found it closed.

Main Street, which also crosses Center, makes a triangle with West and Center, and in that triangle is the older of two formal cemeteries, this one going back to the 18th century. There is a shrine, or altar-place, in the center of it, made of wood and with wooden shelves in it for flowers. The names, those of which have not been worn off the stones or covered by lichen, are of the old—the first—families: Attean, Neptune, Mitchell,

Lolar, Sockalexis, Sockabeson, to name but a few. It is here, also, that Joe Polis, Thoreau's guide on his third and definitive trip here, and the source of his most complete and telling experience of the Penobscot Indians, is buried alongside his wife Mary.

Polis, whose name is pronounced "Porus," which means "little Paul," served in the Civil War after Thoreau's death. He returned to the Island, minus an arm, and occupied what is today perhaps the most interesting house on the Island, from whose front steps, over the door of which is a very strange carved wooden structure that looks more like a dark-green mantelpiece than a door decoration, you can look back down over the ground you have covered. It's a large, white-frame house, longer and narrower than most, and I would judge it had been built in the late 18th century. In 1857 Thoreau described it as "the best looking that [he] noticed there, and as good as an average one on a New England village street." Polis left it to his stepson, Peter Ranco, and it is now in the possession of the Nicola family, another of the oldest among the inhabitants.

West Street mounts finally to a hill which overlooks the river and Orson Island, as well as the entire wooded area of Indian Island stretching back for more than a mile, and is not inhabited. Main Street takes you back to Center. Across from the main entrance to the cemetery, down some fifty feet on the right, is the Lovarama laundromat, recently opened by the Love family with the assistance of the Penobscot Indian Corporation and Operation Mainstream. There are about a dozen machines and driers packed into one room, redolent of bleach and cigarette smoke and full of the talk and banter of women and girls. I never got beyond the big front window. I thought it would be like barging into someone's home, violating their privacy: yet there was always such gaiety inside—maybe some at my expense.

Behind the laundromat is another new business, built likewise under the aegis of the P.I.C. and Operation Mainstream. It is Pherson's general store, and it has its own parking lot to its right before you come to the dike on the right side of the Island which overlooks Old Town proper. There is a dike along the left side of the Island as well, a long, smooth hard-packed walkway, the dirt as hard and dry as if it were concrete, from which you look out across the river to a housing development beyond Old Town and finally catch a glimpse of the Old Town Municipal Airport. Naturally small planes zoom over the Island constantly, and it's a common complaint here that "if they're not trying to asphyxiate us with the pulp mill stink, the noise pollution from the airport will do it."

Center Street's a hill now, rising steadily, gently. On the right is the brown and tan asphalt-shingled Indian Island Baptist Church, which used to be the Tribal Hall and over the entrance to which is painted: CHRIST DIED FOR OUR SINS.

It was in this building that the Devil appeared in the guise of an alluring stranger one evening during a dance. A girl became his partner, and they were afterwards seen leaving the dance: no trace was ever found of her. After the dance, the mark of a cloven hoof was discovered, burned into the floor. Afterwards several people claimed to have heard a noise like the sound of chains rattling in the cellar during the dance.

On a glass-covered sign outside the church, where the service times and sermon titles are listed, it says:

COME AS YOU ARE

HOW ELSE CAN YOU COME TO CHRIST?

There is a new one-story parish hall and community center at the rear of the church.

Across the street from the church is the home of the present Governor of the Tribe, Francis J. "Bunny" Ranco. His wife has a small variety store in the front of the house. It is here that Bridge Street drops from the right of Center Street, down a hill, past a body of water commonly called the Pond, and becomes River Street—sometimes, River Road. Here you find yourself directly above the river on the right-hand side of the Island overlooking Old Town, the fields of Milford, and the Bangor Hydroelectric waterworks and dam. Again, dwellings are scattered along the road or to the rear of it. And there is another moccasin and souvenir shop, this one operated by Ernest Goslin. It sits in a yard of rich, green grass, laced all over with pumpkin vines.

Back at the corner of Center and Bridge is Indian Island School, grades one through six, an old wing and a new one with its combined cafeteria and gymnasium whose windows look out upon the "new" cemetery. Continuing down Center there are more houses, a few merely more elaborate tar-paper shacks, some derelict cars, grass poking up around their tireless wheels. Where Center curves to the right around the back of the Pond you find, to your left, a majestic willow, twenty feet in circumference with great long, low inviting branches. The kids sit here and dangle their legs or swing as they watch the games on the ball court to the right and rear of the tree. This place between Center Street, the Pond, and a swampy area at the margin of the Pond is called Mosquito Valley. Here Center Street curves up sharply on the right, becomes a steep, asphalt-smooth hill and joins Oak Hill Road on the left side of its crest, which takes you straight back to the last dwellings on the Island and the woods. On the left-hand corner of Oak Hill Road and Center, just before the hill crests, rises the partially completed Nedabeh or "Friendship" coffeehouse, project of draft-resister Martin Neptune. At the very rear or woods side of Oak Hill Road is Mildred Aiken's Indian Room souvenir shop, and across the street one called Ed Val's, which advertises Indian artifacts for sale.

Oak Hill is named for the trees, which in 1605 Champlain reported in abundance all the way up the Penobscot from the present sites of Bangor and Brewer. If you take a sharp right where Center and Oak Hill Road join, you will be doubling back down toward River Street. This is the highest point on the Island, looking down again toward Old Town. On the left above the river and near some of the few contemporary or split-level dwellings on the Island is the site of the ancient burial ground, now called Oak Hill Cemetery. There are no stones here, as in the place where Joe and Mary Polis lie, nor any wooden crosses with hand-painted names as in the new cemetery. It is just earth, gravelly, dusty, stubbled over with weeds and set with an occasional oak. But underneath all this are the striations of red ocher in which the first men in America buried their dead, in some cases first burning the body and then making a paste of bone ash and ocher dye (*olamon*, for which an island to the rear of this one, the primary local source for the stuff, is named), forming it into a ball and placing that in its ocher bed along with artifacts and personal belongings, or later, in clay urns which were then placed in the earth.

These first Americans in Maine, called either the Red Paint People for their use of the dye or the Moorehead culture, after the late archaeologist Warren King Moorehead, whose *Archaeology of Maine* (1922), is the first report of work at the burial sites, were once thought to have been a discrete culture or people. Now they are generally believed to have been the ancestors of the present people, who first inhabited the Island nine or even ten thousand years ago. Their burial places have been unearthed at Ellsworth Falls, as well as in the Rockland and Blue Hill areas. A superb collection of their relics exists in Bar Harbor at the splendid little Robert Abbe Museum in the center of Acadia National Park. Other relics can be viewed in Rockland at the Farnsworth Museum.

It ought, incidentally, to be mentioned that the Indians of Maine are at their most bitingly sarcastic on the subject of what they generally regard as the despoiling of their sacred places, and especially, the placing of the "labeled" remains of their first parents in glass cases to be gawked at by white tourists in bermuda shorts and sunglasses. There is a movement in Maine, part of a national one, to have the remains of the Indian dead returned to their final resting places. Activists are quick to point out that "there would be some hell raised" if they took pick and shovel and began to "go at it" in the graveyards of the whites, no matter how old and overgrown.

"If we did it," one remarked, "it would be called 'sacrilege' and we'd go to jail. A white does it and it's called anthropology or archaeology and he becomes famous and holds a university post where he teaches other white people how to do it!"

Here, then, is a good place to end a walk you might take on Indian Island. What is left out is the people themselves, of course, who appear elsewhere in the book, and an exact description of a myriad of houses and flora, dogs and doilies, which you might see for yourself if you go to the Indians.

One white man came this year and wrote this:

A VIEW TOWARDS INDIAN ISLAND

It is
pristine
apparently
across
the green bridge
on a cool day
in spring.
The Church:
St. Anne's,
looks a part of it . . .
a toy village
and a good place.
Crossing
changes that.
The streets wind in agony,
and a scream
of shame,
our shame,
is everywhere.

I cannot go
        as a tourist.
Even the trees ask me,
'Why have you come?
What can you do for us?'
Wooden crosses
        set crooked
in the graveyard
        reject me.
I go back quickly,
but I cannot forget.
I am the stranger here,
and I live on stolen ground.

Theodore Enslin
From *The Aroostook Indian*
May, 1971

DOCUMENTS 1

THORVALD ERICSON'S EXPEDITION
TO VINLAND

Now there was much talk about Leif's discovery of Vinland, his brother Thorvald maintaining that the country had not been thoroughly enough explored. Leif said to Thorvald, "You shall go to Vinland in my ship if you want to, brother."

On Leif's advice Thorvald made ready for this expedition with forty men. They fitted out their ship and put to sea, and there is no account of their voyage until Thorvald came to Leif's base in Vinland, where they laid up their ship and passed the winter in quiet, catching fish for food.

In the spring, however, Thorvald said that they were to put their ship in order and that some of them were to take the ship's boat along the western coast and explore there that summer. They found it a pleasant wooded country: the woods ran close down to the sea, there were white sands, and also large numbers of islands and shallows. They found no trace of habitation by men or beasts but on an island to the west they found a bark hut or dwelling. Not finding further human handiwork they turned back, coming to Leif's base in the autumn.

The following summer Thorvald set out to the east in his trading ship and sailed along the more northerly part of the coast. . . . Afterwards they sailed away eastwards along the coast and into the mouths of the nearest fjords and to a projecting headland which was all overgrown with woods.

A. W. Lawrence and Jean Young, "The Flatey Book," *Narratives of the Discovery of America* (New York: Jonathan Cape and Harrison Smith, 1931), pp. 32–34.

When they had anchored their ship and put out a gangway to land, Thorvald and all his crew went ashore and he said, "This is a fine place: I should like to make my home here." Then they went back to the ship, and on the sands in beyond the headland they saw three mounds. Going up to them they discovered they were three skin canoes with three men under each, so they divided their party and captured all the men but one, who escaped in his canoe. They killed the eight and then returned to the headland, and looking about saw within the fjords certain mounds which they concluded were dwelling places.

After this so great a heaviness came over them that they could not keep awake but all fell asleep. Then a cry was uttered above them so that they all woke up. The cry was, "Awake Thorvald and all your company if you wish to save your life. Go to your ship with all your men and sail from the land as quickly as possible."

Then countless skin canoes made towards them from within the fjord. At this Thorvald exclaimed, "We must put our war-shields along the side of the boat and make as stout a defence as we can, but offer little attack." They did this, and the Savages after shooting at them for a time fled away, each one as fast as he could.

Then Thorvald asked his men if they were wounded in any way, but they replied that none had been hurt. "I'm wounded in the armpit," said he. "An arrow flew between the gunwale and the shield under my arm. Here it is and it will be my death. Now I advise you to go back as soon as possible, but take me to the headland where I thought it would be excellent to live. When I said I should stay there for a time I may have been speaking the truth. Bury me there. . . ."

Now Thorvald died, and after carrying out his orders his men went away to join their companions. They told one another what had happened to them, and spent the winter there gathering grapes and vines, with which to load the ship. In the spring they made ready to return to Greenland and arrived with their ship in Ericsfjord with great news for Leif.

In the summer of 1004 he headed Down East. Attracted
by the heights of Mount Desert, Thorvald set course for
it, landed on what in all likelihood are the shores of Somes
Sound, a fiord, like those of his homeland, that penetrates
Mount Desert Island. Thorvald and his crew were probably the first Europeans to set foot on Maine soil.

Maine; A Literary Chronicle, W. Storrs Lee, Ed. (New York:
Funk and Wagnalls, 1968), p. 2.

CHAMPLAIN NAVIGATES THE PENOBSCOT RIVER

5th September 1604. . . . The same day we passed also near
to an island about four or five leagues long. From this
island to the main land on the north, the distance is less
than a hundred paces. It is very high, and notched in places,
so that there is the appearance to one at sea, as of seven
or eight mountains extending along near each other. The
summit of the most of them is destitute of trees, as there
are only rocks on them. The woods consists of pines, firs,
and birches only. I named it Isle des Monts Deserts.

The next day, the 6th of the month, we sailed two
leagues and perceived a smoke in a cove at the foot of the
mountains above mentioned. We saw two canoes rowed by
savages, which came within musket range to observe us. I
sent our two savages in a boat to assure them of our friendship. Their fear of us made them turn back. On the morning of the next day they came alongside of our barque and
talked with our savages. I ordered some biscuit, tobacco,
and other trifles to be given them. These savages had come
beaver-hunting and to catch fish, some of which they gave
us. Having made an alliance with them, they guided us to
their river of Pentegouet, so called by them, where they
told us was their captain, named Bessabez, chief of this
river. . . .

Voyages of Samuel de Champlain (New York: Charles Scribner's
Sons, 1907).

As one enters the river, there are beautiful islands, which are very pleasant and contain fine meadows. We proceeded to a place to which the savages guided us, where the river is not more than an eighth of a league broad . . . I landed to view the country and, going on a hunting excursion, found it very pleasant so far as. I went. The oaks here appear as if they were planted for ornament. I saw only a few firs, but numerous pines on one side of the river; on the other side only oaks, and some copse wood which extends far into the interior . . . We saw no town or village, but one or two cabins of the savages. These were made in the same way as those of the Micmacs, being covered with the bark of trees. So far as we could judge the savages on this river are few in number . . . moreover, they only come to the islands, and that only during some months in summer for fish and game, of which there is a great quantity. They are a people who have no fixed abode, so far as I could observe and learn from them. For they spend the winter now in one place and now in another, according as they find the best hunting, by which they live when urged by their daily needs, without laying up anything for times of scarcity, which are sometimes severe. . . .

[T]he savages who had conducted me to the fall of the river . . . went to notify Bessabez, their chief, and other savages, who in turn proceeded to another little river to inform their own, named Cabahis, and give him notice of our arrival.

The 16th of the month there came to us some thirty savages. . . . There came also to us the same day the above-named Bessabez with six canoes. As soon as the savages who were on land saw him coming, they all began to sing, dance and jump, until he had landed. Afterwards, they all seated themselves in a circle on the ground, as is their custom when they wish to celebrate a festivity, or an harrangue is to be made. Cabahis, the other chief, arrived also a little later with twenty or thirty of his companions, who withdrew to one side and greatly enjoyed seeing us, as it was the first time they had seen Christians. . . .

I directed the men in our barque to approach near the savages, and hold their arms in readiness to do their duty in case they noticed any movement of these people against us. Bessabez, seeing us on land, bade us sit down, and began to smoke with his companions, as they usually do before an address. They presented us with venison and game.

I directed our interpreter to say to our savages that they should cause Bessabez, Cabahis and their companions to understand that Sieur de Monts had sent me to them to see them, and also their country, and that he desired to preserve friendship with them and to reconcile them with their enemies, the Souriquois [Micmacs] and Canadians [New Brunswick Malacites] and moreover that he desired to inhabit their country and show them how to cultivate it, in order that they might not continue to lead so miserable a life as they were doing. . . .

I presented them with hatchets, paternosters, caps, knives, and other little knick-knacks when we separated from each other. . . .

JOURNAL 2

May 7, 1971, 11 A.M.

Spring morning in Maine, and Augusta is a peaceful city, built on hills, green: pastoral prospect from the State House and State Museum looking down on green lawns, away from the center of the city, the—quotes—Business District—where it becomes indistinguishable from every city of its size in America in the havoc of urban renewal, the loss of its original architecture. It's always been a place for me to come through on the way down to Mt. Desert Island; rarely do I stop except for Ho-Jo's or a tank of gas. At the new Bureau of Indian Affairs Office an Indian girl working as a secretary gives me the census lists of both tribes and the names of the governor, lt. governor, and representative at Indian Island, neatly and crisply typed on a blue file card in the latest Olivetti. There are handouts, historical pamphlets, and mimeographed material on economic develop-ment. She asks me what I'm doing; I tell her; she smiles and I go out and wander around the Maine State Museum, where I copy out the geological descriptions—"Maine occupies a small area on the surface of the large space vehicle which we know as the planet Earth. . . ."—figuring I can work them into the book in some ironic way before setting off for first reconnoiter of Bangor, Old Town, Indian Island.

3 P.M.

Indian Island. A few minutes from downtown Old Town. Houses overlook the back or river side of the Penobscot Shoe Company and are themselves overlooked by a row of late-18th-century and Victorian mansions, typical of the river towns of New England—Haverhill, Lowell, and more elegantly, Newburyport. Greek revivals: still white from a distance; up close the paint peels and the thick glass of floor-length windows is going yellow.

Governor Ranco won't be back until "supper," his wife tells me. Most of the men are still at work. A few kids roam the streets. The trees are still largely leafless; the place looks bleak, empty. I drive all the roads on the Island feeling strange, alien. Couple people look up, maybe hear the chronic rattle coming from beneath my car. I never can find the source. Go up Oak Hill Road to dead end. Ed Val's Indian artifacts. Knock on door, closed. Across the Street, INDIAN ROOM. Likewise no answer. On the way up to Oak Hill—all the other shops closed "for the Season" so no public place to barge into, start asking questions, rapping, foot in the door—flashes of cemeteries, the two churches I was on the lookout for. Where's Mainstream? Where is everybody? Where do the Thompsons, the editors of *Maine Indian Newsletter* live? Here? In Old Town? I'll look them up in a phone book over town; do; it says Center Street. I go up to Ken Thompson's law office over the Rexall, but it's no longer occupied. Call the number, no answer. I go back to the Island, drive around, feel foolish with no one to see. It's getting late, and I have to find accommodations for next time. The Y director in Old Town—nice elderly gent, as always they know someone in Gloucester, very helpful—says they don't have rooms, why don't I go up Stillwater Avenue to the Anchorage Motel? (What am I doing here, casting backward glance at the Island sitting there in the river: I don't belong here, I want to turn tail and run, yet think: there's a pull. Right over there on July 21, 1857, Thoreau stepped off the batteau and went up to Joe Polis, visited the Atteans, old Governor Neptune, came on the Island out of nowhere, strange bearded Yankee in old clothes, talking broken Algonquin he'd cribbed out of Father Rasles' dictionary, the pages of which were found scattered round the Priest's house in Norridgewock, those on the table where his head was laid all bloody—his own blood, the old man working up to the last second, or maybe just interrupted in his work by the door opening, English long rifle leveled at him: *bap*, it's all over—and the English trying to pass it off as an "Indian massacre."

In the same year, 1724, an expedition was conducted under Hammon and Moulton against Norridgewock. They attacked and destroyed that village, and killed a number of the Savages, with Ralle [sic], a Jesuit, who resided there. This and the battle of Captain Lovel, were of great consequence to the people of the province of Maine. These tribes were all Savages which remained of the numerous bodies who once inhabited that territory. These held their villages as resting places for the Canada Indians, and were themselves the guides of the scouting parties who came from thence on our frontiers. These decisive actions, relieved the people from great apprehensions, and saved the frontiers from great calamities.

James Sullivan,
History of the District of Maine, 1785,
p. 262

I won't run, by Jesus. I want to come back here, my work is honorable—I *think*. I find the Anchorage, get set up for next time. Sun's going down and I head home down the Maine Pike.

15 Vine Street
Gloucester, Mass. 01930
May 18, 1971

Governor Francis J. Ranco
Indian Island
P. O. Box 210
Old Town, Maine 04468

Dear Governor Ranco:

I am writing a book on the Penobscot Nation to be published in 1973 by Beacon Press of Boston. One of the things I'm most interested in is having some of your people tell their own stories in their own way and on their own terms. I am anxious to show the reading public, especially in New England, something of the richness of your culture and history while giving as full a picture as possible of your present way of life.

I plan to be in Old Town during the week of May 24, 1971. I should like very much to discuss my project with you, and I hope that you will not mind my calling to make an appointment to see you during that week.

Yours very sincerely,

Peter Anastas

May 25

Anchorage Motel, Old Town. They had an "efficiency apartment" ready for me; outside: trees, piney woods, and the smell of grass (Larry, the owner, had said on the phone, "Come on down, it's really getting pretty around here!"); inside: you could be in any motel in America. Once I closed the door, I closed myself into that nowhere plastic of printed shower curtains and Formica tabletops, wrapped drinking glasses, postage-stamp soap, and disinfectant, as though everyone who used these rooms had a deadly disease and you had to perform some sort of scour/scourge act of ablution every time they check out.

Larry watched me carry in typewriter, tape recorder, pile of tape reels, books, and paper. He caught sight of Munson's awful Penobscot crib-book, my old Federal Writer's Project guide which I swear by, and my Speck and asked me what I was "writin'." I told him I was doing some "research into the history of the area for a book." "Well, there's a lot of history around here, that's for sure—and they should forget most of it," Larry said. He put his finger on it. Nice guy, really friendly, youngish, obliging— perfect person for a motel owner or manager, not too solicitous, not too inquisitive, but friendly with a bit of Yankee distance I am so used to from Gott's Island and Gloucester.

Old Town with a Main (or is it Maine, like in Brunswick?) Street, deserted at 6:30 P.M., when I called home from the Walgreen (not Rexall), shy little girl behind the counter, telling me it was her second day as cashier and she had to call a boy over to oversee while she made change and pushed the, hopefully, right keys. That's at the bottom of the long hill down, Stillwater; and the town itself is in this river basin. At the top, a shopping center or Plaza w. Grant's, First National, Cinema 1 and 2 w. appropriate clean (family) and dirty (everybody) films. (Two boys got turned away from *There's a Girl in My Soup*. I offered to sneak them in as my "guests," but manager said he'd get in trouble; later had to give me long explanation about how he hated to turn them away but "they could close him down." Of course film practically innocuous, a bit of tit and a shot of Goldie Hawn's sleek flanks, quickly diffused by gauze curtains). Ate at Grant's restaurant—lots of old ladies as usual—looked out the window at the half-built quality of the place, nothing but parking lot; Grant's quite empty, some kids for clerks, just jawwing, one guy reporting to his friends that Bobby Seale and Erika "you know her name" got acquitted . . . barrage of color TV's with a million David Frosts in all sizes of face and tone of color letting some gay-sex-rock twins into Old Town, along with London and cunnilingus w. Peter Sellers next door.

MISTRIAL CALLED IN SEALE CASE/ NORTH VIET ASSAULT TROOPS
HIT U.S. CAMP NEAR SAIGON
Bangor *Daily News*

It was "Buck Nite" at Grant's—fried chicken or fish fillets w. cole slaw—and I could look into the store itself from my table: no customers, actually very few goods on display: just a vast room of concrete blocks painted grays and greens, with even the heating pipes and electric wires showing; posters pasted up here and there. But sad in a way, depressing. At least Main Street has an intimacy, but you need another Edward Hopper to paint shopping-center America, tho' it's really quite all of a piece.

Earlier I'd gone to Brewer
on the way here to look for Fannie's house on Wilson Street, took sharp
left after Bangor-Brewer toll bridge (15 cents) and found, going off at
parallel lefts, Spring Street, Maple Street, School Street (every NE town
must have them). I ended up in South Brewer at another shopping plaza,
just blew my mind, for it must have been gorgeous fields once in Fannie's
day. Still couldn't locate Wilson, came back north to Union and State but
nothing. Went over to Brewer Auction Rooms to see if they had any of
her books. Naturally they didn't but found for 10 cents a copy of *Human
Destiny*, which Walter Solmitz had given us to start off our philosophy
course, Bowdoin 1956.

[Professor Solmitz, my god, harried out of Europe
by Hitler, chain-smoking at 8 A.M. with the texts of the pre-Socratics in
Greek, German, French—commentaries, glosses—he'd open a green book
bag and tumble them out: pronounced Kant, "Cunt," rode to class even in
winter on a battered bicycle; stayed up half the night in his office, pacing
the floor; you could see him framed by that office window of a long, deep
autumn night from your dormitory or as you returned to it from the railroad
station after mailing a letter to the girl you thought you loved then. He
taught us philosophy by making us philosophize not process data; the
dummies complained they weren't "learning anything" but he taught me—
"Meester Anastas, to feel is *not* to theenk!"—some of the things that saved
me from the death-in-life of a rural campus in the 50s, tag-end of McCar-
thy America. How did you end up here, Walter: in Maine of all places?
How you must have suffered, I never knew. Drank lemonade with you and
your wife August, 1962, on my way back from Europe, came to your
funeral that September as I was about to take my first teaching job. But
you gave me books to read; you showed some of us there was another
life which was not grubbing for money or tenure or notoriety. You said
that to want to write was a noble thing. You killed yourself alone one summer afternoon in the bathroom with a razor blade, College Street, Brunswick, slashed your wrists because you felt your mind was going and you
wouldn't be of any use to your students any longer/ Walter I remember
you from Brewer, Maine/ you were of use/ you were a beautiful person/
I won't forget you/ I remember you, *here*, in my Indian book, a place
for emigrés, especially the internal ones, like the Indians—and ourselves/]

The clerk at Brewer Auction didn't know anything about Fannie's house
but told me Wilson Street was this one, running from toll bridge up a

hill I'd already come down. I couldn't find a note or sign or plaque on a single one of the old houses to tell where she lived, but I did stop to imagine how it must have been here in a 19th-century river town looking across the Penobscot to Bangor, white houses on the hills: everything quiet, and Fannie in such a house on elm- and oak-lined grassy street, kids coming home from school in cool autumn afternoons, Fannie poring over her books and pamphlets, her birds around her, living alone in one of her father's houses—there's even a Hardy Street here in Brewer—while her sister lived in the other/

She was widowed in Providence in 1899 (year my father born in Sparta, Greece) so Munson says: "moved to a comfortable story and half house her father bought her on Wilson Street; there she was to carry on for 47 years her studies of Penobscot history." I make it, she died year after *Old John Neptune* came out (privately printed). I can see the street and her father's house: there was a gate and Governor Neptune coming to it after her grandfather, his ancient friend, had already died, and Old John came tottering on foot down the 12 miles from Old Town to verify the death, up to the gate, the old Indian Patriarch come to find out if the news of the passing of his old white companion, Patriarch Hardy of old Maine family, was so.

Let Fannie tell it herself:

My father saw him coming slowly up the street and watched, himself out of sight. He saw Old Governor turn to enter the yard of our home, then hesitate, then turn back, and he heard him saying to himself, "No, no; no live um here; Hardy no live um here; no, no." Until he was at the door he could not realize his old friend was dead. Six months later he was gone himself.

Old John Neptune, p. 14

Fannie poring over her books, her stories of Indians sitting by her grandfather's fireplace or Franklin stove, in their top hats and frock coats: Molly Molasses about whom Thoreau wrote, "as long as she lives the Penobscots may be considered extant as a tribe," who bore three of John's children, and old Hardy not even knowing that she and Old John were *M'teolin—Shamans!*

I come back to Bangor and stop by Mr. Paperback before proceeding to Old Town via Veazie and Orono. Bookstores are good places to get some sense of a city: but not much of interest here besides fad books—Hesse, encounter psychology, Vonnegut's sci-fi Hemingwayisms—and girly mags being avidly thumbed by elderly men and business types, *Playboy* yearbooks, and calendars; few mild freaks roaming the streets, women in white trenchcoats shopping. Used to be you'd find Maine a year or two behind Boston in fashions, us behind the Coast, New York esp. but now flash from coast to coast and everyone looks the same: little jr. high school fascists in wire-rim spectacles. So no Revolution in anything but marketing as you always have in Amerika.

Set out for Old Town and get the smell from the paper mills: sickening heavy sour smell, air all filled with the smog of it. In Old Town, boxes of cut flowers and bouquets in front of a cut-rate store which used to be the railroad station. They were covered with cellophane, their own moisture clouding the inside so you could see the flowers but dimly, some pinks here and there, boxes all lined up, laid out, as if ready for a funeral.

America is dying; she is dying as the towns and cities die, the small places, the old places. The land around them is leveled and surfaced, and shopping centers of no account and little commerce are put up and the earth is stifled. People are bled out of the towns, towns out of the landscape. A place that does not know what it was has no future.

And here we are in Gloucester getting ready to "celebrate" the 350th anniversary of the planting of a fishing colony w. fake pageants, carnivals, salesmanship—fish and chips, the fish coming from Poland, the chips, frozen, too, from S. Africa, for all we know, even the breading and the fat suspect! There's scarcely anything left in this once New World—nothing at all but robots and highways and junk heaps. A few Indians huddling by coal stoves in the winter; a few remain of the original dispossessed.

I go to bed reading *Human Destiny* (on the table Shulamith Firestone's *Dialectic of Sex,* I bought—yes, at Walgreen's—for my wife). Tomorrow morning I go to the Indians.

May 26

Called the Governor—had he got my letter? Yes, he thought he had, he was very busy. I told him I wanted to see him. Did it have to be this week? He seemed surprised I was in town. Tomorrow he had to go to

Bangor; no, his wife reminded him he was going fishing. Maybe we could meet this evening someplace as he had no office, had to see people in his home. I told him I'd be free after lunch. Finally we agreed on 1 P.M. "a little after," with some hedging on his part. Had I contacted anyone else on the Island. No, I said, I hadn't; but I was about to dial Kenneth Thompson's number and decided not to mention it; then I felt guilty. As it turned out the Thompsons couldn't see me until later in the afternoon when the day's business was done, his secretary told me. When I didn't give my name I heard him say to her: "Well, I haven't got a lot of time to waste talking to somebody who wants to know about Indians." She came back on and I told her I'd been subscribing to the *Maine Indian Newsletter* since the beginning and I was doing a book for Beacon Press in Boston etc., apologized for not having written but I thought a call would be appropriate. Secretary came back telling me Mr. Thompson would be happy to see me; I was to drive to the top of Oak Hill and I'd find two trailers; one he lived in; the other was his office.

I met Governor Ranco in his wife's little store on the corner of Center and River (soda pop, chips, candy, few canned goods, long counter well-washed, polished down, even the holes shiney; signs:

NO CREDIT

NO SWEARING OR OBSCENE LANGUAGE ALLOWED;

few penciled drawings of Indians in chief's regalia, not Penobscot) and told him my father had a store like this once. He said he set his wife up after she retired from working in a shoe factory. She came in later to see a salesman; she was short and well coiffed, with white-blue curls, reminded me of Nana Lasley in my family, my mother's sister's mother-in-law, French-Canadian and Chippewa Indian from Saginaw, Michigan, that speech mix of Yankee and middle-west, bit of French-Canadian in the accent; in the case of Mabel Dana Ranco, Abenaki intonation.

The Governor, nearly 70 but looks much younger, somewhat nervous, smiling, had plastic rimmed glasses up on his forehead, well-barbered and shaved, in immaculate green short-sleeved sport shirt. Very articulate, told me one ought to study the history of the tribe through the families of the chiefs—he went back to the Sockabesans, his great-grandfather an important chief. Mentioned he knew Dr. Seibert at Penn., who had been working for years on the tribe, also a Donald Fields, someone else who sent him a draft of a chapter on Abenaki history going, presumably, "way back."

Was critical of Mrs. Thompson for "rocking the boat." The Penobscots were getting more from the State than ever before; after all, he said
the State was educating her children. Felt it was foolish to ask for "corn,
wood, grain" even if they would give it, under the treaties. He expressed
concern that what I might write would disturb their relationship with the
State. I told him, as of my letter, that I wasn't there to start trouble, set
one faction against another, but merely to walk around, observe, talk, and
mostly listen—that I planned a series of taped interviews with people who
might possibly represent the various views and life-styles on a present-day
Maine reservation. That's all. I assured him that everyone would have his
say—if he wanted it. He said if I came back "later this summer" we could
talk some more. But it was hard to continue, he behind the counter, me
leaning on it. I didn't want to whip out a notebook and start asking questions, I thought I'd wait. Certainly the tape recorder would scare him off!
I told him I'd be in touch.

My impression was of a pleasant man, really talkative though a bit
wary, sort of torn between wanting to help and getting pleasure at the
attention, allowing his own historical sense some play, dropping a name
or two—"I'm studying some of these things for the first time, myself"—
but warning me indirectly, yet with a certain firmness, to tread carefully.

6 P.M.

Left the Thompsons' pretty near talked out, elated, sobered. Complete
opposite of my talk w. Gov. Strange, is it the generation gap or what?
I walk in, Jean's behind the typewriter in the "reception room" of the
trailer where Ken's had his law office since he shut down in Old Town—
"I didn't just want to climb the social ladder." We start talking and stop
only to draw in others as they appear: Pete Anderson, old Bowdoin class-
mate from Bangor who's taking over some of Ken's cases as Ken phases
out his law practice to concentrate now on tribal law and do research and
proposal writing for Mainstream; Ken's secretary, lovely Indian girl whom
he feels sorry about having to let go now that he's giving up practice,
will sell one trailer; they'll live in the other or in their camper and then
in their new house which is going up in back, foundation down already;
Jean (Eugenia) herself, big with her fourth child and rapping—"it's not
depression around here that's so bad, it's *oppression*"; Jim Sappier, Mainstream director who didn't speak to me at first, very diffident, then: my

book would be just another piece of paper—"What do the Penoscots get out of all this?" Said I ought to take all the "pieces of papers" from the years of white man's writing and put them all together and see what I came up with. I like Jim; he's angry and interested at the same time: fiercely local, I think, in the sense of wanting to protect his people; his anger includes, subsumes theirs; he was barely holding it in, went out of trailer without saying good-bye to me; I went to the door, looked out, said "Good-bye" to him; he mumbled it halfheartedly; finally, Ken: short, well-built, balding on top, with full red beard.

No formalities, I walk in and we start talking. I tell them what I want to do, they tell me about themselves and their work. Ken remarked that it was understandable, the Gov's reticence: "He does speak for many of the older residents, proud they have nine-to-five jobs. They can leave the Reservation at 7 A.M. and return at 5 P.M. in their own cars." Proud they can hack the hours as against old myth of shiftless and lazy Indian living in "Indian time." "They want essentially to live like whites," Jean added, *"be* white."

I like the Thompsons immensely, they are just a few years younger than I am, but, I feel, more buoyant, flexible; they've thrown off middle-class values and attachments much easier than I've been able to. They are more of the voluntary poor in America—a new class that eschews the rewards of professionalism the culture holds out: Ken gets a law degree, Jean supports him during law school; he works for the Indian Affairs office in Augusta; Jean gets a Ford Foundation grant to visit as many Reservations as she can in the U.S. and Canada, so Ken leaves his job and they travel together. They come back and he sets up his law practice, then gives it up to live here on the Island on some of Jean's land: they raise chickens and rabbits, have a huge organic garden. On the bathroom floor of their house-trailer I saw *Bury My Heart at Wounded Knee* and a Pamper.

On the way out to dinner: glassy water of the Penoscot, reminds me of the Merrimack, soft with the reflection of green trees, edged with brown and gray stones.

May 27

Spent three and a half hours at the Thompsons' tonight with Ken, Jean, Eva Ranco, Wayne Mitchell, Martin Neptune, and for the last hour, Tim

Love, who promised to walk me over every inch of the Island tomorrow morning.

Got the Island in microcosm listening to them swap stories of growing up, the people they know. The oral tradition isn't dead, and you would think it might be, among the young especially. Wayne was trained as a psychiatric aide at MacLean's, can't find a job in Maine even though there's a shortage of trained paramedical personnel. ("So now I'm a professional Indian.") Very acute, fine linguistic sense: tells a story cleanly, with incredible power to render dialogue, nuance, place himself in it. Martin's a good raconteur too: long silky black hair, smooth brown skin; his profile more Mayan to Wayne's Nordic darkness. Eva—full breasts, small waist; pitch-black hair, kept getting up to help Jean serve ginger ale in big highball glasses, put out chips and Fritos, clean up afterwards. She baby-sits for the Thompsons. Tim has a lot of hair, pushed out over and above ears and held down by a small green Tyrolean hat. Army-surplus field jacket he wears inside, too. Wayne and Martin, both twenty (Eva's 16, Tim, 17), lived upstairs in Martin's house last year, with another family downstairs. Then both got married. "We didn't want to have another of those cold winters," Martin said. Martin's family is in Manchester, Connecticut, where they went for the working conditions. His mother has periodic breakdowns, but is apparently doing better living in Connecticut. All four felt a greater tie to their grandparents, a bond of sympathy at least in terms of their grandparents' attempts to preserve the tradition. The old people, they said, were of great help to them in their attempts to rediscover their Indian roots.

They told me that a well-known New England bottled drink company had sent 900 cases of diet soda to the Island "as a gift"—after it was outlawed for containing cyclamates. Thank you, Mr. America.

May 28

Fine drizzle as Tim and I walked over the entire Island. We ended up back at Ken's for coffee and good-byes. Jean's taking everyone to New Brunswick today for the three-day Indian Unity Meeting. "No whites allowed," said Ken, who's staying home to take care of the three kids.

I mentioned to Ken how beautiful and peaceful I found the Island at any time of day but especially in the quiet evenings, and he said: "Lots of times we'll sit up at night with a fire and toast marshmallows and all the kids from the neighborhood, little kids and big kids, will come around.

Other times Jean goes to bed early, I'll go across the street with Matt Mitchell (Wayne's uncle) and we'll sit outdoors. Sometimes we'll have a beer or a can of sardines or kippers and just sit and talk. It's so easy to sit out there until twelve or one o'clock because it's so peaceful and really nice out. Matt told me a couple of nights after I went in, he went back out again. He went in to bed and he got up again and went out all over again to sit by himself it was so nice. . . ."

LEGENDS 2

MASTER RABBIT AND THE OTTER

Of old times, Mahtigwess, the Rabbit, who is called in the Micmac tongue Ableegumooch, lived with his grandmother, waiting for better times. And truly he found it a hard matter in midwinter, when ice was on the river and snow was on the plain, to provide even for his small household. Running through the forest one day he found a lonely wigwam, where Keeoony, the Otter, lived. The lodge was on the bank of a river, and a smooth road of ice slanted from the door down to the water. And the Otter made him welcome, and directed his housekeeper to get ready to cook. Then he took the hooks on which he would string fish when he had them, and went to fetch a mess for dinner. Placing himself on top of the slide, he coasted in and under the water, and then came out with a great bunch of eels, which were soon cooked, and on which they dined.

"By my life," thought Master Rabbit, "but that is an easy way of getting a living! Truly these fishing folk have fine fare, and cheap! Can't I, who am so clever, do as well as this mere Otter? Of course I can. Why not?"

Thereupon he grew so confident of himself as to invite the Otter to dine with him on the third day after that, and so went home.

"Come on!" he said to his grandmother the next morning, "let us move our wigwam down to the lake." So they moved, and he selected a site such as the Otter had chosen for his home, and the weather being cold he made a road of ice, or a slide, down from his door to the water, and all was well.

Then the guest came at the time set, and Rabbit, calling his grandmother, told her to get ready to cook a dinner.

"But what am I to cook, grandson?" inquired the old dame.

"Truly I will see to that," said he, and made himself a nabogun, or stick to string eels. Then going to the ice path, he tried to slide like one skilled in the art, but indeed with little

44

luck, for he went first to the right side, then to the left, and so hitched and jumped until he came to the water, where he went in with a bob backwards. And this bad beginning had no better ending, since of all swimmers and divers the Rabbit is the very worst, and this one was no better than his brothers. The water was cold, he lost his breath, he struggled and was nearly drowned.

"But what on earth ails the fellow?" said the Otter to the grandmother, who was looking on in amazement.

"Well, he has seen somebody do something, and is trying to do likewise," replied the old lady.

"Ho! come out of that now," cried the Otter, "and hand me your nabogun!"

And the poor Rabbit, shivering with cold, and almost frozen, came from the water and limped into the lodge. And there he required much nursing from his grandmother, while the Otter, plunging into the stream, soon returned with a load of fish. But, disgusted at the Rabbit for attempting what he could not perform, he threw them down as a gift, and went home without tasting the meal.

MASTER RABBIT AND THE WOODPECKER GIRLS

Now Master Rabbit, though disappointed, was not discouraged, for his one virtue was that he never gave up. Wandering one day in the wilderness, he found a wigwam well filled with young women, all wearing red head-dresses—and no wonder, for they were all Woodpeckers. Now Master Rabbit was a well-bred Indian, who made himself as a melody to all voices, and so he was cheerfully bidden to stay to dinner, which he did.

Then one of the pretty girls, taking a woltes, or wooden dish, climbed a tree so swiftly that she seemed to run, and while ascending, stopping here and there and tapping now and then, took from this place and that many of those insects called by the Indians apchel-moal-timpkawal, or rice, because they so much resemble it. And note that this rice is a dainty dish for those who like it.

And when it was boiled, and they had dined, Master Rabbit again reflected, "How easily some folks live! What is to hinder

me from doing the same? Ho, you girls! Come over and dine with me the day after tomorrow!"

And having accepted this invitation, all the guests came on the day set, when Master Rabbit undertook to play woodpecker. So having taken the head of an eel-spear and fastened it to his nose to make a bill, he climbed as well as he could—and bad was the best—up a tree, and tried to get his harvest of rice. Truly he got none; and succeeded only in bruising his poor head with the fishing-point. And the pretty birds all looked and laughed, and wondered what the Rabbit was about.

"Ah!" sighed his grandmother. "I suppose he is trying again to do something which he has seen someone do. 'Tis just like him."

"Oh, come down there!" cried Miss Woodpecker, as well as she could for laughing. "Give me your dish!" And having got it, she scampered up the trunk and soon brought down a dinner. But it was long ere Master Rabbit heard the last of it from these gay tree-tappers.

MASTER RABBIT AND THE BEAR

Now, truly, one would think that after all that had befallen Master Mahtigwess, the Rabbit, that he would have enough of trying other people's trades. But his nature was such that, having once set his mighty mind to a thing, little short of sudden death would cure him. And being one day with the Bear in his cave, he beheld with great wonder how Mooin fed his folk. For having put a great pot on the fire, he did but cut a little slice from his own foot and drop it into the boiling water, where it spread and grew into a mess of meat which served for all. [This is an allusion to the bear's supposed ability to live during the winter by sucking his own paws.] Nay, there was a great piece given to Rabbit to take home to feed his family.

"Now truly," he said, "this is a thing which I can indeed do. Isn't it recorded in the family wampum that whatever a Bear can do well a Rabbit can do better?" So he invited his friend to come and dine with him, the day after tomorrow.

And the Bear being there, Rabbit said to his grandmother, "Set your pot on to boil!" And, whetting his knife on a stone, he tried to do as the Bear had done, but little did he get from his small, thin soles, though he cut himself, sadly.

"What can he be trying to do?" growled the Bear.

"Ah!" sighed the grandmother. "Something which he has seen someone else do."

"Give me the knife!" said the Bear. And getting it, he took a slice from his sole, which did him no harm, and then, what with magic and fire, he gave them a good dinner. But it was many a day ere Master Rabbit's foot got better.

ANEBEES

"One time dere was a fella call Anebees. Dat means Ant. Well, Anebees was a curious fella, and one day he decided to take a trip so he said goodby and went away and didn't say where he was going. Dat way nobody knew where to go to look for him. Anyway, Anebees went away an' he was gone a long time. Two or three year maybe. He was gone so long everybody said, "Anebees is dead. Poor Anebees." An' dey forgot about him. Den one spring morning the people look up an' dey see someone comin' down the road. It was Anebees comin' home after all dat time, an' he was dressed in furs an' had rich things around him an' he looked good.

"Now, as soon as somebody recognize that this is Anebees, he comes up an' says, 'Hello, Anebees. We thought you was dead. Where you been all this time?' An' Anebees says, 'I been a long way. I seen a lot. Why, I been clear to. . . .' An' another feller comes up an' says, 'Hello, Anebees. You been gone a long time. Where you get dem furs?' An' Anebees says, 'I been a long ways. I been. . . .' Then somebody else break in an' ask him 'bout his business.

"Right then Anebees holds up his hand an' says, 'Wait, come to a meeting tonight. Then I tell everybody where I been. I'll tell you all at once. Everybody come.' With that he starts down the path to his old woman's, and everybody asks him where he been and so on an' he say, 'I'll tell you tonight.' Well, Anebees goes into his wigwam and his woman asks him where he been all dis time an' he tell her what he tole the others an' then he goes to sleep.

"Dat night everybody is at the meetin' an' they all want to hear where Anebees has been. By an' by when everythin' is ready, Anebees comes through the crowd an' takes his place by the fire, but he has caught a ver' bad cold. Anyway he clears his throat an' stan' up an' say, 'You all know me. I am Anebees. I have been on a journey. I have been a long way. I have been to,

Suzy Dana (Mrs. Andrew Dana), Horace P. Beck, *Gluskap the Liar, and Other Indian Tales*, Freeport: The Bond Wheelwright Co., 1966, pp. 110–111.

to, to, t—kachooo!' Right then Anebees sneeze. Ki, what a sneeze! He had a ver' big head this Anebees an' a ver' small neck an' when he sneeze he sneeze his head clear off his neck. Now nobody don' know where that fella been."

HOW MASTER LOX PLAYED A TRICK ON MRS. BEAR

Don't live with mean people if you can help it. They will turn your greatest sorrow to their own account if they can. Bad habit gets to be devilish second nature. One dead herring is not much, but one by one you may make such a heap of them as to stink out a whole village.

As it happened to old Mrs. Bear, who was easy as regarded people, and thought well of everybody, and trusted all. So she took in for a house-mate another old woman. Their wigwam was all by itself, and the next neighbor was so far off that he was not their neighbor at all, but that of some other folks.

One night the old women made up a fire, and lay down and went to sleep Indian-fashion,—witkusoodijik,—heads and points, so that both could lie with their back to the fire.

Now while they were sound asleep, Lox, the Wolverine, or Indian Devil, came prowling round. Some people say it was Hespuns, the Raccoon; and it is a fact that Master Coon can play a very close game of deviltry on his own account. However, this time it must have been Lox, as you can see by the tracks.

While they were both sound asleep Lox looked in. He found the old women asleep, heads and points, and at once saw his way to a neat little bit of mischief. So, going into the woods, he cut a fine long sapling-pole of ow-bo-goos, and poked one end of it into the fire till it was a burning coal. Then he touched the soles of Mrs. Bear; and she, waking, cried out to the other, "Take care! you are burning me!" which the other denied like a thunder-clap.

Then Master Lox carefully applied the end of the hot pole to the feet of the other woman. First she dreamed that she was walking on hot sand and roasting rocks in summer-time, and then that the Mohawks were cooking her at the death-fire; and then she woke up, and, seeing where she was, began to blame Mrs. Bear for it all, just as if she were a Mohawk.

Ah, yes. Well, Master Lox, seeing them fighting in a great rage, burst out laughing, so that he actually burst himself, and fell down dead with delight.

In the morning, when the women came out, there lay a dead devil at the door. He must indeed have looked like a Raccoon this time; but whatever he was, they took him, skinned him, and dressed him for breakfast. Then the kettle was hung and the water boiled, and they popped him in. But as soon as it began to scald he began to come to life. In a minute he was all together again, alive and well, and with one good leap went clear of the kettle. Rushing out of the lodge, he grabbed his skin, which hung on a bush outside, put it on, and in ten seconds was safe in the greenwood. He just saved himself with a whole skin.

Now Master Lox had precious little time, you will say, to do any more mischief between his coming to life and running away; yet, short as the allowance was, he made a great deal of it. For even while jumping out his wits for wickedness came to him, and he just kicked the edge of the pot, so that it spilled all the scalding hot water into the fire, and threw up the ashes with a great splutter. They flew into the eyes of Dame Bear and blinded her.

Now this was hard on the old lady. She could not go out hunting, or set traps, or fish any more; and her partner, being mean, kept all the nice morsels for herself. Mrs. Bear only got the leanest and poorest of the meat, though there was plenty of the best.

One day, when she was sitting alone in the wigwam, Mrs. Bear began to remember all she had ever heard about eyes, and it came into her head that sometimes they were closed up in such a way that clever folk could cut them open again. So she got her knife and sharpened it, and, carefully cutting a little, saw the light of day. Then she was glad indeed, and with a little more cutting found that she could see as well as ever. And as good luck does not come single, the very first thing she beheld was an abundance of beautiful fat venison, fish, and maple-sugar hung up overhead.

Dame Bear said nothing about her having recovered her eyesight. She watched all the cooking going on, and saw the daintiest dinner, which all went into one platter, and a very poor lot of bones and scraps placed in another. Then, when she was called to eat, she simply said to the other woman, who kept the best, "Well, you have done well for yourself!"

The other saw that Mrs. Bear had recovered her sight. She was frightened, for Dame Bear was by far the better man of the two. So she cried out, "Bless me! what a mistake I've made! Why, I gave you the wrong dish. You know, my dear sister, that I always give you the best because you are blind."

VOICES 1

SIPSIS—JEAN THOMPSON

I was born on Indian Island thirty years ago. My mother's father was a Mohawk, but his mother was a Penobscot, Elizabeth Ranco Philips. Then my father's mother is a Penobscot Indian, my father's father was a Chippewa Indian, John Thomas from Michigan, so if I follow my grandmothers back I'm a Penobscot, if I follow my grandfathers back I'm a Chippewa-Mohawk.

Both my mother and father were registered Penobscot Indians. My mother, due to financial difficulties—probably emotional difficulties, too, I don't know, left my brother and myself alone. I was two; my brother was five. My father and my grandmother and aunt took care of us. Then when I was about thirteen I left with my aunt to live in Gardiner. She is a white woman, still living in Gardiner. She married my father's brother. She brought us up, and I went to high school in Gardiner and college.

The only consciousness I had of being an Indian was, "You're an Indian and you should be proud of it." That's the statement I remember. But you know you can say, "You're a nurse and you should be proud of it." Being a nurse, you know, you have certain qualifications, certain things you've got to do. As far as being an Indian, probably what's expected of you is wearing feathers and living in a teepee. That's what was expected of me as I was going through school—here I am, I look like an Indian and I wear braids—so when I was in college there was this young fellow next to me and he said, he says: "Let me ask you a question. I've been sitting next to you for about six months now. Do Indians still live in a teepee?" I thought he was pulling my leg, you know, so I says, "Yeah, I live in a teepee. As a matter of fact, in the fall my brothers go out and hunt deer, and they use the skins to cover the teepee." He believed me for about six months. It was at the end of the school year he come over and he says, "You know I was talking with your neighbor in Gardiner (which is not a reservation you know—it's about six miles from Augusta) and she said you don't live in a teepee; you live in a house just like us, just like she does." He said, "I won't believe you after this."

So I went to high school in Gardiner and I went to Gordon College in Massachusetts. Of course I was the only Indian there. Everything seemed so, so—like there was a circle there and I was outside looking in. It seemed so unrelated to myself. I was brought up in a Christian atmosphere. You go to church every Sunday, young people's fellowship on Saturday night, read my Bible every day and pray: say grace before every meal, no swear words, don't drink beer or smoke. . . . Christ was the center of your life, Christ was the center of the universe, of everything you do, so when I got away from the college atmosphere and got back to reality I found the education I got didn't really relate to what was real; and the thing that is real and had been real for years and centuries was my people's lives. . . . These things which I'd never read about were very real. The only thing I knew about Indians was you're an Indian, be proud of it. What the real things were that my ancestors did, that I *should* be proud of, I didn't know. I'd never read in school or in my home about Indians. Ken knew more about Indians when I met him than I did.

I had a bachelor's degree in psychology. You can't do very much except social work. . . . After I went to college I came back to Maine and worked in Augusta. I lived in Gardiner and did social work. I met Ken there. He was doing social work, too.

KEN THOMPSON

I'd already graduated from Colby. I was born in Sarasota, Florida, but I came to Freeport with my family who were from Freeport originally. I grew up there. When I graduated I was doing social work. It was just a coincidence I was living in Augusta because I really wanted to be in the Portland area. I wanted to get ahead. In order to get ahead and become a supervisor, I'd had to get a master's degree in social work, which was two years, but I didn't really want to spend the rest of my life in social work. I was thinking twenty years ahead, and I hated to think I'd spend twenty years doing what I was doing right there or in a supervisory capacity. You know it's like a lot of jobs. You think you're going to work with people, but the better you are, the higher promotion you get, the further away you get from working with people and pretty soon you have—I really think Health and Welfare is more concerned with paper work than working with people—the whole bureaucracy. I couldn't see it so I thought one more year and I could go to law school. Even if I didn't practice law, at least it would be beneficial for the things I did.

We were married about a year after we met, in 1964, and then we went to Portland where I went to law school. I graduated in 1968. Then we moved to Gardiner. I was Deputy Commissioner of Indian Affairs for that one year, 1968–1969, under Ed Hinkley. He was the Commissioner of Indian Affairs, actually the first commissioner after the department was set up. That was after we'd started the *Maine Indian Newsletter*. We started it in 1967 when I was in law school, and in 1968 when I graduated, we had it going.

JEAN

We did the newsletter mainly long-distance from the Island, although I'd come back to vote in the tribal elections.

KEN

Indians are franchised for county, state, and national elections but not local, unless for example they live in Old Town and not on the Island. . . . Indians were made citizens of the U.S. in 1924, but it wasn't until the 1950s for all reasonable purposes that they were made citizens of Maine, because they were given the right to vote in every election except the House of Representatives, and it wasn't until 1964 or 1966 that the legislature gave them the right to vote in House elections in the state of Maine. Many Indians don't vote in state elections because they feel they're giving up their Indian citizenship. Many of them feel they're Penobscots first and U.S. citizens second.

JEAN

I retired from doing social work for the state of Maine after five years. I said I was going to return to homemaking. So I had another baby, Susan, and she was born in April, and about two weeks before she was born this fellow had contacted the Indian Affairs Office where Ken was working, wondering if there were any Indians interested in a leadership development program designed for Indians, or anybody in the whole Northeast here, to spark some sort of innovative programs in education among rural youth. So for Indians it was highlighted because Indians are part of the rural area, plus they wanted more Indians because they figured we might need the incentive and the spark, I suppose.

So Ken came home and told me about it, and they contacted Paul Jenkins who was coordinator of the program. He came to see me the next day and talked to me about it. I was telling about my experience leaving the Reservation and getting an education. If I had remained on the Reservation, my education would have been somewhat less because of the circumstances—maybe economic, maybe social, maybe psychological—all those factors could have entered into preventing my getting an education. So we thought that would be a good topic to pursue if I were going to be engaged in the program. Find out why Indian kids drop out at a higher rate than white children.

I made out my application and was accepted for the program. The baby was born, and I was nursing and would have to take her with me wherever I go. I went to New Brunswick in July before the program started. There were about sixty Indian kids there who had dropped out of school and were interested in education. They got together and pushed all the adults out and decided they were going to do something about forming a school or do something about their Indianness, their Indian traditions and language and culture. This is what they thought was missing in the present school system. I stayed there a week with Susan and came back home so excited by all this talk. I asked Ken if he wouldn't come with me. We could travel together and go as far as the money went and share these experiences together.

We were still living in Gardiner so for the summer of '69, from July on, Ken and I traveled; we traveled until November—gosh, thirty thousand miles I guess in a Volkswagen bus, from Nova Scotia across Canada to Saskatchewan, to Manitoba six hundred miles above Winnipeg and down to New Mexico and Arizona and Seattle. We established contacts in Akwesasne in New York State. This is where the traditional people live who are still holding on to their languages and customs. So we pursued the contacts they had given us, starting out in Nova Scotia, and we found differences in reservations all over the country, very slight because of the division between the Indian who has gone the white man's way and the Indian who remains traditional, even though he doesn't know it, but still holds on to the way of life, trapping and fishing. (The Micmacs are in Nova Scotia, the Malacites in New Brunswick, but generally speaking there is a great deal of overlapping and intermarriage like among the Penobscot and Passamaquoddies.)

After we got to Manitoba we thought if we were ever going to do something for the Indian the best place to be would be where it all started, on the Island. So after we finished traveling we settled on the Island in a rented house, and Ken set up his law practice in Old Town. We collected all our thoughts and decided if leadership was going to be developed through this particular program, or an idea started so that people could be stimulated, it would have to start on the Reservation, and I couldn't very well do it in Gardiner. That's what propelled us back—well, myself anyway—Ken had never lived there—to continue to be a stimulant on the Island as far as getting the Indian school dropout question settled there.

The very basic thing in school dropouts is your Indian identity. You didn't find it in textbooks or in courses, but your Indian identity was something passed down to you from your relations and your neighbors on the Reservation. They felt in school that it was denied them, very much so, and those students who denied themselves this identity and took on another identity—a white one—were the ones that were able to succeed, and those that tried to take two identities found it very difficult. And because the school system didn't relate to their identity, they preferred to drop out. And even though they could say it was basically for economic reasons, I felt it was related to their identity. So in order to attack this problem of identity I chose a rather extreme method: returning—you know, coming back and being very much a stimulant of Indian thought—agitation, in order to get young people thinking along these lines.

In all my courses in college except for sociology—the only one in which Indians were mentioned briefly—I never learned anything about my people. My American history course was very boring to me—about all those *Indian* wars! So I had to feel isolated from it; I put up a shield so it wouldn't offend me. I'd ignore them; maybe *they* ignored me. It occurred to me it was my own people they were talking about, Indian marauders, Indian slaughters. So for years I would stand up and salute the flag, pledge allegiance, and sing the national anthem not realizing what I was doing. . . .

When the kids were invited to go to Waterville to celebrate Maine's one hundred fiftieth birthday last year, Penny Norwood and about four or five other students and myself were asked to be a part of this program, and there was going to be a senator from the legislature and several of the businessmen in the town and a college professor from Colby and the mayor, all those "dignitaries" on the platform—then us. So they had a little program they passed out, and we're sitting up there in native dress, leather and beads and headbands and feathers, talking things over, and the kids were whispering. So they ask me, "Look here on the program.

It says 'Salute to the Flag' and then it says 'The National Anthem'," and they said "Are you going to be standing up for these things," and I thought, "Well, gee, that's right. I'm supposed to be part of this, but I guess I won't be standing up for these things," and they buzzed back, "Well, we won't either." So the woman in charge of the program come over, and I asked to talk with her, and I said, "It may look funny to you, but on this particular part of the program you may see us sitting down because we're Indians." So she says, "Okay." So she went over to talk to the principal of the school, and he come over in a hurry, and he says, "I understand you won't be standing up," and I says, "That's right, we won't be," and he says "Well, would you mind explaining it to the audience?"—there were about four hundred students and about two hundred townspeople—and I said, "I'd be glad to." So I did. The kids in the audience were whistling and cheering.

I said a few words in Indian—words I knew!—and then I explained maybe it looked funny to you to see us sitting down, but, I says, "You know we're original people; this is our land here, you know. You people are *new* here. This is your allegiance to your flag, this is your song, and we respect you for it, we listen to you, but we're going to show you something. We're going to show you our way of doing things. This is our national dress, and when we'll be dancing, we'll show you our traditions. This flag is your tradition. And another thing," I says, "don't applaud us, you know, because we're not monkeys; we're not performing for you; we're just showing you that we can live together peacefully." I shook my war club and went on dancing. So afterwards those kids that were there just seemed to come alive in their seats, and when it was over, they wanted to come over and touch us and see if we were real!

The Negroes and the other minorities want something that has been denied them, which they say is equal rights, of which the white people have more than the Negroes have. They want equal opportunities, for education, for employment, social graces, so to speak. They want to be treated as brothers. And the Indian, speaking for myself that is—I've been treated equally. The only place I've experienced a coldness, a rejection is down south. The white people down there feel this way about anybody that's not a lighter color than they are or who don't wear the same clothes they wear. So far as the Indian goes, this equal rights has a basis in their land. If they had received legal equality, if the white law had given them equality, treated them as brothers instead of savages, instead of ignorant people, then we'd still be holding onto more land than we've lost, and we could be very wealthy tenant holders, leasing our land to these big lumber companies, chemical plants, electrical companies all up and down the river. And if they had treated us equally in that one respect from the start, this would have made all the difference in the end. But they didn't. And this is what makes a difference between us and the Negro people and other minorities; that the land question is very basic. They are not aboriginals. The Indian was the original owner of America—and still is. It has an economic basis, too. The Indian lived off the land; it was his means of living; ecologically and educationally, to be able to do this without showing a profit. It was very economical and very spiritual at the same time. I can't picture myself as taking back Manhattan because it's a jungle now. What use is it there now, all covered over with pavement and garbage on top of that? But Maine isn't. Some professor down here at the University of Maine, I think he made a slip of the tongue, but he says the Penobscot River's a gold mine.

What he meant was if we clean up the river, the salmon will come and we'll all make a profit. You know the islands in the river here are just like owning a supermarket. The vegetables and fruits and nuts and berries we can live on. You can survive up there. But you get some nut who doesn't know anything up there, he'll probably kill himself.

KEN

There are about one hundred and forty-seven islands in the Penobscot. They run from Indian Island all the way down to Matawamkeag. About three weeks ago I got a chance to travel upriver by plane with four University of Maine students: Earleen Paul, Ricky Mitchell, Paul Francis, and George Tomah. They're all Penobscots doing research this summer on the tribe.

When you're working with the islands and reading about them, if you see them, really know which ones are which, at least how they look and what they're like it's a thrill. There's so much land there! The pilot flew around Indian Island several times so we could take pictures, and anything we wanted to look at he'd circle around.

Two of the students are working strictly on research with Tony Kayliss in Bangor, who has done some research on the Passamaquoddies. Basically it's that he's had experience in research and he's trying to teach them how to avoid the pitfalls. The other two are doing a combination of research and some practical work for the tribe out of the Mainstream office. At least one of them is attending every meeting and function that takes place on the Reservation, mainly to try to coordinate everything. If they can get it together, they can swap information with everyone. It seems like you could go to a meeting every night on the Island, there's so many.

One of the basic issues on the Island is the new Tribal Hall. That's very important to them, to have a meeting place. The Tribal Hall now is in very bad condition. Of course employment is always a problem. Housing— a lot of people have to live in very inadequate housing and yet they have a feeling of security because it's theirs; nobody can kick them out. They don't have to pay property taxes because there are none. Education is always a problem: the kids always tell that when they *do* mention Indians in school it's always how the Indians raided a village or a wagon train and killed everybody, and everyone in the room will turn around and look at the Indian in the class, and he'll have to apologize for being Indian, saying, "We don't do that now," when actually that's only half the story. They were protecting their homeland!

JEAN

If you talk with individual people, you find individual grievances. Some may be with the Agent's Office, some with the Priest's house, some with the Mainstream office. As many people as you talk to, you'll find grievances.

I think my grievance would be the intervention of the white—well, the foreign—let's not color it. Let's call it the intervention of another person's philosophy or way of life which has been going on now for almost three hundred years and which is almost impossible now to change, impossible even to talk about. As a result our people have become foreigners to their land, to their traditions and their language, so any mention of these things would cause the bristles in their backs to jump up. They become very upset at the mention even of any one of these things. This is your basic grievance. All other things tie into it.

There would have to be a very basic individual desire to return to these traditions. . . . The return to the land would supply all the foods. Everybody could live off the land so they wouldn't have to be dependent upon anybody else. Then your language is next because the old people would still have it, so it would be easier to return then to your traditions. But the land itself would be the easiest thing; there's plenty of game. 'Course, once you let the word out you'd have ten thousand game hunters from New York coming up! But we're really talking about a school of thought not particularly a school or a teaching system. You're talking about a whole different way of learning things. Learning how to *survive*, really.

KEN

Of course if you talk to many of the Indians who are assimilated, many of them *want* to live like white people. These people want to have schools that teach Latin, etcetera. I think the most difficult group is the middle-aged group that overlaps with the one that was too young when the Second World War came but were of age during the Korean War, and so they were there. For instance you could even trim it down to the ones that belong to the American Legion and the VFW. Some of them are *very* Indian; some won't vote in elections, but they feel that everyone should serve in the Army and no one should dodge the draft. . . . I never would have expected to find that on a reservation, but one fellow told me that with all the things wrong with this country, the countries he visited during the Second World War, like Burma, those areas of French Indochina, Thailand, and India—he mentioned that no matter how bad things are here, they could have been an awful lot worse like they were over there. This is his reason for supporting the government, and it's a lot more reasonable than the fact that the government says we hate somebody this week so we're going to have a war against them and everybody has to hate 'em and next week we'll be friends with them and hate somebody else. That's not his reasoning, which is that we're pretty fortunate in living where we are. But *he* was pretty fortunate, or at least his people were, before the white man ever came.

So it's the old people and the young people—the New Indians—who want to do it, the others don't seem to want to be Indians.

Speaking of the old people, I met a woman who's ninety-eight years old in a nursing home in Orono—Mary Jane Mitchell Loring. I'd never met her before. She's very much alert and alive. She used to smoke a pipe when she was younger, and she said—she was talking Indian, so her family were telling me what she was saying—the thing she kept saying was, "If I could only go home and smoke my pipe I'd be happy." She can say a few words in English. She can understand you, but the few English words she can say are "Thank you," and "That's nice," little things like that.

Her grandson—he's a grandfather himself—he was telling me that every summer he used to bring her home for a few days for a visit, but he said it got so it was impossible to get her back to the nursing home. She just said, "Well, I'm not going." She's very smart. It's a shame. There are several Indian women over there—at least two who died this winter—and Jean's grandfather died, too. He was a Mohawk, but he came here as a young man. He was in a home in Bangor. And all these people, when they get old—they've lived their whole lives on the Island, and it means so much to them, and they stick them in a nursing home off the Reservation, and there they spend their last years when they could be having friends dropping in and memories of houses and things around them, and they can't do it.

I suggested to two, three people that we ought to try and get a nursing home over here. It wouldn't be a big profit-making thing, but at least it would keep the Indians over here. It's such a shame, you know. You take a woman ninety-eight years old, think of the changes she's seen. She lived here when just about everyone was *all* Indian, before everyone was intermarried, and yet now she's over there and all she sees is white people. And these other Indians who were in the nursing home she couldn't get to see because she was too old to climb the stairs, and the others sometimes wouldn't be themselves; they wouldn't know who was around them. Sometimes she knew they were there, she knew one of them was there, but she didn't get to see her. The same with two other people, Pauline Shea and Teddy Baer; they were pretty near, across the hall. It's like taking someone—say they grew up in England and say they shipped them over to France and made them live the rest of their life in France with a foreign language and a foreign way of life, a foreign way of doing things.

The Indians used to look after their old people. There used to be a place for the elderly at Pauline Shea's on Orson Island. Pauline used to take old people in. Even with these exceptions I think Indians do take care of their older people much better than white people do. I guess that's also true of colored people, too. In fact the Chinese do, too. White people—the first thing they think of is getting them in a nursing home, getting rid of them. They're building these homes like in Florida where they can all live in a village or something.

One of the things that made the young people conscious of being Indian was becoming aware all of a sudden that there were other reservations and tribes. Whenever we traveled, we'd take as many as we could with us, even when we lived in Gardiner. When we got up here, of course, we took even more. I think the newsletter helped—we'd print a lot of news from other reservations. Many people have been to some other reservations, but there's a lot of people here who really didn't have any other contacts except Tobique, Peter Dana Point, and Pleasant Point. Aside from those Malacite and Passamaquoddy reservations they just didn't know anything about other reservations. Some may have visited them earlier, but they'd either forgotten or it didn't have any meaning for them. So this traveling and meeting other Indians is important. And of course there are more and more Indians coming here from other places, stopping by people's houses. And some people here are making regular trips to Akwesasne and Onondaga, to some of the Iroquois reservations, which is pretty good. In fact, some people who had traveled years ago and who had stopped are starting up again! I think this is really opening their eyes when they meet other Indians who are proud of being Indian without having to wear it on their sleeve and keep saying so.

I found it good to go to some of those meetings where there are just Indians. I'd be on the grounds, but I couldn't attend. It seemed good they were very natural about it, about white people not being allowed at the meetings. Some of our people felt pretty good when they discovered there were people still doing that, because you'd go to some of the meetings here and the Priest was at the meeting—a tribal meeting where the tribe conducts its own business—they'd have the white Priest there or they might have the white Commissioner of Indian Affairs for the State of Maine or his Deputy, or the white Indian Agent, always somebody white there to sort of guide them and tell them what to do. A lot of these kids here, especially, they went to other places where there were just Indians and nobody else—there might be white people like myself around, you know—but just Indians at the meetings, and I really think that had a big influence on some.

JEAN

One of the things the North American Traditional Indian Movement wants is to bring about unity among the people. I'm not speaking about all the people. I don't mean let's all grasp our hands, we're brothers, or rally around the flag, that type of thing. It's to open up thinking along traditional lines so those that have the inclination and energy can channel their efforts into helping restore or revive traditions and return to the land—there seems to be a real feeling for the land up in this area that also involves taking cases to court, etcetera—or even if they want to, return to basket making or starting language classes.

I see the Penobscots as two people, as a nation and as a tribe that's dependent upon somebody else. The nation is still in its embryonic or infant stages, so to speak. There can't be independence now. People aren't even aware they can be independent. Those people who think we can be independent are looked upon as nuts, probably all doped up. So you have two frames of thought.

You know, one of the nicest memories I have of growing up on the Island is being able to run through the woods freely without cutting your feet on glass and swimming in the river without getting impetigo all over you. There was one year when we started getting impetigo, when I was ten years old. I have scars on my legs from it, but before that we all swam in the river. Yes, running through the woods and living out there from sunup to sundown, and picking berries—this is what I remember most. Being free and able to go anywhere on the Island. In the city or in another community you couldn't do this, there might be some kidnapper or child molester lurking somewhere, or some other danger you weren't aware of. Living in a community of say eight thousand people like Gardiner you never know who lives there and what they're like. Here you knew who the people were—some of them were your relatives.

KEN

First I ever knew about Indians was when I was in eighth grade. It just happened there were two Indians who moved to Freeport that year from the Island—Joe and John Davis. John and I got to be pretty good friends. They were twins, but Joe was a year behind, and he and I had the same girlfriend. She lived near me, but he had to walk two miles to go down to her house and of course I'd be there! That type of thing. But it turned out they were Jean's half brothers. 'Course I never knew that back then. But we started studying the history of Maine, which is full of Maine Indians, and I never remember the book as being such a bad one. There seemed to be more dates and statistics, rather than editorializing about how bad the Indians were, saying the savage Indians did this or that. But it was even more interesting having these Indian boys there because they used to tell us about different things.

After I met Jean we'd come up to the Island, and in law school I did research for my thesis on the Penobscot treaties. So gradually I learned more and more about Indians. I'm aware of so much more material than

I've had the time to read. You can know *where* to find all these things, but to read them would take hundreds of hours. It was really a gradual thing, but there was a point after I met Jean when I felt I wanted to learn as much about Indians as I could. I didn't want to be one of these experts like you see at the University of Maine in the anthropology department, where you go and ask them and they tell you it has to be this way because this is what I found, and you go to the next one and he says it's has to be *my* way, which turns out to be the opposite of the first guy!

JEAN

Three young white kids come by last week and wanted to know all about Indian herbs—in one evening, you know. And I says, "Look, it's going to take you a lifetime to know all there is to know."

KEN

They were just passing through, but if they ever come back I was going to tell them if they want to know anything about Indians they should change their approach. They should come with the idea of meeting people and talking with them and not pushing things. Let the Indians decide when they want to tell them something. They came, and here I was right in the middle of something—two guys from Mainstream were helping me put up the floor on my house, put up the foundation. It was a chance to really get some work done. We were lacking the sand; we had to go after that, and Jim Sappier come up and said he'd help us get the sand so I could get it finished right up that night or the next morning. We had the cement bags all opened and ready to use, and this kid come up and starts talking to me about Yin and Yang, you know Japanese philosophy. I told him I was familiar with all that. I was a philosophy major at Colby, and I had just come across a book that day on Yin and Yang, and he was telling us a lot of stuff we knew because we're as interested in organic farming as anyone.

JEAN

He wanted us to grow rice! . . . John Stevens sent him down here. He said "Go down and see the Penobscots." So this kid starts right out, "I know you're very busy but I just want to ask you a few questions."

KEN

If he'd waited an hour—he'd been around a couple of hours; I'd seen the car there—if he'd just waited until we finished.

JEAN

I don't know where he was from, and I don't know where he was going either. You give them a couple of hours of your time, you know, and then they up and go. You never hear from them, never see them.

KEN

They visited Martin Neptune for a while. Martin was over helping me two days later; we were putting those cross pieces on the two by sixes up there, and he was waiting to get the mail because his check was supposed to come in. He hadn't been paid for three weeks, and so all of a sudden he looked up and he says, "There's a white Volkswagen going by, looks like that group that was here the other day." He was afraid to go home and check the mail because he didn't want to get involved with them. So I said I think if they come back again I'll tell them their whole approach is wrong.

JEAN

I think I told them.

KEN

That's probably why they didn't come back! Then Martin said, "I wish they would come back now when my check hasn't come." He was really mad because they told him it would be there at least by two weeks and here it was three weeks and he hadn't got paid. Well, you know he's gotta live. And he said, "I'll give them an example of the Indian temper when it gets worked up. All this frustration on the checks—I'll take it out on them!" But it wasn't them as it turned out, it was somebody else.

JEAN

I think I told them; I says, "We got a book here that says the white man will wander the earth and he won't be satisfied until he steps on everybody's land. . . ." I says, "You're heading west, aren't you?" And he says, "Yeah," and I says, "What you gonna be doing, wandering the rest of your life?" He says, "Well, what can we do to settle down and find out?" And I says, "You've got to be adopted by Indians, I suppose!"

KEN

One of those kids wanted me to read this book he had on organic gardening, but it was mostly in Japanese, so I told him; I said, "I just wouldn't have time to look at it because I'm reading a lot of legal things during the day," and I said, "I'm doing some work for the tribe, digging up old deeds, and I'm working for Mainstream, and I have my own interests in reading. I read *Organic Gardening and Farming*, and we have a couple of books on it, too, and those are the things I either want to read or have to read." I said it wouldn't be fair for him to leave the book because I just wouldn't get around to reading it, so he said he'd leave it anyway!

You see, this guy, that's good for him, for what *he* wants. Like with me, I'm very interested in organic gardening, and that's what I want but I don't force it on other people. Both of us—Jean and I—thought this independently because we both talked to him. Jean talked to all three, and Martin did, too, and all of us agreed they seemed like fanatics. You know you see these religious fanatics no matter what you're talking about, no matter what you're doing; they always seem to get you onto religion. This guy was a real fanatic on grains. You know, this Yin and Yang. You have vegetables on the one hand which are feminine, negative; meats which are positive; and grains are in the middle. If you eat grain supposedly you've got it made. He told me he'd been living on grain for four years, and he was very healthy and had never had a cold; yet to look at him—no muscles at all and skinny. It would be insulting to him if I said it, but I really would like to have told him that he couldn't be doing this kind of work we were doing right then—the four of us standing there—looking the way he does. I mean if he could eat that way and do the work that we were doing, then it would show it's healthy, but when you look as white and anemic like he does, then either he should be eating more grain—

JEAN

and doing less reading! I doubt that he even grew his own grain; he said that he just bought it. This type of religious fanatic is able to speak the language and be all excited and pass it on, but to do it, to actually get right down living this type of a life—this is what they were looking for. This is what they were heading west for, wandering from place to place.

KEN

When we were on our trip out around Santa Fe where they have these big communes, we stopped at a gas station and these hippies came over and started talking. I'm sure they took one look at us and said, "They're some of us." One kid said he was evading the draft and leaving for Canada, and when we got to Canada, they saw our Maine plates on the camper, and every kid we ran into it seemed would give us the peace sign.

Like the Hopis—they asked these kids why they were there. And some of these kids actually answered that they thought *they*—the Indians—had something and they wanted to find out what it was. That's the thing, they see the Hopis like that as "having something," but the Hopis are out in that hot sun planting corn, and they have to plant it about a foot deep so it won't grow too high. And they're out there planting their melons and their food, and there's no shade, and that's how they live; they don't live just sitting around and talking; they go out and do a lot of hard work.

JEAN

But these people that wander are searching for something, searching for an identity. The Indians have an identity already, but in a way this interest helps the young Indian people to return because it's a fad—even the long hair because they say, "Well, that's the way Indians used to look so that's all right for Indians!" For example, there's a Catholic high school in Bangor that a lot of Indian kids go to. So Carol Dana, Lolar now—she graduated this past June—she wore this paper headband to class one day, and the assistant principal said, "You'd better take that thing off," and he tore it off her, and she says, "I don't think I should because I'm an Indian and it's part of my native dress." So he says, "You put it on and I'll report you to the principal." She put it back on again, and she told the principal why she was doing it, and they had a meeting, which I went to, with Lou Doyle, who is Director of Human Relations for Indian Services here in Maine, out of the Diocese there. Carol talked with them so they finally decided that only *Indian* kids could wear headbands to high school!

The Indian people that know me know *me*. The white people would only want to know I'd been to college and have a bachelor's degree. There was this woman from Limestone that come down to see me because she had heard there was an Indian woman down here who knew something about something. This to me is the thing I'd like to be known for—an *Indian*—and I think this is a personal thing. As far as psychology goes or social work of the educational system or federal intervention or the salary of each person on the Reservation, I don't care to be expert in those areas, and I wouldn't want to be looked upon as the encyclopedia of this particular bit of Indian information. I'd want to hold special information for special people. If not special information then to be aware of special things: if I want to know about a different medicine, there's a person that knows about it, and some people would say, "Well, gee, I got an illness here. Is there anybody you know?" and I'd say, "Well, *she* knows something"—just pass the information on this way; or like Martin Neptune's grandfather knows a lot about medicine—I'd want to stimulate him to share it. Just to know that among the Indians there are people aware of these things, that there's a certain network among the Indians: we all don't know it all, but each one knows a little bit. To me this is a very basic feeling that I have—that I don't know it all and I never would be able to—but the fact that I'm an Indian is enough. I'm part of a community and part of a land that has a great heritage and history, and the fact that centuries have proven this out as compared to centuries of roving and wandering on the part of the white man—the fact that I'm a Penobscot, in other words—is the most basic and most important thing to me. The second is that I have Penobscot children. And the third is that I've married a white person. People say, "Well, if you're an Indian, how come you married a white man?" I don't know. Maybe love. Maybe it's a coincidence of events that come to be. There's people living together on a common land; we've got to learn to live together and love one another in order to protect ourselves and protect our land, and preserve it.

KEN

I don't feel alienated not being an Indian. It's a funny thing but sometimes when I first lived here, people would tell a story or they'd say something or make some comment about white people, and they'd always excuse themselves in front of me. But after a while they got so they'd just do it anyway, knowing how I'd feel. I could sympathize with them, and I could appreciate why they've developed these feelings and resentments, and I think you have to start now with what they *have* now.

Somebody asked me a year ago when I was going to be accepted on the Reservation, and I told him I was accepted already among people I considered important. As far as the young people go, I'm pretty well accepted—and many of the older people and the people who mainly didn't accept me aren't ones I'd consider real Indians: they're the ones I consider white people like myself, although they do have Indian blood in them, but they're people who are very ambitious and economic minded.

I wasn't going to do anything to be accepted; I was just going to be myself. I feel pretty good here; I really don't feel out of place. At first I did, but now I feel right at home here, and I'd rather live here than any-where else. It's a different type of life. Things are quieter. You can go to a meeting, and you don't have to get all dressed up. In fact, if you do dress up, people will comment on it. People here are carefree and easy-going, and yet you get some people who seem to be bitter enemies, but the minute one of them gets into trouble of some kind, everybody's right there to help him.

I didn't come here with the idea of helping anyone, but if there's any-thing I can do for anyone, I always try to do it.

MARTIN NEPTUNE

It's her nerves and her heart. She has strokes sometimes, and other times it can just be her nerves. Like this time they didn't know which it was, her heart or her nerves. The doctor said he'd treat it as a heart attack. She was in intensive care in St. Joseph's in Bangor. They just took her out yesterday. Both times she said she could hear that death rattle. My mother's about forty-nine, fifty. She just worries a lot. She's always worrying about us kids. I think she really likes it better down Connecticut; then again she misses her home. She don't really care for the Island up here. I don't think she cares for the place, but she likes to visit. She said she really doesn't want to stay here. She was born down to Pleasant Point, down in Perry. That's where she was when she had that attack, the day before. This woman that come up with her—they went down, and she said she woke up that morning, went right down and brushed her teeth, and she went back upstairs and opened the window. She said the air was just so fresh up there. She opened up that window, and she said it just felt so good to feel that ocean air. She hasn't been down there maybe once or twice in the past six or seven years. I think she really misses it. When she come up, she was telling us she'd really like to move back down there when she retires. She'd kinda like to go back down. She's Passamaquoddy; my father's Penobscot. He come up overnight and stayed one day. She was getting a lot better then so he went back.

I've got three brothers and two sisters. We all moved to Manchester, Connecticut, in September of 1967. We went down because of the work. That's why my parents went down. I didn't want to go down at all, but I was under age and my mother told me back then—I was kinda rowdy, always getting in trouble—and she said she'd worry about me and she'd feel a lot better if I went down so I says, "Okay, I'll go down and I'll try to go back to school and see how it is."

We got there a week before school opened, and I went in first day. Down there they have to be all dressed up in school. Coming from Maine, I had on jeans and a jersey, just the way I always went to school. I go walking in, and I seen all these kids just looking at me like I was a freak or something. I went in one class and sat down, and the teacher introduced me. She said, "Well, we have a new student. His name is Martin Neptune; he's a Penobscot Indian," like that, and everybody turns round and just stares at me. I really felt like a freak down there. In the second class they did the same thing. In the third class I seen the teacher; she turned around and looked at me; she says, "Oh yeah, we have a new student—" As soon as she said that, I walked right out; I didn't go back there again.

I couldn't understand it. They called the teams at the school the Manchester Indians. That's what they have on their basketball suits, and there wasn't an Indian at all in that school. The same here in Old Town. Just recently they put that banner up in Old Town High School in the gym—YOU'RE IN INDIAN COUNTRY—and there's hardly any Indian kids that go out for any teams in that school. Maybe a couple'll go out for baseball; once in a while one will go out for track. Very few finish school. I heard there was something like a ninety percent dropout rate between the two reservations, Passamaquoddy and Penobscot.

I was seventeen when I went to Connecticut. When I first went down there I was just turning eighteen, and I was thinking about whether I should sign up for the draft or not. By then I was starting to realize how much people had done to the Indians as a whole. When I was up here on the Island I was always being influenced by the older people. They were always saying you gotta do this, you gotta do that. You get it all the time. You gotta go in the service; you gotta get a job. You gotta forget your language, forget your culture, and all this stuff. You get that right on the Island. They don't say it outright; they just do it so you don't even notice it. So when I was down there, I could think pretty clearly for myself without everybody around. I used to go out a lot of times just by myself and ride around and just think. And so when I turned eighteen, I had to sign up for the draft—down there. I just kept putting it off and putting it off. I was thinking why should I go and fight for this land, for these people who have taken so much away from us? I really didn't feel like I had anything to fight for, but at the time I couldn't get a good job down there. I didn't have a high school diploma or anything, and I was thinking if I could go into some branch of the service without going over there and fighting, and get a high school diploma or learn some trade, it would be worth it. So I went around to all the recruiters, and the majority of them wouldn't take me because of the record I had, and the only ones that would were the Army and the Marines. The record was intoxication up in Maine; they were both juvenile offenses, and they weren't even supposed to be listed, so I didn't include them in the forms I filled out, but they called to check, and they found out about it so they refused me.

So I went to the Army and the Marines, and they said, "Well, we can put you in a certain field," but they wouldn't let me sign anything that guaranteed me I'd get this or I'd get out. I was talking to this Army recruiter, and he's promising me all this, and he says, "Why don't you go home? As soon as I get an opening—" It was in aircraft electronics, I was thinking about the field of electronics then. He says, "I'll let you know." Meanwhile my parents kept after me: you gotta sign up; you gotta sign up or you'll get in trouble." My mother had had an attack already she was so worried, so I thought it would be better if I did go in and sign up. I went down to the local board—I think it was around October, November—I was late. So they signed me up, and after that I was really regretting that I did sign up, and in the meantime I was working and they didn't call me. They didn't call me when I was nineteen either. I got my high school equivalency in January, 1970, and about that time I came back to Maine. I got in some trouble up here, so then I took off to California, hitchhiked out.

The second time I got caught up here drinking the Judge said, "If I see you again I'm gonna lock you up for sixty to ninety days." He says, "I'll get you for at least sixty days." I'd already been in jail here before for ten days and that was it. After being in there—it just isn't natural; they got you locked up, you can't go anywhere, you can't move. All I could see all day was just the sky; the windows were way up. I almost went crazy. You feel just like an animal locked up in there. When I got caught the third time a guy came and bailed me out for fifty bucks. I had to pay him ten dollars down, and I gave him what I had in my pocket, nine dollars and something, and he said, "I'll let you go for that, but if you don't show up I'll send the police and the State Police." At that time I thought he could so I says, "I'm getting out of here." I went back to Connecticut, and the next day I went over to the kids who were working at the hospital with me, and I bummed about fifty bucks, and I took off for California. I was going to Alcatraz, but I never did make it there.

It took me four days to get to California, and I stayed in Sacramento for four days at this place just for Indians called Friendship House, run by a couple of priests. I called my mother on the way out; I didn't want to worry her, and every time I called she was crying. So when I got out there I told her where I was, and the people there told me I could stay for two weeks and I wouldn't have to worry about a job. They said they'd find me one if I wanted. When I called my mother she said she'd got in touch with a lawyer, and he said they couldn't come out of state and get me, and I says, "You mean I went all the way to California for nothing?" She told me if I'd come back, the lawyer would work on it and not to worry about them coming down to get me 'cause they couldn't do it. So she sent me out plane money, and I took off.

I was 1-A then. And last July when I just turned twenty I got my draft notice. I was joking about it then, I says, "Look what I got for a birthday present." I had my induction notice, so it was after I got that, I says, "I'm getting out of here; I'm going back to Maine; let them come up and get me after that!"

That's when I met Ken and Jean. They were down the house in Manchester. They dropped by the house on their way through, coming back to Maine after their trip. No, wait a minute, it wasn't then. It was in March when I come up, and then I got my notice. My mother sent it up to me from Connecticut. I didn't get it until July. I had pneumonia that spring. I was living here at the house, and that was when I was really thinking a lot about the draft. When Jean come down and told me about their trying to get some of the land back and the treaties, I said, "Wow that's really great." I couldn't believe it. For once! The first time that someone was going to do something. Somebody was going to try to get some of that land back. I'd heard there were some treaties, and I knew we'd given up some land, but we still owned some up at Marsh Island. So once I was living up here, me and Ken started looking into this thing about the draft, too. He said, "Once you get drafted, I'll try and help you all I can." So in July when I did get drafted, we were already working on it. I was writing to different people. And by February of this year I was working in the Island's Operation Mainstream.

I seen that car go by and come down again, and these guys were in suits, and I says, "It's probably them." So they pulled over to the office, and I'm just a little ways up from there, and they get out and went inside, and first this woman comes out who works in there; she hollered to me, "Martin. Couple of men here. They want to see you." And I said, "That's them." I turned around and went back up. When I got up there Jimmy Sappier, the head of Mainstream, is out there trying to talk them into getting the Constable to get an order from the Governor before they can take me off the Island, because they couldn't do it themselves. So when I come over, they says, "We got a warrant for your arrest." I says, "Well, I just want to see a copy of it." And I looked it over and told them to call Ken. Then I asked Jimmy to give me a leave of absence for a while, and they took me over, and we got Ken, and then they took me to the federal courthouse in Bangor for a hearing.

Jim and Ken put up bond for me, and they let me out, and after that, we really started working on it. We were checking on it here in Maine, how we could get the case moved back up here. I knew if I went down there I'd lose it. This draft counselor said if I'd seen him earlier he could have got me out on a CO, but I didn't want CO; I said I wanted to test these treaties because the State had made them with us and the Constitution says no state could make a treaty. We got in touch with some people at Harvard, and Jean put it in the newsletter, and we got a lot of information from different Indians around the country telling about their own draft cases; then we went down to Connecticut. I had something like twenty-five or thirty names, and I'd go and see the person, and everyone was refusing. Some lawyers wanted something like forty dollars an hour to work on the case. They didn't understand me. They were all trying to tell me to do it their way; they could probably get me out on some technicality, but I still wanted to bring those treaties into it, and most of them said it was too involved; it would take too much research.

We finally went to see this Mike Berman. He'd only been in practice a couple of years, and he said he'd be willing to give it a try, but first he wanted to see if he could get some money from someplace to do it. So I went in and rattled on for about an hour and a half. I just kept going and going and telling him every single thing I thought might interest him about it. After I got through, he started asking me questions about the treaties. Ken was filling him in on the legal part of it, and the guy says "It really sounds interesting. If I can get some money on it I'll do it and I'll call you back tomorrow." So he called, and he says, "Look I'm sorry I couldn't get any money," and I said, "You can't get any money? That's pretty messed up. If you've got money you can buy your way out of anything. They say this is a free country, and you can get all your rights and stuff, but you have to pay for them." I says, "That's pretty sick." And Mike says, "Well, it sounds really interesting. I think I might like to do it anyway. Why don't you come over again, and we'll talk some more." So me and Ken went over, and we were talking to him again, and he says, "Okay, I'll take it." So we started in on the research.

You know Vine Deloria's book *Custer Died for Your Sins?* Well, his brother Sam's going to Yale Law School. He headed up the research team, which was a bunch of guys down there. They come up with really a lot of good information. They didn't know whether it would help or not; they'd start on something that looked really good, some law, and they'd find another law that went right against it. And it was like that all the time. It went around in a circle. Something would come up good; then it would turn bad again. They said there were just too many laws pertaining to Indians. Finally we got down to whether these laws pertained to us. We were a nation of our own. Even the federal government didn't recognize us. Supposedly the State of Maine was taking care of us. After a while, we forgot about the old laws, and we stuck right to the treaties, and that's what we've been doing ever since.

We found one case where this kid might of won if he had contested the jurisdiction—these people coming on your land to take you away. This was Seneca, down in New York. That's what we thought we ought to do first—try the jurisdiction thing; then after that it would be all open to bring up questions like that during the trial. The mistake he made was not bringing it up at the pretrial hearing.

I'm not an American citizen—that's the whole thing. The draft laws shouldn't pertain to me. We got into this thing about being born in the U.S., too, being a citizen. I was born in Old Town. A lot of kids were born over town in a house over there. It was a lying-in house, not really a hospital, just a little house right down the hill from Stillwater Avenue. Then came the treaties, whether they were legal or not. We had to bring them in in order to prove that this was Indian land, right here where we're sitting now, and Old Town proper. We told them we wanted to contest the jurisdiction and they set that for two weeks, then another week. Then they said come back in two months. It just kept going like that, putting it off. Now I don't have to go back to Connecticut until September. It's gonna be over seven months, and the lawyer says what they're trying to do is get more time and find something on it, which they are doing, and they probably can't get anything on it. Once they've gone over six months, the judge will have to dismiss it for lack of speedy trial.

We got this one judge down in Bangor; he told this kid he didn't care for Indians at all. He was the one I had, and this lawyer was telling me when I got those ten days—he says, "I didn't think he'd give you ten days, second count like that. I thought he'd probably fine you, and the next time he might lock you up." He said it was a stiff penalty for my second offense. Every time the kids from the Island have gone up in front of him he's always rough on them. Everybody knows that. Even the governor and council over here say he's really strict with Indians, and everybody thinks that he's really prejudiced. He's probably in his forties, his mid or late forties—he'll be around for a while all right.

Governor Curtis says he's pro-Indian and he's been over here, but I think it's because today people are starting to look at the Indian, saying, "What have we done to them," things like that. And he probably figures that's the sentiment now; maybe he can get some more votes, you know. That's all it is, just looking for some more votes.

You know, there's no record of how all that land went out of the Indian's hands. It's now owned by all the big paper companies. Or like Katahdin—Governor Baxter gave that land to the people of Maine, just gave it away. We don't know that he ever had a deed for it, from the Indians. Like my brother and me, we got picked up in Baxter State Park for having dogs in the car, and if we had to go to Millinocket about it I told him, "Ask them for a deed to that land. Ask them who owns that land. Let's take it right into a big land question and find out who owns the land up there, whose got a deed for it."

In Old Town the police, they'd always—if you were an Indian, walking down the street and if just once you kinda staggered to the side—

they'd go right over and pick you up for intoxication and they'd wait until they got you up the station to find out if you really were. But lately since Jean's brought up the land question I've noticed in the past year that the police haven't bothered us. Like when an Indian went over town, even riding around, the police would follow him around and see where he was going. But lately if you were riding around they don't even bother with you. Before you'd be walking down the street, and I remember when I was just a little kid they used to watch me all the time, and all the store owners over there, they all thought the Indians stole: if you was an Indian and you went in a store there was always a clerk or maybe two of them following you all over the store; they always did that. There aren't any Indians on the police force in Old Town, they've never attempted to recruit one. I know of one Indian who's in the State Police around here. He's what you'd call an ideal U.S. citizen now. He don't care about the land question. He wouldn't fight for the land anyway. He'd just as soon be white; I don't think it'd bother him at all—to be white. Me, I can't see any inducements to be white. For him it would mean a job, a pension, early retirement—lots of money!

It's really hard to try and be an Indian and yet live in this time. It's difficult. Like myself, I really didn't care to go to work and work all those hours every day. I'd like to just go up in the woods and try and live off the land, but you can't now; it's all polluted. There's too many people. There's planes buzzing all around. There's no wildlife anywhere unless you go way up in the Allegash. Once you get up there you got a health problem. Somebody gets sick, what are you gonna do? The Indians now, they don't know all the old medicine, like we used to. My grandfather knows a few of them. A few old people, they probably know all of them together, but it'd be kind of hard to take them up there. There isn't much you can do actually. You can fight for your land.

My grandfather's the oldest Neptune alive, he's about eighty-six, eighty-seven. That's what it says on the census list, but my father says he's in his nineties. He lives right below our house, in the old gray one down there. He's kind of senile now, too; he forgets a lot, even thinks I'm his brother. He had a brother named Saul once. Every time he mentions him, he says, "You remember, Saul? Remember that time we went and did this or did that?" I says, "That was your brother; he died quite a while ago. I'm Martin." "Oh yeah, that's right, too." And he'll start laughing. He was living alone for quite a while, and then my cousin and her kids moved in with him. Now his daughter's up here from New York. She's spending the summer. I think she's gonna try and get him to move down with her. But he really likes it up here. I don't think he could stand it anywhere else.

He's one of the oldest. There's him and Suzy Dana, probably Nick Ranco—Nick's in his eighties—Pauline Shea—no, she died about a month or two ago—and another woman. I remember she used to stay down below us there. She was really, really old when I first seen her. She used to stay with Mullean Paul, they called her. It's really Molly Ann Paul. She used to stay there with her all the time till she started getting really bad off. I always thought it was funny, a woman smoking a pipe. And I always used to see her in that window. Every time I went by there she was always rocking and smoking that pipe. She never said a word. She'd always just rock and smoke. Once in a while I'd go in there for my mother. She'd send something down there for them, or send me down with a message or something. The only time I ever heard her speak was in Indian, when she spoke to that other woman. I only heard her speak I think two or three times in all the times I went down there. She's kind of a small lady. When she goes and my grandfather goes and Suzy goes, everything's gonna go with them.

A lot of people say everything's gonna be lost because even now you can't get these people to talk to you. They're afraid to say anything to anybody. Like Suzy Dana won't talk to anybody because she's got an agreement with this anthropologist that she won't tell anybody anything. I went down and asked her some questions and she said, "I can't say anything 'cause I got this contract with Dr. Seibert." He's not young, either. He took over after Frank Speck.

These Indians, they all learned these things on their own, by themselves, by observation. The language may be kind of hard to revive; but everything else, the arts and crafts, the kids all have it in them. You can see it when they're drawing and stuff like that. It's in them; it becomes natural, like if they're carving. They can pick up this stuff, I think. They can get all that back and the knowledge of the woods and different medicines. They'd take a while, by trial and error, the way Indians learned it before, but I think it could be done again.

I think it's gonna take a bunch of kids to move off somewhere, like up in the Allegash, someplace where it's really wild. Maybe take somebody with them, somebody from another tribe, an older person who does know some of the medicines. Like this feller who was up here, Dickie—he's a Mohawk. He went out and tried to find some medicines, and I went out with him and learned three or four of them. He says, "I'll show 'em to you but I don't want you telling anybody." He told me, "I wasn't even sure I should take you up here after you married white. I didn't know if I could trust you or not. I was wondering if you changed any." I says, "Maybe I changed, but as far as being Indian I haven't changed any. I told my wife if anybody changed it would be her, not me." He was talking down the house for quite some time, and he says, "Well, after talking with you I felt it was safe so I thought I'd bring you out." Somebody he knew had a fever, and he was up trying to get some medicine for that, but he couldn't find two of the things we were looking for. If we had somebody like him from roughly the same area, New York State or Maine—where they live it's wooded; it's about the same as up here, the woods and the terrain and everything—I think it wouldn't be that hard for us to get back everything.

As far as the language goes, the Passamaquoddy language is very similar to the Penobscot except for a few words, and I don't think you can restore the Penobscot language, but I think as long as you learn Passamaquoddy—they were part of our confederacy—you've got something. Everybody's always saying, "Well we can't lose the language." I hate to see us lose it, but it's a fact that we are because the older people have forgotten some of the words, but I think there's enough Passamaquoddies and Malacites to teach us.

And the kids' minds are all geared to Indian things, like thinking about pollution. They're against pollution. It's a feeling inside you that eventually comes out as you get older. The middle generation have really tried to suppress it, thinking that it would be best for us. It's there, the Indian consciousness; it just has to be brought out. You could go to visit the Mohawks that are quite traditional, and they can tell you about the creation, and different stories, things that have happened and prophesies, and when they tell them to you, you just feel like you've already heard them. They really make a lot of sense, too. Whereas if somebody white went and they told him the same story it would be really hard for him to understand.

I've seen that happen down there before. Like with Ken, Ken and Jean. Jean was telling me when they traveled around, there was a lot of things he couldn't understand and she understood them fully. She was always kind of suppressed, up until a couple of years ago. Then when she started traveling around, it come right back to her. It's hard to explain; it's just a feeling that all Indians have. It's all there; it's just in you, inborn, that you really are different from white people. You realize that when you're growing up. It's really hard to understand. Lots of time the kids on the Island don't dress as nice as the people in Old Town when they go to school, and their color's different, but other than that I think they really feel something inside different, too. Like when you go to class and you're hearing about this and you're learning about that, they don't see any sense in it. That's why a lot of kids have dropped out. They say, "What do we need English for?" Actually I think more of the kids are interested in something like science, things about life. English has been just about everybody's worst subject over there. I think it's something inside of them that just pulls them away from it, kind of like puts a stop to really getting into it, trying to learn it. When we got into it I slept through most of the class. I thought it was stupid. I says, "Well, I can talk, you know. I can talk English. I can't even talk my own language, so why should I learn English?"

I hope through the coffeehouse I can get their minds reactivated, bring the Indian out in the kids. I think now where I'm leaving it might be good for the kids because so far they've all looked to me. It's like people have always been doing things for them. They don't have any ambition, I guess, to do these things themselves. I think once I leave, there won't be one leader; they'll all work together; they'll all have to work together in order to finish up the building, for one thing. And then they'll get their programs set up inside, like the language and arts and crafts, dancing and songs. I think once they begin to get this back, if they get back enough of this Indianness, I think they'll probably start fighting more for Indian language classes in school, maybe set up their own schools over here, set up their own programs. I hope this will unite the kids because the older people are always fighting amongst themselves, always bringing in grudges and politics. And that's what the whites have wanted, to keep the people completely divided so they're powerless to act in a unified way.

I met my wife tutoring at the school on the Island. She was a student at the University of Maine, and she come up tutoring. I looked in and I saw her, and I said to my friend, "I think I'll go inside and meet her," and he said, "Oh oh." He says, "I know; you're gonna go out with her a few times; you're gonna fall madly in love with her; and you're gonna end up marrying her." I says, "You think so." And he says, "Yeah." That was before I went in the room, you know. Before I'd even met her—that's probably Indian instinct. So I went in; I just went walking in. I'd met the nuns in there before, and one introduced me so I sat down and I started talking, rambling on. Kathy was just sitting there listening.

After that I used to go in there every day, and the kids started teasing us, "She's his girlfriend; you're her boyfriend; you're gonna get married." She was really a good kid, and she was all against what the older people think of—you know, materialism. She was brought up with that. She's from Brunswick. She said her mother was always trying to buy her love. She'd go out and buy her clothes and shoes, things she didn't even need, or give her the money to go buy things. She was taking trips all over the place—they were just traveling all over the place any time she wanted to and she said "That isn't what I wanted. If my mother could have said at least once that I love you, that would have been enough." But she always tried to do it through money, and everything had to be just so. You gotta act like this, do this in front of these certain people. "I always rebelled against that deep inside," she says. "I never said anything, but it didn't feel like what I wanted to be like." After she started going to college she began to get her own mind.

I was talking to her about Indians. She'd done a lot of reading on Indians, and she thought they were just about the best people in the world. She'd read what had been done to them, and that's why she was hoping she could help in some way by coming up tutoring, just as a volunteer. She just believed in everything I believed. The way she said it I realized she felt the same way I did. I didn't say, "I believe in this," and she, "Oh, I do, too." It wasn't like that. I could tell just by the way she'd talk how she felt.

I think Indian girls are just about where we are, too, Wayne and me. The funny part of it is I've always told the kids to marry Indians. The younger kids coming up now; they're all hanging around together, the girls and the guys, because there's so many of them. My own age, there's maybe two girls that were marriageable. It was really hard on the Island to meet other Indian girls. Or you'd visit the Mohawks, and you'd come back, and they'd say, "What's wrong with the girls out there?" And you'd just tell them, "Well, you're not out there long enough." You'd go for three or four days, you can't marry a girl you've only known for three or four days, and they says, "Well, why not? She's Indian!" And I says, "I just can't do that."

I hope through the building we can get people to come up and visit; maybe they won't all be Penobscot and Passamaquoddy, but at least they're all Indians. I think we have to keep up the blood. I hope by the time my kids reach that age they'll meet a full-blooded Indian, or at least a half. I'll come back. I don't plan on going permanently to Manchester. I want to come back. I don't want my kids growing up down there. At the latest I'd come back would be when my kid reached maybe four years old, just before he went to school down there. But I definitely want to come back. I want my kids to grow up on the Island.

DOCUMENTS 2

INDIAN FIGHTS DRAFT, DROPS LEGAL BOMB

HARTFORD, Conn. Martin A. Neptune, 21, a Penobscot Indian from an island off the Maine coast (sic) is refusing to serve in the US Army on grounds his island is not part of the United States.

Neptune's attorney, Michael P. Berman, argued Monday in US District Court that Neptune's home, Indian Island, is Indian territory that never has been taken by US conquest or relinquished by the Indians.

Indian Island is one mile wide and three miles long, and has about 400 Indian inhabitants, according to Neptune.

Berman claimed the Federal government does not have a treaty with the Penobscot tribe and therefore cannot order Neptune to serve in the Army.

"I just want to go back and live on the island," Neptune said outside the courtroom.

The case is being heard here rather than in Maine because Neptune's parents, Mr. and Mrs. Arthur Neptune Jr., now live in nearby Manchester. Their son was living with them temporarily when he registered with the draft board.

US District Judge T. Emmet Clarie reserved decision on Neptune's status to give himself more time to study the history involved in the young Indian's claims.

Berman claims the US citizenship conferred on the

From *Boston Globe,* Oct. 5, 1971, p. 1. Associated Press.

(Editor's Note from *Maine Indian Newsletter* : Members of the Penobscot Nation have been awaiting the opinion of the court since July, 1970, when Martin was arrested and taken from the island by federal marshals.)

Indians, as well as Eskimos and other natives, is not valid because it was granted with the provision that their tribal possessions would not be taken.

The lawyer said Neptune and his people were illegally deprived of their property rights.

Neptune, who was married in June to a white woman, said he is not primarily waging his fight for other Indians in his position but merely to be able to return to his island.

The Penobscots "are kind of afraid to stand up for things," he added, partly because of fear they will lose their welfare benefits.

JOHN NEPTUNE'S LETTER

1825 was the year of the great Miramichi Fire in New Brunswick and one of the most disastrous forest fires ever known in Maine, which was rendered more destructive by the orders of the State Land Agent who commanded that wild meadow hay on Mattawamkeag waters, cut by lumbermen plundering the public pine forests, should be burned, and at a time when the drought was greatest. In these fires a large amount of fine pine land belonging to the Indians was burned and John Neptune dictated a letter which was printed in Peter Edes' Bangor Weekly Register and copied by the Columbian Centinel, Boston, September 21, 1825.

Eckstorm, *Old John Neptune*, p. 12

Now me speak in paper—had timber all burnt up—me seeum Mattiwawcook Island all bare just like my harm no blanket—what meanum states agent send Captin Chase to burnum hay when everything so dry—Indian two township all burn up before rane come—Indian lossum all timber and hay—sartin me now walk general court next winter then me speakum Governor Parris—me hearum he giveum to the agent to burnum all hay—spose Governor Parris speak so he say so—then me speak states agent pay Indian all hay and timber he burn—spose he say so—then Gover-

nor Parris he pay sartin—when Indian haveum all timber
and hay noboddy burnum hay—now state gittum all Indian land but two township then he settum fire to drive
all Indian off—now me haveum no more timber—by by
me be naked just like snake—all indians speak so.

John Neptune

LUGGING BOAT ON SOWADNEHUNK

This is a Penobscot story.

When the camp-fire is lighted, and the smoke draws
straight up without baffling, and the branches overhead
move only as the rising current of heat fans them, then if
the talk veers round to stories of crack watermen, and the
guides, speaking more to each other than to you, declare
that it was Big Sebattis Mitchell who first ran the falls at
Sowadnehunk,—though full twenty years before, John
Ross himself had put a boat over and come out right side
up,—do not, while they are debating whose is the credit of
being first, let slip your chance to hear a better tale: bid
them go on and tell you how Joe Attien, who was Thoreau's
guide, and his men who followed after and who failed,
were the ones who made that day memorable.

And if your guides are Penobscot men, they will tell
it as Penobscot men should, as if there were no merit in the
deed beyond what any man might attain to, as if the least
a man should do was to throw away his life on a reckless
dare, and count it well spent when so lavished. For so are
these men made, and as it was in those days of the beginning, so is it yet even to the present among us.

You will have heard, no doubt, of Sebattis, he who
from his bulk was called by the whites Big Sebat, and
from his lazy shrewdness was nicknamed by his tribesmen
Ahwassus, the Bear. Huge and round he was, like the beast
he was named for, but strong and wise, and in his dark,

Fannie Hardy Eckstorm, *The Penobscot Man* (Boston: Houghton
Mifflin and Co., 1904).

flat face and small, twinkling eyes there were resources, ambitions, schemes.

Scores of you who read this will recollect the place. In memory you will again pass down the West Branch in your canoe, past Ripogenus, past Ambajemackomas, past the Horse Race, into the welcome deadwater above Nesowadnehunk. There, waiting in expectancy for that glorious revelation of Katahdin which bursts upon you above Abol, that marvelous picture of the giant towering in majestic isolation, with its white "slide" ascending like a ladder to the heavens, you forgot yourself, did not hear the tumult of falling waters, did not see the smooth lip of the fall sucking down, were unconscious that just before you were the falls of Sowadnehunk. Then, where the river veers sharply to the right, you felt the guide spring on his paddle as he made the carry by a margin, and you realized what it would have been to drift unguided over those falls.

So it has always been,—the sharp bend of the river to the right, blue, smooth, dazzling; the carry at the left, bare, broad, yellow-earthed. Crossing it forty rods, you cut off the river again, and see above you to the right the straight fall, both upper and lower pitches almost as sheer as milldams, and in front the angry boil of a swift current among great and thickset rocks. So it always stays in memory,—at one end the blue river, smooth and placid, and the yellow carry; at the other, the white hubbub of tossing rapids below perpendicular falls.

One May day long ago, two boats' crews came down to the carry and lugged across. They had lugged three miles on Ripogenus, and a half mile on Ambajemackomas, besides the shorter carry past Chesuncook Dam; they had begun to know what lugging a boat meant. The day was hot,—no breeze, no shade; it was getting along toward noon, and they had turned out, as usual, at three in the morning. They were tired,—tired, faint, hot; weary with the fatigue that stiffens the back and makes the feet hang heavy; weary, too, with the monotony of weeks of dangerous toil without a single day of rest, the weariness that gets upon the brain and makes the eyes go blurry; weary because they were just where they were, and that old river would keep flowing on to Doomsday, always drowning men and making them chafe their shoulders lugging heavy boats. There was not a man of them who could not show upon his shoulder a great red spot where the pole used in lugging boat, or the end of an oar on which barrels of pork or flour had been slung in carrying wangan, had bruised and abraded it. And now it was more lugging, and ahead were Abol and Pockwockamus and Debsconeag and Passangamet and Ambajejus and Fowler's and—there are, indeed, how many of them! The over-weary always add to present burdens that mountain of future toil.

So it was in silence that they took out the oars and seats, the paddles and peavies and pickaroons, drew the boats up and drained them of all water, then, resting a moment, straightened their backs, rubbed the sore shoulders that so soon must take up the burden again, and ran their fingers through their damp hair. One or two swore a little as relieving their minds, and when they bent to lift the boat, one spoke for all the others.

"By jinkey-boy!" said he, creating a new and fantastic oath, "but I do believe I'd rather be in hell to-day, with ninety devils around me, than sole-carting on this carry."

That was the way they all felt. It is mighty weary business to lug on carries. For a driving-boat is a heavy lady to carry. The great Maynards, wet, weigh eight to nine hundred pounds, and they put on twelve men, a double crew, to carry one. The old two-streakers (that is, boats with two boards to a side where the big Maynards had three) were not nearly so heavy, and on short carries like Sowadnehunk were lugged by their own crews, whether of four men or six; but diminishing the crew left each man with as great a burden. A short man at the bow, another at the stern, with the taller ones amidships under the curve of the gunwale if they were lugging without poles, or by twos fore, aft, and amidships for six men lugging with poles, was the usual way they carried their boats; and it was "Steady, boys, steady; *now* hoist her!"—"Easy, now, easy; hold *hard!*" for going downhill she overrode John and Jim at the bow, and going up a rise Jack and Joe at the stern felt her crushing their shoulders, and when the ground was uneven with rocks and cradle-knolls, and she reeled and sagged, then the men at the sides caught the whole weight on one or the other of them. Nothing on the drive speaks so eloquently of hard work as the purple, sweat-stained cross on the backs of the men's red shirts, where the suspenders have made their mark; they get this in lugging boat on carries.

But they bent their backs to it, wriggled the boat up and forward to her place, each crew its own boat, and staggered on, feet bracing out, and spike-soled shoes ploughing the dirt and scratching on the rocks. They looked like huge hundred-leggers, Brobdingnagian insects, that were crawling over that yellow carry with all their legs clawing uncertainly and bracing for a foothold. The head boat crowded Bill Halpin upon a rock so hard that he fell and barked his shins on the granite; that dropped the weight suddenly upon Jerry Durgan's shoulder, so that a good two inches of skin was rasped off clean where it had been blistered before; little Tomah Soc stumbled in a hole, and not letting go his grip, threw up the other gunwale so that it half broke his partner's jaw. Those boats took all the mean revenges wherewith a driving-boat on land settles scores for the rough treatment it receives in the water.

They were lugging that May morning only because no boat could run those falls with any reasonable expectation of coming out right side up. For up to that time they had chiefly used the Wallace boat, built low and straight in the gunwale, raking only moderately at the bow and low in the side. It is related that when the great high-bowed Maynard batteaus were first put on the river, short old Jack Mann . . . looked with high disfavor on the big, handsome craft, and then, rushing into the boat-shop, demanded an axe, an auger, and a handsaw.

"What's that for?" asked the foreman, suspecting that it was but one of Jack's devices for unburdening his mind in some memorable saying.

"Want 'em to cut armholes in that blasted boat," growled Jack, insinuating that the bows were above the head of a short man like himself.

But the old boat,—you may yet sometimes see the bones of one of them bleaching about the shores of inland ponds, or lying sun-cracked in the back yards of country farms,—stable and serviceable as she was, was no match for this handsome lady of to-day. They run the Arches of Ripogenus now with all their boats, and have done it for years; but at the time when Sebattis came down to Sowadnehunk, such water no man ever dreamed of running. It is likely enough that Sebattis, just back from a sixteen years' residence at Quoddy, did not know that it had ever been run successfully.

Be that as it may, when Sebattis and his bowman came down, the last of three boats, and held their batteau at the taking-out place a moment before they dragged her out and stripped her ready to lug, what Sebattis, as he sat in the stern with his paddle across his knees, said in Indian to his bowman was simply revolutionary.

"Huh?" grunted his dark-faced partner, turning in great surprise; "you t'ought you wanted run it dose e'er falls? Blenty rabbidge water dose e'er falls!"

The bowman had stated the case conservatively. That carry was there merely because men were not expected to run those falls and come out alive.

But the bowman's objection was not meant as a refusal: he knew Sebattis, that he was a good waterman, few better. A big, slow man, of tremendous momentum when once in motion, it was likely enough that all the years of his exile at Quoddy he had been planning just how he could run those falls, and if he spoke now, it was because this was the hour striking. In his own mind he had already performed the feat, and was receiving the congratulations of the crowd. It was no small advantage that he knew an audience of two boats' crews was waiting at the lower carry-end to testify, however grudgingly, to the authenticity of what he claimed to have done.

The bowman had faith in Sebattis; as he listened to the smooth stream of soft-cadenced Indian that cast silvery bonds about his reluctance and left him helpless to refuse (Sebattis being both an orator in a public and a powerful pleader in a private cause), the bowman caught the rhythm of the deed. It was all so easy to take their boat out into midstream, where the current favored them a little, to shoot her bow far out over the fall, and, as the crews ashore gaped in horrified amazement, to make her leap clear, as a horse leaps a hurdle. And then to fight their way through the smother of the whirlpool below, man against water, but such men as not every boat can put in bow and stern, such strong arms as do not hold every paddle, such great heads for management, such skill in water-craft as few attain.

This was the oration, with its Indian appeal to personal glory. It was, as Sebattis said, *"Beeg t'ing,"* and he fired his bowman with the desire for glory. The Penobscot man, white man or Indian, dies with astonishing alacrity when he sees anything worth dying for. And the name of "crack waterman" is a shining mark to strive for.

Thus at the upper end of the carry Sebattis and his bowman talked over at their leisure the chances of dying within five minutes. At the other end the two boats' crews lay among the blueberry bushes in the shade of shivering birch saplings and waited for Sebattis. It did not worry them that he was long in coming; they knew the leisurely Indian ways, and how unwilling, though he weighed hard upon two hundred and sixty, and had strength to correspond, was Big Sebattis to lug an extra pound. They pictured him draining his boat and sopping out with a swab of bracken the last dispensable ounce of water, then tilting her to the sun for a few minutes to steam out a trifle more before he whooped to them to come across and help him. It did not worry them to wait,—it was all one in the end: there would be carries to lug on long after they were dead and gone.

So, looking at the logs ricked up along the shores and cross-piled on the ledges, looking at the others drifting past, wallowing and thrashing in the wicked boil below the falls, they lounged and chaffed one another. Jerry Durgan was surreptitiously laying cool birch leaves on his abraded shoulder, and Bill Halpin was attentively, though silently, regarding his shins: there had been none too much stocking between him and that "big gray." The Indians, stretched out on their backs, gazed at the sky; nothing fretted them much. On one side, an Indian and an Irishman were having a passage at wit; on the other, two or three were arguing the ins and outs of a big fight up at 'Suncook the winter before, and a Province man was colloguing with a Yankee on points of scriptural interpretation. It was such talk as might be overheard almost any time on the drive when men are resting at their ease.

"It was French Joe that nailed Billy; Billy he told me so," came from the group under the birches.

From among the Indians out in the sunlight arose a persuasive Irish voice.

"Why is it, Tomah, that when your folks are good Catholics, and our folks are good Catholics, you don't ever name your children Patrick and Bridget?"

And the reply came quick: " 'Cause we hate it Irish so bad, you know!"

Off at the right they were wrangling about the construction of the Ark.

"And I'd just like to have seen that bo't when they got her done," said the Yankee; "just one door an' one winder, an' vent'lated like Harvey Doane's scho'l'ouse. They caught him nailin' of the winders down. 'How be ye goin' to vent'late?' says they. 'Oh,' says he, 'fresh air's powerful circulatin' stuff; I callate they'll carry the old air out in their pockets, an' bring in enough fresh air in their caps to keep 'em goin';' an' that was all they ever did get's long's he was school agent. My scissors! three stories an' all full of live-stock, an' only one winder, an' that all battened down! Tell you what! I'd 'a' hated to be Mr. Noah's fambly an' had to stay in that ole Ark ten months an' a half before they took the cover off! Fact! I read it all up onct!"

Said another: "I don't seem to 'member how she was built, 'ceptin' the way they run her seams. She must have ben a jim-dickey house with the pitch all on the inside's well as on the outside o' her. Seems to me a bo't ain't bettered none by a daub o' pitch where the' ain't none needed."

"'T ain't the Ark as bothers me some," put in the Province man; "I reckon that flood business is pretty nigh straight, but I couldn't never cipher out about that Tower of Babel thing. Man ask for a hod o' mortar, an' like enough they'd send him up a barrel of gaspereau; that's"—

The religious discussion broke off abruptly.

"Holy Hell!—Look a-comin'!" gasped the Yankee.

Man! but that was a sight to see! They got up and devoured it with their eyes.

On the verge of the fall hovered the batteau about to leap. Big Sebat and his bowman crouched to help her, like a rider lifting his horse to a leap. And their eyes were set with fierce excitement, their hands cleaved to their paddle handles, they felt the thrill that ran through the boat as they shot her clear, and, flying out beyond the curtain of the fall, they landed her in the yeasty rapids below.

Both on their feet then! And how they bent their paddles and whipped them from side to side, as it was "In!"—"Out!"—"Right!"—"Left!" to avoid the logs caught on the ledges and the great rocks that lay beneath the boils and snapped at them with their ugly fangs as they went flying past. The spray was on them; the surges crested over their gunwales; they sheered from the rock, but cut the wave that covered it and carried it inboard. And always it was "Right!"—"Left!"—"In!"—"Out!" as the greater danger drove them to seek the less.

But finally they ran her out through the tail of the boil, and fetched her ashore in a cove below the carry-end, out of sight of the men. She was full of water, barely afloat.

Would Sebattis own to the boys who were hurrying down through the bushes that he had escaped with his life only by the greatest luck? Not Sebattis!

"Now you bale her out paddles," said he to his bowman, and they swept her with their paddles as one might with a broom.

"Now you drain her out," commanded Sebattis, when they could lift the remaining weight, and they raised the bow and let the water run out over the slanting stern, all but a few pailfuls. "Better you let dat stay," said the shrewd Sebattis.

It was quick work, but when the crew broke through the bushes, there stood Sebattis and his bowman leaning on their paddles like bronze caryatids, one on either side of the boat. They might have been standing thus since the days of the Pharaohs, they were so at ease.

"Well, boys, how did you make it?" queried the first to arrive on the spot.

Sebattis smiled his simple, vacuous smile. "Oh, ver' good; she took in lill' water mebbe."

"By gee, that ain't much water! Did she strike anything?"

Sebattis helped to turn her over. She had not a scratch upon her.

Then the men all looked again at the boat that had been over Sowadnehunk, and they all trooped back to the carry-end without saying much, two full batteau crews and Sebattis and his bowman. They did not talk. No man would have gained anything new by exchanging thoughts with his neighbor.

And when they came to the two boats drying in the sun, they looked one another in the eyes again. It was a foregone conclusion. Without a word they put their galled shoulders under the gunwales, lifted the heavy batteaus to their places, and started back across that carry forty rods to the end they had just come from.

What for? It was that in his own esteem a Penobscot man will not stand second to any other man. They would not have it said that Sebattis Mitchell was the only man of them who had tried to run Sowadnehunk Falls.

So they put in again, six men to a boat, full crews, and in the stern of one stood Joe Attien, who was Thoreau's guide, and in the bow Steve Stanislaus, his cousin. That sets the date,—that it was back in 1870,—for it became the occasion for another and a sadder tale. If only Steve Stanislaus had held that place for the rest of the drive, it is little likely that we should have to tell the story of the death of Thoreau's guide.

And they pushed out with their two boats and ran the falls.

But the luck that bore Sebattis safely through was not theirs. Both boats were swamped, battered on the rocks into kindling wood. Twelve men were thrown into the water, and pounded and swashed about among logs and rocks. Some by swimming, some by the aid of Sebattis and his boat, eleven of them got ashore, "a little damp," as no doubt the least exaggerative of them were willing to admit. The unlucky twelfth man they picked up later, quite undeniably drowned. And the boats were irretrievably smashed. Indeed, that was the part of the tale that rankled with Sebattis when he used to tell it.

"Berry much she blame it us" (that is, himself) "that time John Loss." (Always to the Indian mind John Ross, the head contractor of the drive, was the power that commanded wind, logs, and weather.) "She don' care so much 'cause drowned it man, 'cause she can get blenty of it men; but dose e'er boats she talk 'bout berry hard."

That is how they look at such little deeds themselves. The man who led off gets the credit and the blame; he is the only one remembered. But to an outsider, what wins more than passing admiration is not the one man who succeeded, but the many who followed after and failed, who could not let well enough alone when there was a possible better to be achieved, but, on the welcome end of the carry, the end where all their troubles of galls and bruises and heavy burdens in the heat are over, pick up their boats without a word, not one man of them falling out, and lug them back a weary forty rods to fight another round with Death sooner than own themselves outdone.

YES VOTE—THEN NO FOR INDIAN SEAT

AUGUSTA—The Maine House voted 67-57 Tuesday afternoon in a non-roll call vote to allow Indian representatives to occupy a non-voting seat in the House, and then turned around in a roll call vote 10 minutes later and reversed that decision.

When lawmakers were forced to signify their votes on the electronic tote board, they voted 75-58 against the order by Rep. S. Glenn Starbird, Jr., D-Kingman, to amend the House rule specifying who shall be seated inside the House railing.

Starbird said Indians hadn't been seated on the floor of the House in a non-voting capacity since 1951. He said the presence of the Indians is "of immeasurable value to us here on the floor on any question involving Indians."

Rep. Theodore S. Curtis, Jr., R-Orono, agreed. Curtis said what the legislature needs is "fewer Indian experts and more expert Indians."

But Rep. Joseph E. Binnette, D-Old Town, said Maine Indians "don't want any part" of being seated in the legislature.

If they wanted to be seated they can run for the legislature like any other candidate, Binnette and Rep. James T. Dudley, D-Enfield, argued.

From *Bangor Daily News,* May 26, 1971.

(Editor's Note from *Maine Indian Newsletter*: And then on the other hand the nonIndian might demand a seat on the tribal council. The principle of this issue signifies a separate citizenship for the people who are still occupying the land of their fathers and grandfathers and who still remain a separate nation. And then if representation were granted, then taxation would be sure to follow. However our economic standards measure up to the Maine citizens, you can be sure that our land is priceless. No amount of money could buy the land, for in case of need, we can rely on our land for sustenance, shelter, and support.)

Maine Indian Newsletter, Summer, 1971.

"But they don't want to, because they feel they can get along better this way than if they were on the floor of the House," Binnette declared.

Rep. John Donaghy, R-Lubec, spoke against the order. If Indians are given seating privileges, he said, the Legislature would be bound to provide space for any ethnic group which demanded it.

Rep. Richard Hewes, R-Cape Elizabeth, raised the question of constitutionality. But Starbird said he had been advised by Atty. Gen. James S. Erwin that seating of the Indians without voting rights can be done by a House order. Any citizen can be so seated, he maintained.

"We should do simple justice and pass this order," Starbird said.

The present Indian representatives to the Legislature, elected by their tribes but having no voting power at the state House, are John Bailey of the Passamaquoddy tribe and John Mitchell, Sr. of the Penobscot tribe.

JOURNAL 3

Saturday morning, July 24

Looks like it's heating up to be a scorcher: less breeze than yesterday, maybe none at all—

I arrived midafternoon y'day at Ken's, his garden exploding green all over the place, so cool and peaceful under his trees; trees rustling, the river blue and smooth, kids playing wildly, and an Indian couple from New Brunswick visiting, the husband taking a nap in a chaise under the oaks, wife jawing with Jean who's about to give birth any day now. Next door Martin's peeling gray house with two cars and some truck parts scattered all around: Wayne's across the street. Suddenly, what is the perfume I smell?—the trees themselves and the earth. The Island is a much more beautiful place to be than Old Town:

Two hours ago, Kitty, waitress in Ho-Jo's in Augusta, starting U. of Me. in Sept., overhears me talking with Liza and Steve, young couple I picked up in Mass., dropped them on the way to Gardiner: "Did I hear you say you were writing a book on the Penobscot Indians? Do they like you? Do they want you up there?" "Some do, some don't. I think I get along pretty well with the young people." "We never should have bothered them—" She has dark-red hair; her eyes flash; she snaps the menu behind the napkin dispenser, "We never should have come here and disturbed them. We took everything away from them, like with the Negroes!" She's from Hallowell, she says, she's going to become a nurse—

One hour ago, stopped in Bangor at State Information Office to ask if they had any literature on the Maine Indians, specifically about Penobscot Nation at Indian Island. "It's just where they live," the girl answers, either bored or put off by my appearance [me, poor old superannuated Beatnik]. She manages to find a postcard: "There's nothing special there," she concludes. I give her a nickel for the postcard that is really one of the pulp mill and the Bangor hydroelectric works, the dam—if you know what to look for you can just barely make out the trees of Indian Island.

I woke up fuzzy-headed after drinking beer last night, first with Ken and Jean at my motel room while I got them on tape, then, as I was dropping them off around midnight Wayne Mitchell came over and said, "Jesus, you've gotta have one beer with me at my house before you go to bed." So we went to his front porch in the dark. "I like to sit here in the dark and drink my beer," said Wayne. His hair's longer, and he has new oval wire-rimmed glasses, yellow sport shirt, blue jeans. Terri's inside asleep. When we go in for more beer we take a peek at six-month-old Jason lying in his crib, toys all around him, mobile overhead, drinking a nighttime bottle, not a word.

Then "Bicou" appears out of the dark to banter w. Wayne. He's about 20, wanders from Maine to California, picks potatoes in the north, hunts, heavily into white counterculture—said he had 16 oz. of grass with him as well as THC, mescaline, acid—"Oh I got all I need." Wayne's put off by this; I shut up. Bicou's got thick black hair, banded around his ears, and just dropping wildly onto his shoulders: red and white checked hunting shirt, torn chinos, hunting boots. He's got a child (or will have soon) in Massachusetts by a white girl and had recently gone there with a younger kid from the Island who got drunk and wandered out into the night from whatever party they were at, entered nearby woman's house, saw a couch in her living room, and just flopped down on it. Woman wakes up, sees this Indian kid there in headband and moccasins, calls the police, and he's booked on charges of breaking and entering and—dig—attempted rape! Naturally some "police brutality" followed, with the kid charged w. resisting arrest.

Bicou has strange, soft, almost effeminate voice (probably a bit high at the moment—him, not voice); says when I go home he'll drive to Mass. with me. I ask him what he does for money. "Oh, anything. I modeled at an art school in Boston."

"You what?" says Wayne.

"Modeled," he says.

"Naked?"

"Yeah—"

"Jesus!"

Then a white VW bug pulled up, baby's bed strapped to the roof of it, disgorging two couples: Tim Love, who has been studying and teaching in a street academy—SASSI Prep—in Springfield, Mass. with his girl Jo Ann and a white couple, the Makwi&zniks, in their early twenties, from Chicopee. Girls in loose jerseys and tattered bell-bottom dungarees; Tim's hair flies out now in thick black wings on either side of his head. He couldn't keep that hat on now I saw him with in May. The couple, very sweet, as we go inside to Wayne's living room: guy with lots of blond hair, a small beard; his wife very gentle with the year-old baby I thought was a boy. Tamara's taken upstairs where Wayne and Ed (Helene's the wife's name) set the crib up; then the baby cries softly and Helene says, "It was a long ride. She'll be all right."

Terri got up and came in with a housecoat over her nightgown. I hadn't met her; slim and blondish, born in Old Town and lived here all her life. She asked me if I knew her relatives, the Porters, in Gloucester, and I tell her no, but it's very common for Gloucester people to have Maine relatives as there was a great coming and going between the two parts, even as far back as the 17th century. Wayne says the Indians visit back and forth constantly, from the reserves in New York and Canada, from New Brunswick to Pleasant Point and Peter Dana Point, where the Passamaquoddies live—"Eva Ranco's mother is Passamaquoddy, and so's Martin's."

Terri's sitting next to the Franklin stove in the only armchair; Bicou's got his back to it (he's suddenly quiet after being so loquacious outside). The couple's on the sofa with Wayne. Tim and Jo sort of come and go arm in arm; she has a floppy peasant blouse on now, with a big black and white serape over it. It's chilly out, which is why we all came in. Tim seems older than he did in May, as though something has pushed him up the notches of life a bit, some experience. He seemed pleased to see me, as did Wayne who immediately invited me to move in, said: "Next time you plan to stay with me. I don't see why you ought to pay all that money at a motel. In fact, why don't you move your things over now?" I told him I'd paid up, which I hadn't, but I was so moved by his offer I immediately got shy about it. He said, "Well, next time you plan to sleep here, you hear me?"

Wayne's an expert storyteller and started in first on Indian language, differences between Passamaquoddy and Penobscot words and uses and meanings of same. His pronunciation is excellent from what I can gather; he seems to have a fair working vocabulary. He got started on the Wabenaki Confederacy and how the Penobscots were considered the leaders, especially effective in decision-making and were always called in, sometimes keeping the conferences waiting several days while they took their time coming in from hunting—how finally Penobscots withdrew through some "hot-head" bringing back their wampum belts and coming into council place here, tossing them down on the table.

Terri, in the meantime, sitting smoking, in profile her face very much of the Anglo-Saxon line you see in Maine and I recognized all over when I was in the North of England ten years ago. Terri just sits smoking and listening to Wayne, who's a very sophisticated talker, a great social adept, very much the master in his own house.

IT CAN'T HAPPEN HERE?

The Times has learned that Old Town received its "regular" shipment of "soft drugs" Friday morning, July 16. Delivery was made direct to Old Town, not through Bangor or Orono.

The shipment, worth about $370 at "going rates," was expected to be "sold out" within the week. It contained approximately:

45 capsules of THC (a derivative of marijuana), which sells for about $1 per capsule;

(Some business in the White-world)

12 to 15 separately wrapped ounces of marijuana, worth $15 an ounce;

30 capsules of mescaline (hallucinogen derived from the peyote cactus), selling for about $2 a capsule; and

25 tablets of LSD (acid), which sells at $2.50 a tablet.

Many of these "soft drugs" are bought by teenagers of 14 to 17, who mix them with alcohol for a weekend "high."

The Penobscot Times, Thursday, July 22, 1971

COUNTER-COUP   COST OF LIVING
SHAKES SUDAN   SPIRALS UPWARD

Bangor Daily News, July 24, 1971

Saturday, July 24, 2 P.M.
Hot. I'm sitting on the bridge. Already July's high flush of green is gone
and the weeds have that late summer tarnish—goldenrod, milkweed, purple
thistle. The river is softly rippled by the breeze. A saw buzzes across the
street in Old Town, cars driving slowly across the bridge for the pageant.
In the summer haze the willow leaves are silvery, but the lushness is burnt
off. Canoes on the river: some new aluminum ones, and also the old
green-painted canvas and varnished wooden ribbed ones, slicing the water
with scimitar bows. The parking lot at the church is full, and people are
walking around the church and down to the grassy yard or "fairground"
behind the church and right on the river where the pageant will take
place.

Met Eva at Walgreen's corner earlier in a white, long-sleeved blouse,
long purple flower-printed skirt, her hair in a bun, sandals: she looked
Mexican. Asked me if I was "up for the pageant," and I replied it was my
luck to get here and find it. "See you there," she waved, crossing the street
with the green light. I would like to get to know Eva better: something in
her I respond to—beyond the sexual, I mean. Oh, yes, she's a very attractive girl/woman, exotic in some ways, ordinary in others. There's a sadness
in her, almost a resignation to it—the sadness and her life—and a drifting
in the way she and so many of her contemporaries on the Island just
hang or hover in time or space: transistor radio at the ear, gum in the
mouth; the filtered cigarette, adornment of the body. I want to say, "Listen,
Eva, what's up? I mean what are you waiting for?" Well, I know, in part:
her options are limited—school, a job, a way out of here; marriage, a
family, a permanence. Today Eva could be sitting next to me as she suddenly appeared with a girl friend, both of them in tight tan corduroys and
jerseys, just plunk herself down with a certain defiance and answer my
silly questions: Is he Jim Sappier's brother? Who's Sammy's wife? How
long did it take to rehearse the Snake Dance? Next year, a husband and
a baby—or a baby and not a husband.

To get to the pageant I walk between
church and convent, down a gravel path, I pay two bucks at a table (to

benefit St. Anne's Sodality) and emerge overlooking the river. Bleachers have been set up just behind the rectory overlooking the dancing place and the river. There are about a hundred spectators, mostly Indians, men in sport shirts, women in bermudas. Those who wear tribal dress will dance. They mingle now. But on the way down: a beautiful thing. Two Indian couples from *India*, wives in gorgeous saris, swirling around them as they walked into Chief Poolaw's American Indian souvenir shop: puff of light blue and pink silk on the breeze, and 5-year-old Bobby Troy Nelson standing to look at the women in absolute amazement, eyes wide as a sunflower's. I leave him waiting for them to come out again.

The pageant begins with Ernest Goslin reading from what sounds like *The Life and Traditions of the Red Man,* a not uninteresting rendering of the creation myths and the tales of Glooskap—*Klose-kur-beh,* as Nicolar would have it—but so thoroughly suffused with Christian, nay, Catholic imagery as to make the grim austerity of the oral legends, collected in the 1850s by Charles Leland, seem like birchbark scratchings to Nicolar's Byzantine tapestries.

Ernest thanks the audience for "giving the young people a chance to wear their feathers for a few hours." And the dances follow in succession—The Welcome Dance, the Green Corn Dance, the Hunter's Dance, the Wedding Dance, the Snake Dance, the Medicine Man's Dance, the Penobscot Death Dance—essentially a finite series of adumbrations upon a single, intense, staccato movement of the legs and body, a jerking, now animated, now grave—most of them done either in a circular pattern or a snakelike one, the circle opening to an undulating line, to the accompaniment of a drum (tom-tom), which of course was not the ancient practice: the Penobscots used a cow-horn rattle filled with shot in the 19th century; earlier, a gourd filled with dried pumpkin seeds, the rattle especially of gourd and seeds in keeping with the basic primal (mythic) thrust of the dances: Nature, the Creation, and the human seasons of conception, birth, growth, union, procreation, and death cognate with the seasons of earth and the movements of the tribe or bands of the tribe through the seasons from winter camp to summer habitation, the harvest, and the hunt.

But the real problem with these dances and latter-day Indianisms is that you begin to wonder if, after so many Indian movies and other white corruptions of native dances and ceremonies, the ceremonies themselves haven't imperceptibly absorbed if not become their corruptions, in a word, the white man's idea or version of what they used to be in reality. So the primal thrust is there in name and probably in form, but what about war whoops and drumbeats: wasn't there really something a lot more complex and indeed more primitive? For one thing, it wasn't a spectacle; it was an intensely personal *and* communal act, the dancing, each person experiencing the rite and the concomitant release, feet rooted in the earth, head in the sky. As for the songs, they are recoverable from Speck and Curtis (*The Indians' Book*)—white sources, white notation, but at least recoverable. (Teresa Sappier, who sang, told me she was taught them by her mother—"but I don't know what the words mean.")

Sunday, July 25

I was fifteen minutes late for services at the Penobscot Indian Baptist Church, Rev. Daniel F. Downs, Sr., Pastor (his wife at the piano: rotund, white-haired lady in blue print dress, glasses, sitting between times alone in left front pew), because I'd locked my keys in the car and had to get a screwdriver to slip in through the vent and open it. But I didn't feel too badly as one middle-aged man slid in ahead of me, parking his car with the two others in the lot of the gray, asphalt-shingled church.

I counted sixteen people, one young man, one old man, two middle-aged men, two little girls, two old women, seven teen-age girls between, say, thirteen and twenty, one teen-age boy. Rev. Downs said, "If I was preaching a social gospel, telling the folks how wonderful the life they're leading is, how everything is just great in America, I could fill the church every Sunday. But what I have to say about the sin in the world and the evil in men's hearts nobody likes to hear. That's not a fashionable message. . . ."

He introduced two "college students" who bill themselves as Ambassadors for Christ and travel all over the country, "sharing Christ, even in rest rooms." One plays a guitar; the other sings: "We see this longing and this need in people's faces. They need to be satisfied." Ed and Ken might pass for fraternal twins; they look more like surfers than "Jesus freaks," and they told a story about how they talked God at a dormitory in Orono on the Maine campus last night while "those students" jeered us, but "one boy came up afterwards and he wanted to know how Jesus would save him. We had a long talk, and he said, 'I knew there was something wrong with my life.'"

Rev. Downs announced a "demand performance" of *Dead Men on Furlough*, "filmed during the Korean War in Korea and shows the real facts of a country taken over by the Commies. Persecution of the Christians brought into being one of the strongest Christian Churches in the world. Don't miss it!"

The day's worship program contained a quotation:

"P. T. Barnum was right: there's a sucker born every minute."

Rev. Downs is a balding Down Easter, wearing a tan and brown short-sleeved summer shirt with an olive tie and what looked like a lodge pin in it. The topic of his sermon was "Reconciliation":

—"We're naturally bad. If you don't believe it, watch a little child from the crib. There's a natural spirit of rebellion there. We don't have to teach children to be bad; they're born bad.

—"We cannot please God; there's nothing good in us, in our own being, that can be reconciled to God.

—"The reason for so many suicides among young people and old people, psychiatrists tell us, is they have no hope.

—"You take one step toward God; he'll take two to you! (A wasp flew in, circling the pulpit, little rustle among the girls who were not the lively beautiful girls who danced yesterday and frolicked by the river; they seemed subdued, in church because they had to be. One girl yawning practically in the minister's face. There was a fan going in the corner and an old suitcase-type movie projector with a screen on the floor near it, these presumably for the movie that night.)

We sang two hymns whose names I've already forgotten. I put a quarter in the collection plate—my price of admission. I was among the first out, beaten only by the gangly teen-ager (a Loring boy, I think) whom I suddenly recalled as being one of the best dancers yesterday.

Sunday, 4 P.M.

I'm on the bridge where swallows sing and dive, Milford to the east, a church steeple. I saw another performance of the "pageant," drank a lot of soda, got tired; there wasn't anyone to talk to, and decided I'd go to the Catholic Mass at 6, after the last performance. Burnell comes up to me, "The pageant bores me!" And there was an Indian, obviously a Vietnam veteran, with a patch on his field jacket, "Vietcong Hunting Club." I wanted to go over and ask him if it hadn't occurred to him that those people he had to pursue and kill weren't fighting the same battle in Southeast Asia that he was fighting—or his people were—right here in the U.S., the same struggle of all the oppressed peoples in the world. Then I thought, "Who am I to bug the poor kid? He was probably glad to get out of there alive."

St. Anne's is a fairly spacious church with an abstract wall hanging above the altar in bright red and blue cloth pieces: the Eucharist, a fish for Christ on top, the wheel of the world below, and a chalice and wafer under all. The Priest, Fr. Rokus, officiates from a thronelike chair; a Sister reads; and it's a folk Mass with one of the Francis sisters, a large, pretty girl about twenty with black hair, dark-brown skin, and coal-black eyes playing her guitar very nicely. The service is exhilarating—and over before you know it. Of course, the church is packed, the dancers having all come in in native dress. High on the wall to the right is a painting of the Crucifixion, by a native artist, done in somber rich colors, pressed in the 19th century as juices from berries. It's been varnished over now, and from a distance looks like a Sienese primitive, which, in a way, it is.

After the first performance, forgot to record an encounter: nicely dressed middle-aged woman with a Boston-sounding voice went up to an ancient lady being wheeled up the gravel path onto the street in a chair. She was bent over, her face all wrinkles.

Woman leans over the wheelchair: "Do you remember Joe Polis?" she asks in a loud voice.

Some confusion, a daughter, I guess, who's pushing the chair, translates. The old lady's nodding. The Boston lady says, "He's buried in that cemetery right over there." Again the old woman seemed to nod affirmatively, but I think it was just that she heard the name "Joe Polis" and recognized it. The Boston lady went off smiling.

Talking with Ken and Jean yesterday, I asked Ken, relative to what he was saying about Indians voting, just how many Indians were registered as living on the Island, and he said about 383 on "or around Old Town." Jean broke right in: "My god, it really doesn't matter. I wish you wouldn't get into numbers. It's quality not quantity. I mean, I don't ask you how many toes you have, but you walk around all right, don't you? You don't have any trouble walking, do you?"

Monday morning, July 26

One of those absolutely still, hot summer mornings. Even the sounds of cars on the road and the cries of the children playing on Stillwater Avenue seem somehow muted. You get a feeling everyone is reserving himself for the rigors of getting through the day. I lie in bed; all around me my books on the Penobscot Indians—Frank Speck lamenting that the next phase in their history to be told, after 1936, would be that of "acculturation."

I was pondering, too, what Ernest Goslin said yesterday in introducing the dances, that "the Penobscot people have been able to withstand the encroachment of forces—terrible bloodshed and war—and survive until now with the help of God." But those forces must include the coming of the white man and the Church, itself, wiping these people's memories clean and their bodies out, plundering their lands and their inner resources; and now it's a question of all of us withstanding these "forces." I really wonder what has survived in these people to hold them together at least as a political unit. They are now so intermarried between tribes, Passamaquoddies, Micmacs, and Malacites with Penobscots, that I think it can now be safely concluded that there are no more "pureblooded" Penobscots, if there ever were. But that's not a negative thing. They've all of them survived in intermarrying, and what did survive was a lot of Indian consciousness, race consciousness, family consciousness, as these people are intensely familiar, and that is a major "force" in itself. It used to be the clans; now it is the family as clan—not the Bear clan or the Otter clan, but the Neptunes as clan, the Mitchells as patriarchy (or matriarchy?). I'll have to talk to Wayne about this.

11 A.M.

I drove up to Wayne's, called in through the kitchen screens, then walked through the kitchen (toast shards scattered in the plates, coffee cups on the table) to find Terri changing Jason, who was six months old yesterday (he gurgled and grabbed my finger, stuck it in his mouth), and Wayne, sitting bare-chested at the telephone table, on the phone to the State Police. Last night a car full of whites, men it looked like, not kids, with Maine plates had driven up Oak Hill, and the men had shouted threats: they would bomb some of the houses tonight.

Wayne said the police hadn't heard anything about it and wanted to know who he was.

"I told them I was a resident of Oak Hill."

"Well, I'm not staying around here," Terri said, still in her dressing gown. Wayne sat down and started to play with Jason. He said he'd just been on Bangor radio. A talk show. Apparently the talk-master had wanted some discussion of Indian problems, and Wayne phoned in.

"I told them about the threat last night. I said, 'That's just about the way you treat Indians around here. You'd love to exterminate us.' Only one other person called, a woman. So they wanted to discuss Indian problems, and they got two calls, both from Indians. I gave them an earful. I filled them in on what's happening around here."

I told Wayne I'd gone to the Penobscot Baptist Church yesterday morning and found 16 people in attendance and that I'd been amazed at the reactionary attitudes, political, social, even religious, that were either expressed or implied in the service.

"No wonder they never get any more than forty people there," I said.

"Well, it's mostly one family," Wayne said, "the Lorings."

I told him I'd gone to Mass at 6 P.M.

"You had yourself a busy day," he laughed. "I wouldn't speak to the Priest. I was right there at the Pageant, and Father Rokus come up to me and laid his hand on my shoulder. 'How are you, Wayne?' I didn't say nothing, just turned to the guy I was with, and started discussing the dance. 'Father's talking to you,' he said. And Father goes, 'Aren't you going to say hello, Wayne? Not even hello?' And I says, 'I don't give a shit who's talking.' I used those words, too—"

"He's right in the thick of the Tribe's politics. He supports one faction against another. He wouldn't support us in running our own program this year. I went to him this summer and asked for a donation toward the program to help feed the people who were here. We had Indians from the Mohawk reservation in New York, some from Canada, and he said he didn't have any money, that I should donate to help support him. I said, 'Don't give me that bullshit, Father. I know how much money you make. You get your food and your fuel free, and you get a salary, too!' "

" 'The Church is very poor,' he said."

" 'Like hell it is, Father, like hell.' "

He was bouncing Jason up and down, and he asked Terri if she was going to feed Jason any cereal. (Earlier she'd gone out to prepare it.) The men are very patriarchal.

[Later, Wayne's father, sitting at the red picnic table out in front of his house two doors down from Wayne's, working on the generator from his daughter's Mustang; all the women coming and going around him hanging wash, tending kids, cooking inside; the entire family humming quietly around Norris; and him sitting in great serenity, a profoundly philosophical man; black hair getting longer over the ears (Wayne told me *he'd* been kicked out of his father's house for having hair as long as his father's is now), dark-red shirt, blue jeans, nut-brown hands stained with car grease, chain-smoking Marlboros: "We're acculturated. That began with the first white man setting foot in Maine, like that helicopter going down there in the Philippines, the minute it landed, *acculturation*. We're acculturated but not assimilated. One time some white man visiting here from New Jersey said we should all enter white society; that would solve all our problems, and I told him: 'White society in America is about the most rigid class and caste system I've ever studied, worse than any Indian one. Now you tell me where am I going to fit in that system!'"]

"He refused to marry us, you know. He said he didn't want to be party to a mixed marriage, one that wouldn't last a year. Well, it was a year yesterday."

Wayne bounced Jason, who was dressed in a little one-piece blue suit; he bounced him up and down on his knee:

"And you know what? Three months later he married another couple, mixed—right in front of everybody. There's your politics. No, he should leave the people alone. He should keep his nose out of the tribe's business."

Wayne said he'd take me over to his father's before he himself left for his uncle's camp, which he was about to do. I asked him if his father would mind my having a tape recorder around in case I wanted to record our conversation.

"Hell, no," he said. "He's got one himself he uses when people come to talk to him."

I excused myself, pissed off that I'd forgotten to stick the recorder in my car, rushed back to the motel (hot as hell going and coming), and when I got back to Wayne's, Terri said he was down at his father's, so I drove over, parked off Oak Hill Road. I saw two women and called up asking if this was Wayne Mitchell's father's house. They said yes, but Wayne wasn't there. I got the tape recorder out of the car and started up the hill. Wayne's father was seated at his red-lacquered picnic table with built-in benches, hunched over that generator, scraping away at the rust on the edges of it with a yellow, plastic-handled screwdriver. I asked him if he were Norris, and he nodded. I asked a girl in orange top and white shorts if she was Wayne's sister, and she said "Yes" very curtly and hung the few pieces of wash and left.

Norris continued to scrape for a while. Then he looked up at me, his handsome face (he resembles an older, wiser, sadder, more intelligent Richard Boone) set in a serious mask:

"I see you haven't read Vine Deloria."

He has very strong hands, and a dark skin like Wayne's that has a certain burnishment, as of copper. He must be in his early fifties, but he could pass for forty: coal-black hair, a tiny stubble of mustache and beard which he hadn't shaved that morning.

I started to get nervous:

"I have," I said; "you mean where he talks about keeping anthropologists off the reservations? Well, I, er, understand. I *know* it's a problem, but I'm a friend of Wayne's, and I'm not an anthropologist; I'm a writer!"

"If I remember correctly he says beware of white man—any white man—with a tape recorder."

"Of course," I said, "I realize it's a problem."

"There was a fellow come up to see me, and he had it in his pocket. He didn't think I saw him reach in and turn it on. I said, 'Now wait just a minute; what do you think you're doing with that thing? I don't mind *talking* to anybody—' "

"It is an invasion of privacy," I said, "a terrible one."

"Hell, I mean it's all in Vine Deloria. You can't trust a white man, even after all these years. You don't know what his intentions are. You try to trust him, but then you find out you can't."

[Norris raps at great length, in the most engrossing manner, about exploitations, cruelties; he's well read in total American Indian history . . . I'm going crazy because I have no way of getting it all down, I'm not Truman Capote with that fabled tape-recorder memory he supposedly developed for In Cold Blood: *I'm caught because the content of what Norris is laying down is so completely absorbing. What do I do, try and listen to listen—for the benefit of my own head—or try and listen to memorize; in which case I'll fuck up anyway. I give up, succumb to Norris' language.]*

"Intentions, I mean we're speaking of genocide," he concludes—must have been an hour of absolutely prime observations, deductions that would make a white academic historian or anthropologist look sick—"of the extermination of a whole race of people, a whole way of life. I get peeved when I read these histories about how the white man came here and found a handful of Indians encamped on the Saco River or on Mt. Desert

Island and how he said there were only a few hundred Indians—Savages!—around here. Well, you know damn well there were hundreds of thousands. They just broke up all over the East into family groups and smaller camps so they could be comparatively free from raiding parties. But just the notion that from having sighted a few camping parties there were only a couple hundred Indians in North America, well, that's what I mean—"

"The white man's first view of the Indian was colored by racism, wasn't it? He was prepared already to see what he saw. You just look at the names of the Indians: Norridgewock, Wawenock, Abenaki, Aroosaguntacook, Sokoki, Pennacook—Christ, those aren't the names the Indians had. The white man gave them those names. You talk about tribes as cultural entities, those names don't tell you anything. I subscribe to the theory that these were just family groups scattered all over the terrain—"

[Notes:]

1. *Try to describe setting, all the cars in the yard, old weather-beaten Cape Cod house on the hill; as we talk, the sun on my back, Norris looking right into it, smoking, talking, working on the generator, the smell of the pulp mills omnipresent.*

2. *Our discussion of place, environment, and assimilation—"You assimilate the Indian and it's all over."*

3. *Norris talking about his way of life—"I work when I can." His studies, experiences at U. of Me., almost up to his BA degree, was scheduled to teach in Abenaki Studies program but wanted it to come under the Dept. of Anthropology so that when funding ends the Penobscot part of it won't die with the entire program. Lots of people come to talk with him; at University he is considered more of a resource person than a student. Got onto Thoreau.*

Apparently there's a Mrs. Sherwood who lives over in Milford, a Thoreau nut, who talks constantly about being able to look out on the river Thoreau and Joe Polis paddled on, always pushing Thoreau, she is, a regular Thoreau fanatic; Whatever T. said must have been true.

"Now this Joe Polis is a very shadowy figure," says Norris. "Mrs. Sherwood told me he was a bear, that he'd carved his sign on a tree, but nobody I know verifies that. If you asked any of the old people around here who Joe Polis was they'd just shake their heads. I can show you where he's buried, right down there in the old graveyard on Center Street, he and his wife. There's a bell on the stones, but as to who he was, nobody seems to know. A very shadowy figure, I'd say. He might have settled here from someplace else. Maybe he was Malacite. He's no bear."

July 26, 5 P.M.
Wacked-out. I spent all afternoon in Bangor at The Golden Era of Logging on the Penobscot exhibition at City Hall. Unbelievable. I could write a hundred pages on it, describe in detail the ingenious models and facsimiles of that early technology, excerpt from the booklets and handouts. But just dig on this copy.

—*PRIME MOVERS/*   Out of state *proprietors, David Pingree, 1795–1864, Wm. Bingham, 1752–1864:*

Through land ownership and development these men greatly influenced and assisted the tremendous growth of lumbering in the Penobscot Basin. They were wealthy, influential, held diversified interests. Representing these investors were local agents who were intelligent and industrious and of great integrity. The interests of these men included not only timber lands but railroads, ship building, shipping, banking, manufacturing and mercantile establishments. Their paths crossed as neighbors, business men, community leaders, competitors, friends and enemies. One in particular was Rufus Dwinell, 1804–64, second mayor of Bangor: dashing, ambitious, aggressive, he had the faculty of doing more business successfully with a given amount of capital than almost any other man of his time—

OK. Now, here we go:

In 1820 Maine and Massachusetts sold PUBLIC lands in excess of 11 million acres to speculators, viz:
>   1820   *14½ cents an acre*
>   1824   *45 cents an acre*
>   1831   *50 cents an acre*
>   1875   *$1.23 an acre*

Next: pay scale of the workers in the lumber business:
>   *Boss—30 to 60 dollars a month*
>   [Just imagine how much wealth they produced for the out-of-state owner.]
>   *Chopper—20 to 26 dollars a month*
>   *Swamper—12 to 15 dollars a month*
>   *(cut roads to forest)*
>   *Loggers,*

cooks,
other
camp
help—12 dollars or less a month
[Men died by the hundreds because of the hazards involved in this work.]
"Never mind the men but be careful of the Peaveys (logging hook);
they cost three dollars!"

Reprinted as "logging humor"

I'm looking all over the place for references to the Indians, who played
a major part in the logging operations as expert choppers, boatsmen, river
men, loggers etc. Nothing, not even a photograph. I look for Mrs. Eckstorm's *The Penobscot Man,* a collection of stories and recollections of
just this activity; the girl at the desk tells me they "couldn't find a copy
to borrow" for the exhibit.

I'm simply staggered by this lighthearted, civic-minded celebration of
the exploitation of the land, the Indians, the working men of Maine . . .
it's almost a paradigm of the nationwide process that left Maine by the
end of the 19th century—formerly one of the most potentially wealthy of
states—a depressed area, which it has remained to this day.

On the way out I catch sight of a plaque that says it all: the exhibition has been sponsored by THE JUNIOR LEAGUE OF BANGOR.

8 P.M.

I went up to Ken and Jean's—Jean looking very well, still hasn't gone
to the hospital—who were talking with the Sapiel sisters, Mary, married
with four children, and Teresa, who sang at the pageant. I asked Teresa
who taught her the songs. She said her mother had them from her own
mother, but she added, she wasn't going to sing anymore. "I don't want
to be an Indian no more, just a white person." She laughs, very jolly.
Then she apologizes for being "negative," says she isn't the right person
for me to talk to. She's studying medical technology in Waterville, and
she never wanted to see the Island again. "You want to know what this
place is, a great big security blanket for everyone who was born here.
They can always come back and have a shoulder to cry on. They know
there's one place in the world that welcomes them."

Mary lives with her husband and children in Old Town. She and her
husband are both shoe workers, both on strike since last spring—they
struck; then the company locked them out. Then her husband went to

work in a pulp mill. We talked unions, and she said that although she and her husband would vote to have one, they weren't very strong in Maine. Mary said her children didn't have any trouble in school, and we all began to talk about whether living on the Island stigmatized you. Mary said, "The further away you get, the more you're accepted. People go to cities, and you tell your neighbors you're an American Indian, and they think it's great, but around here, no." Mary's a very pretty small, dark woman, quite shapely in denim shorts and white blouse, her hair in a short permanent; Teresa in stretch pants and blue jersey, square, modish wire-rims for glasses. She's plump and jolly and volatile, complained about all the singing she had to do, but I think she liked the sense of having been in the pageant and the fact that I told her I liked her singing, which I did.

Tuesday morning, July 27

Couple of things I want to take note of before I get up to Martin's to talk with him before he goes to Manchester, Conn., for what looks like a year at least. His mother is sick again, had a seizure while visiting Martin and Kathy here on Saturday, is now in Bangor in intensive care, and last night Ken told me Martin decided to go to Connecticut to be near his mother. Ken and Jean will move into Martin's house next door to them. (Later, last night when I went over to Martin's to find Wayne there in the kitchen, and Martin's cousin, an interesting-looking woman, and Martin all sitting around an oil lamp talking, Martin said he wanted Ken to be in the house because he knew it would be well looked after. Apparently Martin will turn the work of the coffeehouse over to some of the younger people. The Thompsons and Wayne are very sorry to see Martin go, and I am too, as I always look forward to seeing him when I come. Martin has been invaluable in helping me to get to know people. I hope he comes back—and stays.

TV cackles, and I can't get over the immorality of an 8-million-dollar electric dune buggy—a fucking car!—being dragged up to the moon and about to be driven across it. We've learned absolutely nothing in our 400-year rape of the New World, and now we are about to leave our debris on the moon's surface and all over outer space, not to mention whatever planets in the solar system we are going to defile next. I think of the first white men who came to North America and what they did to the land and the people—slashed the woods and burned them out, kidnaped "Savages" and brought them back to Europe to be gawked at and die of smallpox. Then the settlers, the fishermen, farmers, and trappers—

the beginning of the end. (And implicit in every account you read—Champlain, Rosier, Pring, Levett—the white man's uncontestable right to what he found in the New World.) No wonder every single Indian I've spoken to up here in the past five days has mentioned the discovery of the Tasaday Tribe—the "Stone Age" people of the Philippine rain forests, the Manube, who have been described as having no knowledge of rice, corn, salt, sugar, or pottery; no contact with the sea; and maybe the only people in the world who don't know anything about, or use, tobacco! They just know what's going to happen to them now that the white man has "found" them: they just feel it in their bones; it's part of their racial memory. It's uncanny how everyone brings the conversation around to the Tasaday Manube, even one kid—was it Burnell? And I'm not unaware of what role I play in it. I can't come on as the dispassionate journalist recording the living, oral history of the Penobscots. As Norris pointed out yesterday, or implied, I'm here to exploit, too, tape recorder on or not. I'm here to snoop around and peek into houses and into souls if I can. I'm a white exploiter. After all I'm the one who's being paid for the book, and it will be published under my name.

Noon

I checked with Wayne about the "threat" the night before to see if anyone did come up. Apparently Wayne wasn't too disturbed if he was going up to his uncle's camp. It turned out he didn't stay the night there, but came back. It was quiet on the Island last night, the police cruised Oak Hill and "downstreet," but no trouble. Come to find out the threat grew out of a brawl in Old Town two nights before. A resident of the Island was involved, everyone apparently drunk. But I told Wayne a threat to bomb houses proceeding from a thing like a fist fight was a bit heavy. "Well, it's coming to that," he said.

Wednesday, July 28

I drove down the Maine Pike with Bicou this morning—blazing hot from Bangor to Augusta; then it started to rain. By the time we hit Portsmouth the highway was like an ocean. Bicou smoked incessantly and drank beer from two king-size six-packs he picked up in Old Town. He offered me some, but I refused, told him beer gives me a headache, especially when I'm driving. He talked some on the Maine Pike, then subsided into occasional remarks, was sleeping by the time I got to his stop on Mass. Route 1. He said he'd spent the night before at Senabeh's because the police had been looking for him for some unspecified reason—dope? He was drunk, and Senabeh always has an extra mattress for him, said he was Senabeh's nephew, and occasionally they went out into the woods together. He says Senabeh's knowledge of medicine is excellent and that he can cure himself of practically anything. "He drinks, but why do you think he doesn't get sick? He has medicine for everything."

Bicou had a red canvas bag with him and just the clothes he was wearing, was going to visit "some rich friends," then maybe see his "woman." He'd be back on the Island by mid-August, and then he wanted to go north for potato picking. On the other hand he was considering going back to California, where his brother, age 30—"now there's a hell-raiser"—was involved in an Indian culture program. Bicou is sarcastic when he refers to Red Power people or the Indian nationalists on the Reservation, those he's met in New York State. "The real Indian lives off the land."

I asked him, since he seemed so heavily involved in the white counterculture if he wasn't trading on his Indianness. "Aren't you a symbol to the people you hang with, especially if they're white?"

"I just have a good fucking time, man. I just groove."

VoICES 2

WAYNE MITCHELL

Bucky Andrew used to live in this room, and across the hall was my great-grandmother's room, my grandfather's mother. My grandmother told me one time about Bucky Andrew when he came in drunk, and if you coulda seen pictures of my grandmother when she was younger, you coulda seen how big she was. So one time Bucky Andrew come in here and started harassing her, and she told him, she says, "You get your arse the hell up them goddamn stairs," she says, "or I'll throw you up there!" He says, "You ain't got the goddamn gumption to do it." Jez' Christ, my grandmother's a big woman, so she grabbed him right by the seat of the pants and the neck of his shirt, and she threw him right up the stairs, and he landed on this landing out there and sametime he hit the floor she was right behind him and she threw him again. She threw him in here!

Her name was Mildred, Mildred Mitchell. She was a McKinnon. She was a white woman from over town, and when she got married—she and my grandfather married in 1917—when she married my grandfather, her whole family disowned her because she married an Indian. And of course back in them days, you know, it's when the Ku Klux Klan was quite strong in Milford. And the whole family disowned her, so she lived over here for fifty-five years. When they first got married, she used to live down street, and she used to bake bread, pies, and all kinds of pastries and baked beans and things and sell them on the weekends, just so that they could have money to fix the house with. This was before my grandfather inherited this place. Then after about two years down street my great-grandmother, my grandfather's mother, asked them to move here, so they moved up here. When they did move, Dan Mitchell, my aunt Hilda's first husband, who was no relation to us, he's a "Daylight Mitchell"; that's a different clan; we're the "Bears." (Each clan was given a name, like the Bear, a very fierce animal who can be very gentle sometimes; but also, a bear is a great hunter and fisher. Or the Eel—an eel's very swift, very slippery, very quiet, and could be treacherous at times. Martin's clan are the Eels, the Neptunes. Then there's the Cat, or Lynx, or Bobcat, clan, because of their slyness and their great speed. It all goes with the animal. What the animal's

115

attributes are that's what the clans identified themselves with, or represented themselves as being. They were given these names, but you had to earn it, too. And the point was to live according to all these attributes and share the world out there with all the other animals and people the way their namesakes did.)

So Dan Mitchell moved them up here with a team of horses and a buckboard. Lawrence was a baby then. He was the oldest son, and he died when he was fourteen years old. He died of spinal meningitis. Most of the kids slept downstairs. The room where Terri and I sleep now was my grandparents' bedroom, and some of the children stayed in that room. Then there was a little room where my baby's room is now which was the other kids' room. This living room downstairs was a combined living room, bedroom, work area. 'Course the two rooms up here were inhabited by Bucky Andrew, who was no relation to the family, but my grandmother and grandfather took quite a liking to him, so he lived in this room until he died, and by my great-grandmother, who lived across the hall.

My grandparents lost three children in all, Lawrence from meningitis, and Adeline and Mary both died of ptomaine poisoning from grapes. My Uncle John, who is past governor and now representative of the tribe in Augusta, ate some of those grapes himself and almost died from it, but he didn't have enough of them in him. So they lost three children—in fact in those days everyone lost children, and the children were laid out in the homes of course.

The family made baskets all the time. That's how they lived. They'd sell them. My father told me they used to make these little, little tiny baskets, my great-grandmother did, and she'd sell them just so the kids could have money to go to church with, to put in the collection. My grandfather would make mostly laundry baskets and pack baskets. My grandmother made shopping baskets, and that little basket sitting right there she made. She also made what they call barrels, little round wastebaskets. That tent that's rolled up over there used to be outside. It's a huge tent, bigger than this room. They used to work in it, and they'd have all their baskets on display for tourists. Every summer they'd go to the coast and spend the whole summer there; then they'd return in the fall and start in all over again making baskets, using ash wood and, of course, marsh grass.

This house is quite an old house. This part of the house was floated down from Sugar Island about seventeen miles upriver. It's about a hundred fifty, a hundred seventy-five years old. So they floated it down on barges, the Indians did back then, and they really knew the river. You

Wayne Mitchell

know it took about sixty men to get this house up here. At that time Indians lived on all the islands, on Orson, Orono, Black Island, Twin Islands, Long Island, Sugar Island, Hemlock, Birch, Big Bratsky, Little Bratsky, Moon, Cow, Lincoln—I don't know all the names, but every family owned land there. We own seven islands, the Mitchell family does. There wasn't an island didn't have two, three houses . . . quite huge homes, too. Everyone lived on their land and made use of it, but now they just live and that's it. They don't live for the land but for themselves.

We have over here what we call the Knitters Group, and that's a sort of minority that goes against everything that comes up. That's what we've named them, the Knitters. They represent their own interest, and they conspire against the gains that we're all trying to make. They're mostly middle-aged; some are people that have run for office and been rejected. Oh, they're very Indian: they're for what they call the old ways of living. They don't want to see anything new come in here because everything's changing and going to what they call "the dogs." We're trying to better the community in certain ways, and they'd just as soon see it stay the way it was because it's the way they've always been themselves.

The difference between my interest in Indian ways and theirs is in teaching the children those ways. Their interest is not to teach the children. Now you take my parents; they both speak Penobscot and Passamaquoddy and I know neither or very little of both, and what I've learned I've picked up since I was fourteen years old mostly on my own. But I've been able to identify myself and make myself proud that I'm an American Indian of this American continent and that I know I had a purpose and still have a purpose if I wanted to fulfill it and gain a certain knowledge because they can take everything else away from us but one thing and that is our knowledge, and the more I have the more my children will.

But I think the biggest reason why the Indian has survived and can survive on what some people think is so little is that he can think on two planes, two plateaus. He can think his own way, the Indian way, and he can think the white man's way, and he can conspire with each so there's a certain thrust there for himself. He can thrive more successfully because he knows the ways of each, he's *had* to know them.

For instance, take this pollution problem that we have today. The white man can think of industry, money, but the thing the Indian can think of above everything else is preservation—self-preservation and the preservation of his surroundings. And the reason for this—this goes way back—the Indian has always worshiped everything. Everything had its purpose, every living thing; everything that grew, everything that breathed, has always had its place and its purpose. No matter how minute they were, they always had their purpose and they were worshiped for that purpose, and who are we to destroy that purpose? Now the way the white man would think is, Jesus, they were put here for us to take. We take, but we don't return. The Indian will take, but he will return what he has taken. He will return just as much. This is his way of thinking.

Being in the psychiatric game, especially in white society, has taught me they can only think one way. This is where it gets back to that. White people are too proud to bring themselves to another level of thinking in order to clear things up. Now one of the reasons for this is the circumstances of the country, the situation it's in: the daily routine, the hustle and bustle, you might say. Do this, do that. Don't make a mistake or else. If you do it, don't do it wrong. It's the way of living, the place they're in, the speed of everyday life—it's the money situation. Their one concern is, how the hell am I gonna make my next buck? Instead of thinking, well I know I'm gonna have a hard time making my next buck so I'm gonna make the best of this time in order to survive and survive fruitfully.

Because you don't see too many Indians in a mental institution. Hardly ever you see an Indian there, and nine times out of ten if you see him in there it's because of something like multiple sclerosis or alcoholism. And Indian alcoholism is different from white alcoholism. Anyone can become an alcoholic, depending on their life situation, but the reason for the Indian's alcoholism is because of stress and prejudice reflected upon him. A lot of Indians just can't cope with that. Another reason, if I want to go into the medical part of it, is because of chemical makeup. The Indian is very sensitive, and alcohol has always had a poisonous effect on him from the very beginning when the white man first came.

I've been on my own since I was fourteen, and I've had to learn how to survive. It's just like planting a garden; it depends upon how well you baby it and help it grow, and if you do that you get a good fruition from your plants; you get a beautiful harvest and I figure it's the same way with life. How you put yourself in certain situations and help yourself and develop your mind, the more of a chance you have of surviving and the better your harvest will be.

I've always gone to Indians, the old ones, a lot of them. Mary Jane Francis, who's ninety. Well, I used to go visit her when she was eighty. The day she turned eighty was the first day I ever set foot in her house. She lives down street; she's still living there. She speaks English and she speaks Indian. I used to go down there and talk with her by the hour, and I'd look at her surroundings and I'd look at the way she lived and I'd look at her, *herself*, her expressions and the life on her face—you could see how hard a life she's had and how she struggled through it and how she's still trying to survive. And other people like Russell Joseph, who was a carver on the Island and who's dead now, and Senabeh and Leo Francis and a lot of old Indians now that are just about ready for the grave that I've talked with and enjoyed their company.

There's nothing I love more than to sit down and talk with an Indian that is an Indian. They don't talk like white men. A conversation between two white men always ends up in a power struggle—what I know more than you, what I can do better than you. But these Indians I've talked to are just earthy people. They lived for the earth and they lived for themselves to make a better life for themselves and they've tried and they've struggled, and what they've attained now is just a small amount of what they hoped to attain, and they know it.

Now a white person would come here; they'd see Senabeh; they'd see Leo; and they'd say, "Well, they're a couple of drunks." This is the only way they can see. They can't see *through* anything different. What makes Senabeh such a great man is his vast knowledge. He's an individual who can be classified as an individual. He is the one person that knows what *Senabeh* knows. And he's just the person that knows what life is about, what living things are about, what purpose they have and how they can help you. It was just passed on to him, that's all. It's gone out with my parents' generation, but the generation before him knew everything there was to know. Senabeh learned it all from his mother—and also from his father. Each Indian has his own certain way of thinking, and if both parents pass down to the child what both their life-styles were about, this child has a remarkable development of life ahead of him because he's learned two ways of living. And then he has to live his own way, and plus he knows how to live the white man's way. So he has four ways of surviving that he knows of!

Senabeh lived alone in the woods and on Hemlock Island for quite a few years. He's quite an odd man and he thinks on the Indian level more than he does on the white man's, but he can think the other way, *that* I know and have seen. And it's good. Now I'll go into the woods myself, sometimes for two, three hours. Maybe a whole day I'll be gone. Terri won't see me. You just get away from civilization. An Indian has to have solitude in order to think. And an Indian thinks a great deal, and he analyzes instead of being just skeptical. You can take the woods away from an Indian, but you can't take it *out* of him.

I was born in my father's house next door. My father was born in this house and he went to school at Old Town; he went to school on the Island and over there. He went to the University of Maine for one year, and in the last six years he's been finishing his college. He was tribal clerk at one time but he won't run for office.

When I left high school I felt like a soul wandering in the darkness and coming up against a brick wall and reaching out in any direction, probing, trying to find a way to get over that wall. And I was lost in myself because I didn't know what the hell I was and what I was supposed to do in life—and I thought I had to find it over there, over that wall. I went through several training programs. I tried each one, tried to feel my way through each one and see if it was really the one I wanted to do. I did a workshop program in higher education, but I found that psychiatry was what I wanted to do and still is, even though I went through other things like working on construction and as a mason-tender. I even drove a cab. I just danced around the fire, you might say, and when I found the coal that I thought was mine I took it.

In '69 I went to MacLean's. Before that I worked as a psychiatric aide at Bangor State Hospital and then at Eastern Maine Medical Center. I went through a training program as a medical aide and as a psychiatric aide. After I finished at MacLean's I came back here.

When I worked in mental hospitals I got a lot of criticism because I was bringing myself to my patients. They didn't like that one bit, the doctors. They told me not to get involved with my patients and I told them, "The hell with you, how can you not help but get involved with your patient?" If you think you can help him by not doing it, okay, but it's just the ruination of him if you don't get involved. When you do get involved—in my personal opinion and in the way that I've worked—you get a certain compassion and understanding that can't be achieved in any other way. You have to put yourself in his shoes and try to imagine his experiences and try to help him cope with them. But at the same time you try to get him to answer his own problem. I think I was getting better at doing this because I was getting better at understanding myself by then. And this has been my whole theme on life anyway—how can you understand anyone else if you can't understand yourself? I mean, what the hell good are you to anyone else? Well, that's Indian thinking, too! I tell myself the more furs I have under my belt the better off I am at understanding.

I met Terri, my wife, at a dance one night in Old Town, didn't pay much attention to her, just someone to dance with. About a month later I met her at another dance. Then things started to blossom a little. You might say the seed had germinated and was becoming a plant. By that time we'd known each other for three, four years so the rose is in full blossom now. Why a white girl and not an Indian girl is hard to say. You have to find your mate no matter what nationality. If she has the qualities you're looking for, then that's the person you want—when you get hit by that little arrow there ain't no two ways about it! Of course, there's a history in my family of white people coming into the family. My parents felt the same way I did about it. When you meet the right person that's the one for you.

Mostly what I'd like to do now is get back into psychiatry because I love that work. There's a certain thing each person can do and I think psychiatry is mine. I think being an Indian has helped me in it because many don't have that basic appreciation of life the Indian has. All they can do is take life for granted, and all they care about is their own personal gain—and money!

The ideal life for my people would be to get away from material gains, back to the way of thinking and appreciating life as it is, instead of taking it for granted, being able to appreciate nature and her bounties. My father tells the story of how when they used to log in the river; they'd hear this barge coming down the river, tooting its horn—Toot! Toot! He said you could hear it coming way upriver, and they'd all run like hell up to the head of the Island, and at one time up at the head of the Island there used to be nothing but gardens—gardens everywhere!—just acres and acres of gardens. Everyone had a garden, and they'd run through them and jump into the river and go in and out and meet these barges, swim in alongside of them—and all those logs; they'd jump the logs. But the gardens, everyone had one. You go up there now and you can still see the mounds. Joe Ranco had the biggest. Even I remember his. It was tremendously large, and none of the kids would touch it. They had respect for what he was trying to do. And when he'd harvest, he'd give some to everybody. He'd keep only what he needed to survive for the winter months. These gardens went back to ancient times when people lived on all the islands. They were all inhabited and cultivated; everyone was farming. But you'd be surprised; almost everyone has a little garden still near his house. They do it mostly for the pleasure of it. To know they can still make something out of nothing.

At this point in my life I don't have any regrets. I'm a family man. I've got a nice son, a nice wife. I've got a roof over my head. I could get a job tomorrow if I wanted; there's no great rush. I could drive out of here tomorrow and get a good job—I could earn two hundred dollars a week if I wanted to, but it's the shit you have to take. If you can't be what you want to be, then what the hell's the sense of living? Why go out and buy something like a birdbath or a swimming pool? It's a waste of money. Why should you throw away all that money on a swimming pool when you can run right down the river and jump in—that's nature's swimming pool right there for you. I say you have to live for a purpose and that's not material gain. You have to live not only for yourself but for others. That's what life's about in my mind.

I feel no guilt whatsoever in being supported by the State. It's just something that is owed. It's something that they're paying us for; it's nothing that they're giving. And they'll never reach the price that it's worth because there is no price.

At one time nothing but Mitchells lived up here on this hill, but people moved away and others moved in. But we're all related up here. The Neptune family is part of the Mitchell family by marriage. The Ranco family is part of the Mitchell family. The Philips family *is* the Mitchell family. And there's John Sapiel living up here now, "Sammy." Well, he's part of the Mitchell family. And Jean Chavaree who lives downstreet; she's part of the Mitchell family, and Rita Dana. So really if you want to go back we're all still Mitchells who live up here.

MIKE RANCO

I made the map that's in the school library when I was teaching in the Indian Island school last year. We wanted to have a social studies class and a geography class, and we thought, why don't we teach geography showing our own place?—show the kids the history of Indian Island through its geography. So I started to make the relief map as a topographical one. Of course it isn't finished yet. You've got to put the streets on it and paint in the houses. But the kids already use it. They point to it and say, "Well, this is where I live." It doesn't show it on there yet but they almost exactly know on what hill it is.

I was born in this house myself—it's my grandmother's. I went to school on the Island until the sixth grade. Then to junior high school and high school in Old Town and then to the University of Maine in Orono, where I'm still going part-time. First I was a chemistry major; then I changed to biology; then I felt I was getting further away from what I wanted to do—come back here—so I tried to decide what would be useful to me and also to my own people, and I thought education would be the one so I studied that. I graduated from Old Town High School in 1966, and I had to take a postgrad in 1967 before I went to Maine.

I got involved in Tribe, Inc., from just working here on the Island. I started when I was sixteen in recreation programs, and I saw the kids getting really involved, and I just continued at that and tried to figure out some other programs that would benefit the kids, like the tutoring program I started with University of Maine students.

The impetus for Tribe, Inc., came mainly from Down East, from Wayne Newell and John Stevens, and they had a consultant, Ed Hinkley, from the Department of Indian Affairs in Augusta. Tribe stands for Teaching and Research in Bi-cultural Education. They approached me and wanted to know if I could get away from the Reservation for a while. I worked mostly with the kids down there in recreation. I did some counseling, and I was in charge of student services. Most of the money to start it came from the National Endowment for the Humanities and HEW, and now they've got $76,000 more this year from the National Endowment with the stipulation that they raise $34,000 in nonfederal money, and they've already got $20,000 of it. They're also going to get another grant from the Rockefeller Foundation.

They started in December of 1969—in June 1970 they got the lease, and in July they brought in the first students for a teaching conference. Then they had another conference in September on education. But the kids planned the school—what kinds of curriculum they wanted, what kinds of teachers, Indian or non-Indian. The age group of the students was sixteen to twenty, all dropouts. The main emphasis was on Indian culture. They started mostly with native language. They had a Micmac class and a Malacite and Passamaquoddy one. Some people already knew how to speak the languages, but there was a difference in learning how to write them. This is one reason why ours is dying out. So now we're trying to devise a method for teaching native language.

The Passamaquoddy were originally in on the planning of Tribe, Inc., and Jean Thompson was one of the people who represented our tribe at the meetings. The basic philosophy is to have the education controlled by the Indians themselves. First they asked the Indian students what they wanted. If, for example, somebody wanted to study Penobscot anthropology they'd find someone who could help him with that and the same with anything else. That's how they started out.

The next step is teacher-orientation. Now they're planning a series of conferences for Indian and non-Indian teachers in Maine to help show the non-Indians the problems that exist among the Indians. They'd examine the textbooks the Indians have to use in white schools, and they would include teachers from schools near the reservations as well as white teachers who did teach Indians. They're going to do the same thing with school officials and administrators and finally with state officials and politicians, like Rep. Mills from Eastport who represents a lot of Indians, or the two from this area who kill every Indian bill that comes up. They'd bring all these people together, tape-record and video-tape the meetings and conferences and just let everyone go and talk, and then hopefully they'd show it to the public.

The question is how to find out primarily where the Indian people have to work to get change. Is it the teachers? Is it the legislature? Or is it the school officials? Is it the State Department of Education? We have to invite school-board people, too, because there's such a gap between the Department of Education in the State of Maine and the local school boards: there aren't any guidelines for control over these local school boards. The Department can't tell the local board you shouldn't be doing this or that toward the Indians in your district. When our kids go over to Old Town we have absolutely no say in what's taught them over there, and yet we come under the Maine Department of Education just the same. They almost throw me out on my head every time I show up there in Old Town!

Last spring they were supposed to have an Indian Studies program at Old Town High School. I don't know if it was a token thing or not, but I invited myself several times to speak, and I told them, "You shouldn't have an Indian Studies program without Indian consultants." It's useless when you have a white teacher teaching a culture that she doesn't know anything about. She's a new teacher, not from this area—not even from Maine—and there she was sitting up in front of 40 kids talking about Penobscot Indian culture! That's no good.

So here was a person, not from around here, not from Maine, not even an Indian—plus the fact that they really didn't even teach Maine Indians. They had a book about the American Indian today, and they were trying to teach about three hundred different Indian peoples in one hundred pages! You can't do that. All they wanted was for it to look good when they had to face the Department of Education. They had a Black

Mike Ranco

Studies program, too. And all it shows is that "See we're keeping up with the times, don't worry about us here in Old Town." Not even one Black person in this part of Maine!

I remember when I was in eighth grade they actually turned down one Black student from attending that school. Come to find out this Black became an all-American. His father was stationed near here at the Air Force base at that time. He didn't get into school in Old Town, but they eventually took him in Bangor, and he went on to become a great football player . . . Yet there's this banner at Old Town High School, "You're in Indian Country." But they really don't mean *Indian* country—they mean it in sports. They call themselves The Indians! I mean, how do you change that? I'd love to change it!

Of course Tribe is one way. The only problem is they're working up there in Bar Harbor, and we're down here, and there's this gap in between. One thing that could fill it up is Tim's Indian Academy, which Tribe is very interested in. I gave them the proposal this weekend. They're very interested because in order for them to establish credibility in the community they have to run on a two-way avenue. So they're willing to give us the technical assistance with our program here on the Reservation. I have my own program I'm interested in, and the Indian Academy and I are going to get together. Mine has primarily to do with resources: we're planning an Indian culture program including films. Then we have a remedial reading program for kids here who have reading problems. In order for them to compete—in quotes!—in a white society they have to play their game so we can teach them these "white" tools. We feel we can still deal with skills for getting along in the white world, but at the same time we can do it in the context of Indian culture. It has to be that way. We can't revert back, and what you do have for Indian culture now is in a transitional stage. They're trying to decide "Who am I, which way am I going to go?"

The Passamaquoddy started a bilingual program to preserve their language. Right now it's too late for us to do that. So we have to try to preserve the other things we have. The values. To me to be an Indian is to be *here*. It doesn't matter if you wear the clothes. But I think the time has gone by for the language. We're going to have to do a lot of reviving if you want to get the language back. A lot of people are going to have to make a lot of sacrifices. At this point there still are people who speak the language, but to get them to sit down and do it, I don't know. Of the people who still have a grasp of the language there's Senabeh, Suzy Dana, my grandmother. But Suzy's got a contract with Dr. Seibert that she can't reveal anything. What's going to happen is once she dies, or he dies, it's going to come out in *his* name. And *he* can speak the language because he was taught Penobscot by her husband, Andrew Dana, who died.

Now it's true that some of the old people complain about the young, that they're too much on the go, they won't sit down and take the time to listen. That's the whole thing. The Indians now are sort of shifting away from Indian values—non-time-consciousness to time-consciousness. They don't want to make a basket now; they'll say how long will it take me to make it? You have to have that dedication to learn something. I learned how to carve, but I didn't say, "How long will it take me to make this?" I just sat down and watched and watched. You have to sit down and watch someone doing something; that's the only way you can learn. You can't teach something like carving or basket making verbally. The only verbal communication is, "Do it this way."

You also have to accept the older people who could teach just as they are. Now Senabeh is a very traditional person—the way he speaks; he speaks broken English and you get the kids making fun of him, which is wrong. If you listen to him he's got a lot to say, and the way he talks is simple and straight to the point, none of that double-talking. I sit down and talk with him a lot. It really bothers me: I'm twenty-four now, and our age group was the last one to have any contact with the culture around here. We learned it from our parents and people like Senabeh but now you walk up the street, and there'll be about twenty or thirty kids standing around doing nothing—*talking* about how to preserve the culture! And a lot of them still have their grandmothers. Everybody could just pay attention in their own houses. Now, our resources program uniting with the Indian Academy, one big organization—we could have some influence.

As far as I'm concerned the kids don't have to "make it" in the white world, but they do have to live in this kind of environment, predominantly white. To me you've got to have that Indian base first. A stable person must have that identity; he must have that pride in being Indian. If he doesn't have it—just that pride—he's going to be a very confused Indian, and then it gets back to your typical Indian in a bar. You see a lot of this, like with the older people. Like with the men here—they drink heavily, some of them, but essentially they're all good and valuable human beings. If you just went up and talked to them you'd discover that right away.

Like Senabeh, there should be a lot of kids down there every day listening to him talk. Or there's Louis Sockalexis, my uncle; he should have a lot of kids with him. But they're traditional: they'd rather have the kids *come* to them. One of the things I'm thinking about when we have the center here is just bringing in the older people and letting them talk, start them off with a few questions like, "What can we do to help our kids have an Indian consciousness?" and some of them will tell you right away, "Well, all they think of is having cars and riding around!" But maybe the kids don't really want this. Maybe they want to set down and talk to the older people, too. But how do we get them together. Maybe we have to change the way we get them together *ourselves*.

One of the things we're trying to do is get a video-tape machine. The Aroostook Indians have one, and they rent it out for ten dollars a day. We'd like to tape a lot of things—have an older person sit down and make a basket from scratch; then we'd show it to the kids. Then maybe bring that person in afterwards to talk to the kids about how she did it. That's why we need this resource center. A place where you can sit down and find out how you make a basket, what goes into pounding ash or gathering sweet grass—finding out how to pick the best piece of ash for what kind of basket you want to make. We'd teach Indian medicine, too, which is becoming a lost art. And we'd have money set aside to photocopy all the Indian books you can't buy, Speck's and Mrs. Eckstorm's—Suzy Dana helped contribute to a book about Glooskap. We'd have it all available for the kids to come in and read on their own because now they're scattered all over the place—the University of Maine; the Peabody Museum, some of them; the Abbe Museum at Bar Harbor. We'd even copy the archives in Boston and Augusta, have all the relevant books and materials and documents right here. We could photocopy all the original treaties, make the kids aware that these things are the basis of where we are today.

Now Speck, he came in here and lived among the Indians, like an Indian himself. He was accepted here and he gave a true account of their life. But he put his name on it, as if to say, "Now I made it with the Indians." I feel that if there's any more anthropology going to be done on the Island the Indians should do it themselves. Just like the Council here gave their okay for Dr. Snell the anthropologist to come in here and dig, for the stockade supposedly, and they never saw the stuff afterwards! That was two summers ago, and the condition was that if he wrote up a paper he'd give a copy of it to the Penobscot Indians and also turn back any of the artifacts he found, and it hasn't been done yet. We keep writing letters—well, he hasn't worked on anything yet. The site is right over here on the other side of the swimming pool. They found a lot of coins, and even some muskets! This was a trading area among the Indian people.

I was fortunate enough to have a grandfather, Gabriel Polchies, who I could sit with for hours and just watch him and listen to him. He died when I was about ten. That's why I say if you get these kids when they're six or seven or even younger because they're naturally inquisitive—that's all I ever did with my grandfather, who was a carver. I kept on asking questions: "What do you do with this knife?" Things like that. I was carving with a razor-sharp knife when I was five years old. That's what's wrong with education today. They don't let you experience anything or come in contact with, say, people who take drugs. They take you away from everything, and they put you in a very sterile environment, away from life, and you can't wear long hair; you've got to wear neat clothes. You've got to have your hands clean. They never tell you why you've got to have your hands clean or you can't wear your hair long in order to learn something. They just tell you, "You can't do it."

If you go to any Indian community they let you experience it. It's not a restrictive life, and it's not permissive either. It gives you a little more leeway—they let you experience something and then they tell you why. Education is still *doing*. You take the kids here on the Reservation. They get a lot of experience just from everyday living. Once they go over Old Town in a completely new environment, what they've learned has no counterpart in that culture. That's why they have problems. When a kid leaves elementary school here it's a difficult period for him, a transitional period. He says, "Well, I'm not a baby anymore, but I'm not an adult either." And if there's no way he can even be an Indian, he's going to be a very confused person. Between the 6th and 7th grades if he starts sinking and becoming negative towards his own community he's going to be confused, and once he grows up, he's going to stay here and still be in trouble.

One of the reasons I came back here is that I remember the teachers over in Old Town saying, "Well, you've got to get a good education so you can get a good job and move away from the Reservation." That's what I didn't want, but you keep getting this kind of feedback. You get kind of sick of it. Like in the 8th grade we had to take Maine history, and there were pages to read on the Indians, and you know it's all wrong—but what do you do with an eighth-grader who's confused, in a strange world? How can he say, "That's wrong!" He's only one in three hundred people, and that's what they use against him. They say, "How can you have something to say when you're only one out of three hundred?" That's what's wrong with that Maine history book; that's why I want to change it as soon as I can.

I've wanted to do what I'm doing ever since I was practically in junior high school. I was elected to the Tribal Council last year, but I had to step down, because I went up to Tribe. I was pressed into stepping down, too. I wasn't the youngest person who ever got on the Council. There was someone twenty-one on it before, but I was the youngest elected chairman of the Council. But this is part of the biggest paradox over here. Everybody wants their kids educated, but they don't want them educated to come back! That's kind of confusing. When we start coming back they're confused. They feel their security is threatened. No reason why—maybe it's just for the sake of power. You noticed at that meeting they just shrugged off Timmy and me without even thinking about it. I don't think they intended to do it purposely; it's just something they have to cope with. I don't think they understand what we're doing.

I think white politics influences them indirectly in their thinking that people in power should have the power and people on the outside are secondary. But then, too, they're struggling with themselves. People on the council are geared to economic development above everything else. You know, business development. Some of them are talking about opening up the whole place. To me, I think they should clamp down, like some Indians in other places, and close the river to any use. Like Martin, he brought that up at the Council and he got turned down. He wanted to close the Island to non-Indians. Everybody jumped on him, and they said, "Well, I'm married to a white person. My in-laws, they should have the right to come over here." So that was a conflict, and then on the Council they didn't want any young people because that was against the tradition.

They pictured being on the Council as being old—aged—which is a stereotyped thing. To be on the Council you must have wisdom, and wisdom comes from experience and age. Well, experience, yes, but not age. Age doesn't say you have the wisdom. You see people sixty, seventy years old who have no wisdom at all, and that's what I brought up when I ran. I said education just speeds up the process, even though experience does count. Education just hastens the awareness. This is why you have more young people at meetings than before—they're concerned. When I was teaching at the Indian Island school in social studies you'd have kids talking about why we need housing over here—or why we don't—and we had a debate going on of kids only in the 3rd grade. This is an awareness. These kids are conscious of what's going on around here. They know the social problems; they know the economic problems; and they want to do something about them. Nobody listens to them. I got a big kick out of that—Sister did, too. Parents calling her up, calling me up, too, saying, "Why did you let these kids argue about this thing?" Well, because they're not supposed to know about it but they do. A kid maybe 5 years old, but he hears people talking about housing. It seeps in. What can you do? That's the educational process!

We feel a certain kinship with white kids trying to change the system, but I keep teasing Timmy Love because he used to be involved in a lot of groups at the University against the draft and against the war, and I keep teasing him, telling him he's got to decide which battlefield to be on. I say, "Are you going to go over there and fight their battles for them, or are you going to stay over here and fight our battles?" Of course I do it jokingly to him, but I think he understands what I mean.

I think the Indian people here would rather work within the system to change it. But I don't vote anymore. I did the first time, but not anymore. Maybe we should but what good is it when you've got a President saying he'll promise all these things to the Indians and they don't come about? You go back to thinking maybe we lack the numbers for change, but in Maine I think it's going to change. Not only do we have the numbers but we have the voice. We're going to have the first Indian Commissioner. Everybody thought that was impossible; now we're going to have one, the first *Indian* Indian Commissioner, the first one that is Indian, John Stevens, who's Governor of the Passamaquoddies. It's going to be publicly announced tomorrow [September 20, 1971]. That's taken a long time, but now we have it.

I expect to stay here on the Island and work. I'm married, with a little boy, eighteen months old. My wife's name is Livingston. She's white. We met in college. That's another problem. There's so much intermarriage going on because there's no contact. When we were growing up, the boys outnumbered the girls. Now I'm married to a white. So's Jim Sappier, so's Jean Thompson and Wayne and Martin and Timmy—or he will be. And still all these people are active. John Stevens, the new Commissioner, he's married to a white woman. Now Earleen Paul is active, but she's got a conflict; she's really up on education and she wants to leave the Island to work. She's worked with me for a couple of years on the tutoring program, but this year she's really fired up and working on her own on the Reservation, but it's her senior year in college and she's talking about getting away for a while. She said, "I'm going to come back here but I just want to get away for a year and think."

Everybody wants to come back, but it's not withdrawal. They come back for a need. We have an influx every year at elections. People come back to renew their family ties; they come back at Easter, at Christmas and Thanksgiving. It's that reassurance. And every time they come home they experience the desire to stay home. Some people would like to make that move back, but maybe they've got good jobs in other places and if they come back here they've just got to struggle, and I think it's a personal struggle, too. I think I could go out there and get a good job, but I stay. I could go away and get a good job by white standards, or I could stay right down at Tribe if I wanted. To me that was useless. I wasn't involved in any changes. The only change I was doing was on paper; it looked good on paper, but if you can put it in effect that's different. That's why I came back here.

With people coming back this is one reason we want a housing program—for the sake of our own people, our own resources! Now we're at optimum; we're stagnant; we can only allow 300 people or so to live on the Island, so even though we keep that same attainment, we have to shove off everyone else. We'd be building mostly houses, not apartments, because people like to live in houses. There's already a list of people who would be willing to come back here and live.

If people would only start thinking about themselves. A lot of people don't—they just go through the motions of living here; they don't know why they're living here or why they're contented here. You've got to have an awareness, like why are you giving your kids an education? Right now we're only living on one-fifth of the Island. We're just creating a system within itself like the country as a whole—there's too many people being born. But we want this. The Indian birthrate is five times the national average. Right now we're feeling the pressure. In the last two years we've had 26 marriages, four of them have been Indian to Indian. The rest have been Indian to non-Indian, and out of twenty-six marriages only three young couples are living on the Reservation—that means twenty-three of them are living off the Reservation, twenty-three couples who could be active. I'll be moving off soon because there's no place for me to live with my family. If we had housing we'd all be back. The idea is, the input is only limited, so if you don't expand, if you shove in more, it's just going to explode.

I don't want economic growth, I want population growth—the more people here the greater the selectivity. Every election it's the same people running for office. No change. Everybody may vote for somebody different but the same thing goes on. You've got people on the Council who don't even speak up. It's always the same few, and what happens is, they send out the minutes and somebody reads the same names that have been there for twenty years, and they say, "Well, gee, they've got beautiful leadership." But people don't have any other alternative to vote for. Even twenty years on the Council isn't any good if you don't implement it.

Like the other night the Council voted to go after the money from the Diocese. They voted to do it. The Diocese promised $33,000 for a new Tribal Hall, and nobody did anything about it for a long time, but now that they've even voted to do something, still nothing's been done about it as of today.

The Council's looking at the young people like through a microscope. They're waiting for us to make a mistake, then "Ah ha!" But they don't make mistakes. They just try to please everybody. But if I start a program and forty out of sixty want it, I figure that's forty people I've got, but the Council won't vote for a program for thirty people out of seventy. Like a lot of people are against the Indian Academy. They think we're bucking the Old Town school system, but you've got ten kids walking around out of school already—dropouts—and school's only been in session a week. What are you going to do for those ten kids? Ten out of ninety. But isn't it an adult responsibility to make sure that these ten get an education— or some alternative approach? This is why I'm so glad that Timmy's going to start the Academy. We talked about it a long time ago when we were both in Neighborhood Youth Corps here and I was one of the group leaders, and he had this idea, and I said, "If you want to do it, do it and we'll give you the support."

But I'd like to stress one thing; the Indians aren't taking any money from the State of Maine or the people of Maine. Money that goes into the Reservation is the income from trust funds set up when the Indians sold their lands to the State and from the various treaty agreements and obligations. The State likes to think it's providing welfare for the Indians, but the money is legally ours for the well-being of the Indian people. Just the same, people are going around saying, "We're giving the Indian free education, free medical care." But it isn't true. The State is only living up to the treaty agreements: it's just another interpretation of the treaty. The State couldn't live up to its obligation of fifty barrels of molasses, fifteen hundred blankets, so many pounds of chocolate a year. The Indians felt there was a different need other than those so it was agreeable to both parties to start accepting other things, like getting medical assistance, making scholarships available for Indians; it's just another form of the treaty. But how do you convince people of this? Even the State of Maine doesn't tell the people what is taking place—*not* that the Indian is living off us, but this is how we're obligated to *them*.

LEGENDS 3

GLOOSKAP AND THE BIRCH TREE

In naming the birch tree Glooskap is said to have asked it to take care of the Indians. But once he found a straight birch tree which he wanted to make into a canoe. When Glooskap cut the tree down it fell in such a way that he was almost killed. In addition to being angered by this narrow escape, Glooskap was further provoked because he had an exceedingly difficult time in extricating himself from its branches. Being extremely enraged, Glooskap took up a stick and beat the birch as hard as he could from one end of it to the other. He then commanded the marks which he had made to remain as eyes so that the birch would never again kill, or almost kill, anyone. The Indians still call the lenticels in the bark of the birch tree eyes. Some they call long eyes, and others, short eyes.

GLOOSKAP AND THE FROG

Becoming bored with home life, Glooskap bade farewell to his grandmother and went out to inspect the rivers. He paddled along in his stone canoe reducing falls and clearing rapids and in general making navigation less dangerous. At Castine he disembarked and left his canoe (where it remains to this day) and proceeded on foot until he came to a village full of distressed people.

Oglebamu, the frog, the people told him, had taken over the water supply and would let the Indians have none. They were dying of thirst. Glooskap went to the spring, and there sat a huge frog. All around the trees and grass were dead, and the frog swallowed all the water as fast as it came out of the ground. "Give the people some water," said Glooskap. "They-can't-have-any," replied the frog. Then Glooskap called Mikumwesu. Immediately Mikumwesu was there, and as soon as he understood

Horace P. Beck, *Gluskap the Liar, and Other Indian Tales*. (Freeport: The Bond Wheelwright Co., 1966), pp. 69–71.

what the matter was, he told the frog to give back some water, but instead of complying the frog swallowed Mikumwesu. At this Glooskap became furious. He stamped his feet and roared with rage. He grasped his axe and swung it as if it were a feather, bringing it down with all his strength upon the back of the monster. So great was the blow that it broke Oglebamu's back and caused him to vomit up all the water and Mikumwesu along with it. Mikumwesu appeared soiled, angry, and wet, but unharmed. Still furious, Glooskap seized the frog in his hands and squeezed him small. At first Glooskap was so angry that he denied the poor creature any water, but Oglebamu pleaded so hard that the giant's heart was softened and he told the frog that henceforth he could live around the edge of ponds and in wet places but could not have all the water. (In a modern version of the story Glooskap made him change his cry from "They-can't-have-any" to "Jug-o-rum.") To this day you can see across the frog's back the results of the axe swung with such fury so long ago.

When the water gushed out of Oglebamu the Penobscot River was formed and many people, in their joy, plunged into the stream and were transformed into various aquatic creatures, from whence spring many family names in use today.

GLOOSKAP AND THE WITCH

N'karnayoo, of old times; once it came to pass that Glooskap met with an evil witch, and she had made herself like unto a fair young girl, and believed that he could not know who she was. And she asked him to take her with him in his canoe. So they sailed out over a summer sea: and as they went the witch sought to beguile him with sweet words; but he answered naught, for he knew well what kind of passenger he had on board. And as they went on she played her cajoleries, but he remained grim as a bear. Then she, being angry, showed it, and there arose a great storm. The wind howled over the waves as they rose and fell, like white wolves jumping while they run, the first lightnings flashed, and the sky grew dark as night.

The Master was angered that so mean a creature dared to play him such tricks, and paddling the canoe to the beach, he

leaped ashore. Then giving the bark, with the witch in it, a push out to sea, he cried to her, "Sail thou with the devil! But never be in human form again, O she-beast!"

Then she, being frightened, said, "Master, what wilt thou that I become?" And he replied, "Whatever thou wilt; that grace alone I give thee." And in despair she plunged into the waters, and became a Keegunibe, a ferocious fish, which has upon its back a great fin, which it shows like a sail when swimming through the water. So the canoe and the witch became one in the evil fish, and the Indians to this day when they see it, cry, "See the witch who was punished by the great Master!"

OF SOME MEN WHO WENT TO GLOOSKAP FOR GIFTS

Now there went forth many men unto Glooskap, hearing that they could win the desires of their hearts; and all got what they asked for, in any case; but as for having what they wanted, that depended on the wisdom with which they wished or acted.

The good Glooskap liked it not that when he had told anyone evenly and plainly what to do, that man should then act otherwise, or double with him. And it came to pass that a certain fool, of the kind who can do nothing unless it be in his own way, made a long journey to the Master. And his trials were indeed many. For he came to an exceeding high mountain in a dark and lonely land, where he heard no sound. And the ascent was like a smooth pole, but the descent on the other side far worse, for it hung over the bottom. Yet it was even worse beyond, for there the road lay between the heads of two huge serpents, almost touching each other, who darted their terrible tongues at those who went between. And yet again the path passed under the Wall of Death. Now this wall hung like an awful cloud over a plain, rising and falling at times, yet no man knew when. And when it fell it struck the ground, and that so as to crush all that was beneath it.

But the young man escaped all these trials, and came to the Island of the Great Master. And when he had dwelt there a certain time, and was asked what he would have, he replied, "If my lord will, let him give me a medicine which will cure all disease." More than this he asked not. So the Master gave him a certain small package, and said, "Herein is that which thou seekest; but I charge thee that thou lettest not thine eyes behold it until thou shalt reach thy home." So he thanked the Master and left.

But he was not far away ere he desired to open the package and test the medicine, and, even more, the truth of the Master. And he said to himself, "Truly, if this be but a deceit it was shrewdly devised to bid me not to open it till I returned. For he knew well that once so far I would make no second journey to him. Tush! If the medicine is worth anything nothing will change it." So he opened it, and the substance fell to the ground, and spread itself like water everywhere, and then dried away like a mist. And when he returned and told his tale, men mocked him.

Then again there were three brothers, who, having adventured, made known their wishes. Now the first was very tall, far above all his fellows, and vain of his handsomeness. For he was of those who put bark or fur into their moccasins, that they may

be looked up to by the little folk and be loved by the squaws; and his hair was plastered to stand up on high, and on the summit of it was a very long turkey-tail feather. And this man asked to become taller than any Indian in all the land.

And the second wished that he might ever remain where he was to behold the land and the beauty of it, and to do nothing else.

And the third wished to live in exceeding old age, and ever to be in good health.

Now the three, when they came to the island, had found three wigwams there, and in two of these were dwellers, not spoken of in other traditions. In one lived Cool-puj-ot, a very strange man. For he has no bones, and cannot move himself, but every spring and autumn he is rolled over with handspikes by the order of Glooskap, and this is what his name means in the Micmac tongue. And in the autumn he is turned towards the west, but in the spring towards the east, and this is a figure of speech denoting the revolving seasons of the year. With his breath he can sweep down whole armies, and with his looks alone he can work great wonders, and all this means the weather,—frost snow, ice, and sunshine.

And in the other wigwam dwelt Cuhkw which means Earthquake. And this mighty man can pass along under the ground, and make all things shake and tremble by his power.

Now when Glooskap had heard what these visitors wished for, he called Earthquake, and bid him take them all three and put them with their feet in the ground. And he did so, when they at once became three trees: as one tradition declares, pines; and another, cedars.

So that he that would be tall became exceeding tall, for his head rose above the forest; and even the turkey-feather at the top of his head is not forgotten, since to this day it is seen waving in the wind. And he who will listen in the pine wood may hear the tree murmuring all day long in the Indian tongue of the olden time,—

> Oh, I am such a great man!
> Oh, I am such a great Indian!

And the second, who would remain in the land, remains there; for while his roots are in the ground he cannot depart from it. And the third, who would live long in health, unless men have cut him down, is still standing.

GLOOSKAP LEAVES THE WORLD

Now Glooskap had freed the world from all the mighty monsters of an early time: the giants wandered no longer in the wilderness; the cullo terrified man no more, as it spread its wings like the cloud between him and the sun; the Chenoo of the North devoured him not; no evil beasts, devils, and serpents were to be found near his home. And the Master had, moreover, taught men the arts which made them happier; but they were not grateful to him, and though they worshipped him they were not the less wicked.

Now when the ways of men and beasts waxed evil they greatly vexed Glooskap, and at length he could no longer endure them, and he made a rich feast by the shore of the great Lake Minas. All the beasts came to it, and when the feast was over he got into a great canoe, and the beasts looked after him until they saw him no more. And after they ceased to see him, they still heard his voice as he sang; but the sounds grew fainter and fainter in the distance, and at last they wholly died away, and then deep silence fell on them all, and a great marvel came to pass, and the beasts, who had till now spoken but one language, were no longer able to understand each other, and they fled away, each in his own way, and never again have they met together in council. Until the day when Glooskap shall return, and make men and animals dwell once more together in amity and peace, all nature mourns.

THE RETURN OF GLOOSKAP

"Is Glooskap still living?"

"Yes, far away; no one knows where; some say he sailed away in his stone canoe beyond the sea, to the east, but he will return in it one day. Others say that he went to the west. One story tells that while he was alive those who went to him and found him could have their wishes given to them. But there is a story that if one travels far and long, and is not afraid, he may still find the great Sogmo. Yes. He lives in a very great, a very long wigwam. He is always making arrows. One side of the lodge is full of arrows now. They are so thick, and when it is all full he will come forth and make war. He never allows anyone to enter the wigwam while he is making these arrows.

"And on whom will he make war?"

"He will make war on all white people. He will expel them from this country. He will make war on all, kill all."

JOURNAL 4

August 3–5, 1971

Mark and I go to the Indians. A grand reunion and some laughs on the Maine Turnpike. We skirt the Bowdoin campus, probably August-lush and overgrown with summer students: it's better to joke about the past rather than relive it. Instead we hit L. L. Bean's and Mark buys himself some bush clothes and cotton shirts (can't stand synthetics, as I can't either) and a Ché Guevara *basque*. The Indians we won't freak out, but a few Maine-iacs look askance at two bearded long-haired "hippies" (well over thirty!) making their progress from Freeport to Auburn by way of Ho-Jo's in Augusta (counter-girl tells elderly couple she lost a hundred eighty nine dollars on the horses on her day off: "I was going to commit suicide!" "Cost more than that to bury you, my dear," the wife snaps back in her face while her husband drools in his coffee over her backside in well-elevated mini-uniform). Mr. Paperback in Bangor, and Jack's Restaurant in downtown Old Town.

We arrive at Wayne's and Mark starts snapping his shutter all over the place: opens Wayne's refrigerator, takes picture of the food. I expect him to open the clothes closets and start in on them. Shoots the breakfast table, Terri's bric-a-brac on top of the TV with the TV on, shoots the photos already on the wall, the house outside, the windows, the outside through the windows, the inside *in* through the windows, the yard, the clothesline ("I don't want anyone taking pictures of my wash," said Jean Thompson last time while talking about how the Penobscot Tribal Council voted against participation in *Land of the Four Directions* photo book—quite nice, actually) the cats and dogs, while I sit at Wayne's kitchen table and sip a beer. Wayne's working as a carpenter in Holden, south of Bangor, building a garage for somebody, he goes down in mid-afternoon and comes back late at night—Terri's left—"The house is yours."

Watching Mark's eye take in everything calls my attention to those photos on the living room wall which engrossed him: Wayne's parents, brothers and sisters, aunts and uncles. School photographs of graduations, armed service shots, weddings or just commercial portraits, the children—

hand-colored things, or sepia tinted. They're keepsakes, reminders of steps attained in the white world, commemoratives. Unfortunately none of them does justice to the remarkable faces of the people. The Mitchells are among the handsomest people I've ever met: men and women—they vibrate with life, they're *there*, all of them, in their bodies and their language (all excellent talkers) right in front of your face: just *being*. Somehow the photographs deny this ("I'm not photogenic," Norris said to Mark, as a statement of fact, not a warning for Mark to put up his camera); they flatten the faces, thin out the color; the taste of the time in glasses and clothes naturally dates the photos, too. But what disturbs me most is that these Indians, in their photographs, are made to appear white, and no doubt they unconsciously, some of them, wanted to, or wanted simply to look like everyone else as this or that step attained—high school diploma, marriage, first baby etc.—is supposed to make them so, rank them as having done things that allow them entry to white society (or if they don't want this consciously, the photo at least satisfies that unconscious desire— or that pressure white society has applied to them). I'm not arguing in favor of flashy photos of them all dressed in leather with beads and headbands etc. In fact any one of the people pictured here would look out of place in native dress. What I do wonder, though, is if they can't be pictured for what they are. (In Bangor, at Mr. Paperback, an Indian man, about 55 or 60 came in, white, short-sleeved summer shirt, summer-weight trousers, and I first thought: "My god he looks Vietnamese," and then of course I realized the Indian aspect immediately—the Penobscots and Passamaquoddies look a lot like Eskimos I've seen in *Akwesasne Notes*. This man's face was softly lined, his skin slightly yellow, his voice soft and deep, just putting down his dime and nickel for the Bangor *Daily News,* and I was wondering if he lived in the city or was going back to the Island from work. At any rate it ought to be possible to photograph him as he is, an American who just happens also to be a Penobscot Indian, as I happen to have a Greek mother and father and therefore what you might call a Mediterranean aspect: small, dark eyes, prominent nose and lips, darkish hair, and decidedly dark complexion—even yellow-brown at times.) For we *are* our origins, our parents; and we are compounded of the places we were born and grew up in; the earth of them, the air of them, their moisture and fiery exhalations: of these substances so are we made *substantial* and nourished, and our cells do carry a memory of that primal matter which is earth.

4.30 P.M.
Overcast, almost autumnal afternoon (Marks says it's a perfect light for pictures, somber, but not bleak or dark), some tourists leaving the shops, people filtering back on the Island after work: a breeze and voices drift up from the street. I'm at the foot of the bridge; Mark's at the head taking pictures of Bobby Troy Nelson and Andrew Francis, who began to follow us around all afternoon as I showed Mark the two cemeteries, the churches, the dikes on either side of the Island. Mark smokes and we decide to take another turn before going for dinner in Old Town.

Down on the dike near Senabeh's shack we meet "Bengun"—Norman Lolar—walking along, smoking and carrying a bottle of beer. He hands it to us; we pass it. Mark lights him up again. Small, almost dwarflike man, probably late forties, a loner, working as a carpenter revamping houses for Mainstream. He has short gray-black hair in a soft crew cut, probably just sheared off by an Old Town barber. He told us about being in the Navy out of Boston in WW II—"A ship sinks only once." Didn't particular seek us out; we met and chatted; Mark asked him if he minded being photographed—"Oh, no, go right ahead." He put the beer bottle in his back pocket—loose black work pants—nodded at us and left. Wayne's cousin Burnell had told us Senabeh was looking forward to a visit from us, but Senabeh wasn't in— we saw a pile of freshly cut logs outside his house, didn't know what they were for—and we decide to go eat at Jack's.

We drink coffee and pore over the *Bangor Daily News* and the *Penobscot Times,* listen to the locals chat just before closing time ("In Maine you don't get ahead," says woman behind us). Everyone knows everyone else in a small town, and this is a real American town in the sense that there's one big central street essentially where the business is carried on and where people meet to talk and trade. Urban people, especially those who didn't themselves come from small towns, don't understand them at all. Jean Shepherd does superbly, but he's a Midwesterner. His "Moose area 18 miles" piece in *Car and Driver,* on the young people driving up and down the main streets of Maine's small towns night after night and going from submarine sandwich to double banana split, from fried chicken and onion rings to coffee and pumpkin donuts at all the local chain and franchise stands—with a couple of hours out at the drive-in for an X-rated movie—hits the nail on the head. It's about all there is to do, or be: next step is work, family, responsibility (which most kids take on early anyway, either through boredom or because they knock their girl friends up)—or jail. The kids aren't even in possession of the most elementary information on contraception and birth control, and the parents are fighting to keep sex education out of the public schools in Old Town with the old and useless excuse that it "belongs in the home." (One woman wrote in a letter to the editor, July 22, Penobscot Times: "Sex education has been given the glossy name of Family Life, but that doesn't change what it is. Teachers will put a proper knowledge on gutter talk, but that isn't going to change it. Sure we have a gutter, we always have and we always will. There are no morals there, and apart from God morals cannot be taught. So we do gloss up the gutter and put it into our schools.") Well, at that rate, it simply doesn't get taught there in a form of anything more than the dogma of "don't": don't for the girls, and "if you can't be good be careful" for the boys, though with no hard information as to "how" to be careful. Naturally the boys are indulged, while the message still comes through to the girls "sex is dirty/duty," and the fulfillment only of "marital obligations"—but it's still dirty; you really aren't supposed to enjoy it, but you can use it, and your body, to manipulate your husband into buying you something or your boyfriend into marrying you, which is at the root of the continual war of American marriage. It lives in the vocabulary— and the psychopathology—of everyday life. The man—I've actually over- heard this in the pizza joints and grog mills of Old Town and Orono— is still talking about "getting it." And the question is always asked of the girl, "Did you give it to him?"

Mailer's brilliant sally on the relationship between the small town and the war in Vietnam in Armies of the Night is a tour de force, really breath- taking—but wrong. He describes the alleged "support" for Vietnam as emanating from the small towns and implies that it really isn't the govern- ment fighting on its own in Vietnam so much as carrying out the mandate of the small towns who see our struggle in Vietnam against the threat of "World Communism" as an adjunct to their own at home against an urban- spawned encroachment upon their way of life, including their own brand of insanity. So Vietnam becomes a metaphor of their resentment, even, as Mailer puts it, the place "where the small town had gone to get its kicks." ("The small towns were disappearing in the bypasses and the supermarkets and the shopping centers, the small town in America was losing its sense of the knuckle, the herb and the root. . . .")

There are plenty of angry reactionaries in small towns, neither are they without a certain small-mindedness, a willful ignorance like your anti- sex/education people. But I've also encountered a good-heartedness in small towns and sometimes a more remarkable understanding of human situations than a lot of paranoid urban dwellers give credit for. Small-town people just move and think differently: they are not intensely political, or even politically aware in any sense of national politics. (Not a single member of the Republican City Committee of Gloucester had ever seen a copy of "Monday"—weekly newsletter and strategy-sheet of GOP Nat'l Comm.—when I mentioned it to them, or knew what it was. When queried, they can't give a coherent account of national party policy; they still operate on the level of friendships and family relationships—as do the Democrats—"I've known Al all my life, our parents got married the same day!" And this isn't stupid or unreal. It's very real if you live in a small town, as I have all my life.)

In the case of Old Town and Indian Island you have two adjacent if not parallel small towns, and societies or cultures of the same. There are some points of similarity, the Indian culture often aping the white, but not consciously: most middle-aged Indians actually "feel" white, think white, in the sense that they just live in white culture. The points of difference are like those between the Greek, Italian, and Portuguese subcultures in Gloucester—a certain foreignness (among older people) in mode of speech, religion (Catholic as against Protestant), food eaten, holidays celebrated, the feel and texture of family life and relationships. (After a while in Gloucester I began to notice that my own life was much more family-centered, more like that of my Italian friends—in fact I grew up able to understand Sicilian and Portuguese from listening to my school friends' grandmothers talk to them in their native tongues—than that of my WASP friends, whose parents always seemed to be with people who were not related to them. We even lived in a family enclave—a kind of Greek ghetto—on Perkins Road, my mother's entire family spread out among half a dozen houses);

What I'm trying to get at here is the question of a "handle" not only on the understanding of small-town culture but the application of that to the sociology, say, of Indian Island, as a cultural and social entity within Old Town, and having its own government, essentially its own social and political hierarchies centering on the Family, the House, the piece of property or Real Estate, the Business owned or operated by the family or within the family, the family trade or occupation, at the basis of which is a continually elaborated oral history as gossip [my friend Peter Parsons presses what he calls the "distinction between 'information-as-gossip' and 'dirt'"] in the stream of which each family moves, past and present, and each member of each family is able—and taught—his place somewhere in that movement: 'You remember Bill, well his Uncle Jack is the one who—' And there it is: granted, it's limited and limiting, and in a sense often tragically deterministic—"Why, no member of the Belcher family ever did that before." Young people hardly ever achieve an authentic identity in such a system, especially if they remain in the town. The image of me that sticks in Gloucester is of the earnest and "active" high school student in ROTC uniform, voted "most likely to succeed," so that when I turn up again in town a "bearded-hippie-Commie-writer"—to some—it blows their minds: "My, how that boy has changed!" I mean I ripped the walls right out of their pigeonhole—a man could go to jail for that, or, at least, suffer ostracism, or, more accurately, find himself bad-mouthed all over—"And he has a wife and three children, too!" No, most "smart people" get out, but they become wanderers, exiles in that global restlessness which America has become: all these people who left their towns and families and who now can't "stay put" anywhere. However, the ones who have left the towns often seem to "achieve" (if only in the eyes of the people at home) the most—some do remain to exploit their fellow townsmen—but they stay away always with a sense they ought really to return, go home, someday, but they can never bring themselves to do it.

Ultimately, their insularity, their provincialism and bewilderment at the outside world are the undoing of the small towns. People hold on to what they have for a long time; then in desperation they let it go. They become prey to outsiders. For example, neither the impetus nor the capital for shopping plazas ever comes from within a town. It's always a national corporation, like the one that built Grant's Plaza in Old Town and then sold it out from under the people's noses to yet another trust. But who needed it? Who needed an immense, empty parking lot with a supermarket, theater, and discount store?—the kind of thing you have in every small town now, surrounding them, circumscribing them even further, drawing the people out of the comfortable residential streets and main thoroughfares into housing developments near them, unutterably boring in their sameness and dullness, people hoodwinked into thinking that's where life lies, in an aping of exurbia. And then whatever did exist of history, family, daily reality in the small town is destroyed as the monuments to it are torn down and allowed to wither away, old houses no longer repaired or restored, "kept up," urban renewal butting out the 19th-century shops and office buildings, each place flattened out toward another: Milford to Old Town to Orono; Bangor engulfing Brewer, the linkages no longer the Main Streets and the families, but the shopping centers and the industrial "parks," until finally they take over the landscape and the human dwellings are so many clusters in their shadows.

Then people's names mean nothing to anyone, nor the names of the streets and stores, rivers and roads. In some cases, even more tragically, there's a commercial attempt to reconstruct local history in the form of an amusement park with a few replicas of colonial houses and some people in "costume"—or in summer, festivals for the benefit of tourists who wander the land anyway looking for what they believe to be history—a series of bad spectacles and odd statistics: this is the world's smallest town; this is the largest mountain in the state. But mostly there's death and decay, and, like a person, a town simply wears away and eventually no one remembers it was ever there. Pretty soon they'll have to cover up the cemeteries, too, to make more superhighways from shopping center to shopping center, or at least in this acid air we breathe the stones will crumble, or like they do in Venice, get their own kind of cancer, so you won't be able to read the epitaphs or names on them. But the names won't mean anything to you anyway. And that's how it will all end, anyway, in America: *amnesia*. Not "civil disorders" or "revolution"—but a vast and neutral amnesia.

Next morning Wayne's cousin Burnell takes us to Senabeh, leading the way on his bicycle. Yesterday's overcast is now light drizzle; the river's gray, a dull mirror to the trees and weeds: the smell of the pulp mills thick now under the cover of fog and mist, down on us. We slept in Wayne's attic in Wayne's grandmother's bedroom-sitting room, ghost of the old white woman in the high, narrow window as a plastic curtain billowed out by the cold night air. Mark pulled a mattress out on the floor—reminder of the days we crashed on Beacon Hill—I take the creaky bed, deep sag in the middle from Mildred McKinnon, who was so strong she threw Bucky Andrew, one of Speck's friends and informants, up the attic stairs. Perfume of the wood of the house and ancient tobacco about us, ashes in the Franklin stove. We bed down early, want to get up for the good light tomorrow. Wayne and Terri will be up late as usual. Wayne got home from work and made himself a gigantic sandwich; we drank some beer, talked. Mark and I were alone in the house earlier; then we shot the shit with Wayne. I brought *Black Elk Speaks* along to read in but was too tired for prose, then, even for talk. The air here makes you sleep well, notwithstanding the pulp mill grunge—the Island itself is compensation for the rest.

Senabeh's puttering around outside by his fireplace; a pile or stack of bricks to one side with a board over them makes a sideboard. Jar of French's mustard there, unwiped knife, bag of Wonder bread. He's got a cold, he says, sniffing. "I'm not so good today," he apologizes. He's hungover, too, takes out a damp Lucky; Mark lights him up. We talk about the names of animals, I tell him I've learned a few from a study of the myths— *Awasis,* "bear"; *Bicou,* "squirrel." Senabeh says, "Good, good." I get embarrassed at my pronunciation; you don't know where the stress goes sometimes, is it *Sen*-a-beh or Sen-a-*beh?* (It means "man"; someone said "old man," but I think just "man," a form of *Arenabe.*)

He says he'd like to receive us inside, as it is on the damp side, but his house is a bit messy. He gestures to a mattress that he had to drag out one night—"it caught on fire"—and now it's soggy from the rain. There's a big black hole in it, probably from a cigarette burn. From where we sit on a log, I can see another mattress inside and some sticks of wood, clothing hanging from some nails. There's also a small pot-bellied stove.

His hair is short on top, parted on the right fairly low, combed down with a bit of length at the back of his neck. Thin, his face is, yellow, long thin nose, hooded eye-lids which palpitate involuntarily as he speaks. How he's somnolent, can barely move to sit down, then as we ask him about the logs which turn out to be ash he's up and with a sort of club he's beating the wood up and down until he can strip a piece right off, just peel it down: these are the strips which go to make baskets, you can tear them any way you want, get, even a few gradations of thickness depending on the kind of wood you use, it apparently peels like an onion. This, he tells us, along with the marsh grass or "sweet grass" Mark and I saw an elderly couple loading out of the back of their station wagon yesterday afternoon on Oak Hill is what your basic materials are. They can be used naturally or dyed.

I tell him I heard he once spent several years (some people have even said 20) alone in the woods. "Yes," he remarked, "after the war. I was stationed in Europe for the war, then I came back here and went into the woods. I still go into the woods when I can—" Mark offers him a Lucky and he accepts with a smile:

"I'm not so good today," he lets the smoke out of his nose, "I'm sorry." He looks in back of him, "I haven't even got any beer to offer you."

"Next time we'll bring some," I say.

A woman in her fifties, stout, quite jolly comes up:

"Listen, Senabeh, someone just called and left a message that someone they know wants a painting on a wall. They want you to make a painting."

"Oh?" he says.

"Yeah, I got the woman's number if you wanna come up. Okay?"

He nods, almost bored.

"Look, you come up the house when you're ready."

"I will." He shakes his head up and down.

"Whenever you want." She smiles at Mark and me. Burnell is just sitting at the edge of the clearing in the underbrush where the shack is, mosly covered with new tar paper. The woman leaves, wiping her hands in her apron.

Senabeh notices me looking at his house.

"Have to get it ready for winter," he says, takes out a Kleenex and blows his nose, excuses himself. "I got an awful cold."

"A summer cold can really get you down," I say.

Mark begins to take some pictures quietly; Senabeh, like Bengun doesn't mind: it's probably a habit now with him to be photographed.

I explain to him what we're trying to do in our book and he nods. I tell him I was pleased to hear they asked him to teach the native language in the school daytime and evenings—

"But they lose interest," he says sadly. "I put some of the words and sayings on tape so the children can go in the library by themselves and listen. We used to keep them on the blackboard too, and if anyone wanted the lesson for that night—the class was on Wednesdays—he could go in and copy the words down and study them. But it's going," he said.

I think he meant the language. It's somewhat of a strain for him to talk; he's really not feeling well. I don't want to prolong the thing for him so I get up and tell him we'll come back again some time when he's feeling better. We go away, the three of us—Burnell wheeling his bike (we scarcely noticed him). I thank Burnell and tell him Mark and I are going to lunch. We walk up to the bridge, don't say much. Mark says he would like to spend several days just following Senabeh around, do a whole series of images of him, talking, cooking outside over his fire, painting, carving, doing baskets, drinking, and smoking. I tell Mark there's something strangely familiar yet otherworldly about the man. Later it comes to me that in reading Carlos Castaneda's The Teachings of Don Juan and A Separate Reality: Further Conversations with Don Juan, I have built up a picture in my mind of the old Yaqui Indian, short, powerfully built, wiry, with gray hair, a man of an indeterminate age (Senabeh could be anything from 48 to 60 years old; I guess he's about Norris's age; then I look him up in the Tribal Census, where he's listed as Ronald Francis and find he was born on September 13, 1914, which would make him 57 years old), and Senabeh fits that picture almost exactly, probably slightly less muscular, though I had Don Juan as not so much a man of visible muscular development as of a hardness all over, a man who had done a certain kind of physical labor all his life, a man who knows how to survive and can and has, but not by a kind or manner of brute force—rather by a certain resourcefulness which his strength merely implements, a man of virtues, and not without, well, a certain magic—what the Indian calls "medicine."

DOCUMENTS 3

PENOBSCOT SHAMANISM

After reading *Old John Neptune* last spring I became tremendously intrigued with the possibility of turning up at least some remnants of Penobscot shamanism or magical practice. My friends couldn't help me—neither Martin nor Wayne, whose own families, the Neptunes and the Mitchells, contained shamans of old, could remember a single instance of the practice in their own time. Martin offered to take me to his grandfather, the oldest Neptune but said he was quite senile now. Then Martin left for Connecticut. Suzy Dana was mentioned as someone who might have a story to tell, but I was cautioned that she doesn't talk to anyone anymore (that famous "contract" with Dr. Seibert—I ought to call him up at Penn. or write him to verify it). Senabeh, of course, practices Indian medicine and told us others did, too. But—granted the fact that old people are very reluctant to talk, and many of the younger people just aren't into this aspect of their own culture [I gave Wayne *The Teachings of Don Juan,* and he seemed very interested but hadn't heard of it, although he's read widely in American Indian culture, esp. in recent paperback reissues and new works]—I wasn't in a position to push this. You really have to be among Indians for a long time for them to trust you and in a way it would be foolhardy, I mean *preposterous,* for someone like me to think that after a few weeks among Indians they would tell me all kinds of things instantly or take me to meet people who didn't know me but who, somehow, would tell me personal or tribal secrets!

Ken and Jean Thompson thought it fairly safe to conclude that shamanism is dead as a practice among the Indians of Maine, that it died a natural death, with its practitioners, since none seemed to have passed on the knowledge, although a knowledge of herbs, medicines, and crafts *is* transmitted through mother and father to their offspring; but they wouldn't exclude the possibility that among a few of the older people a memory of such practices exists.

Leland (*The Algonquin Legends of New England*) describes shamanism as

> the belief that all the events and accidents of life are caused or influenced by spirits. . . . Thus all disease whatever, all suffering, pain, loss, or disaster, or bad weather, is at once attributed either to a spirit or to some enemy who practices witchcraft. The Shaman is the priest or doctor, who professes to be able by his counter-charms, to counter-act or neutralize this devil's work.
>
> The magic of the Passamaquoddy and Penobscot, like the magician himself, is called *m'teoulin*. It is the same effectively as *meda,* which is from the same root. It is a "power," but opinions differ as to how it is acquired. It is certain . . . that some children are born *m'teoulin*. They manifest it, even while babes, by being capricious, eccentric, and malicious. Others acquire the art as they grow older . . . M'teoulin take two forms —one of witchcraft, the other of magic. The former is innate, or may be acquired; the latter . . . may be sometimes inborn, but is generally acquired by fasting, abstinence of other kinds, and ceremonies.
>
> pp. 334–340

Speck and Mrs. Eckstorm point out the tribal familial or clan aspect of shamanism, in which each group, having its own hunting territory, would also have its own shaman to protect that territory from the encroachment of other clans, families, or tribes. Shamans would be employed in family or clan or even personal feuds; Speck cites cases of shamans fighting amongst themselves, as in the case of Old John Neptune's battle with the giant squid, seaworm, or sea monster—whatever it actually was!—called *Wiwilia-mecq'*. Shamans often worked through familiars or helpers, called *baohigan* (in Penobscot literally "instrument of mystery,") whose animal forms they could assume, especially those of otters, beavers, muskrats, porcupines, owls, minks, loons, bears, and wildcats. At any rate a shaman was to be feared—and prized—and his power believed in. It was one of those things, as Leland writes, "which the white man talks about without feeling, and which the Indian feels without talking about it."

Some tales will illustrate—

THE FIGHT WITH THE WIWILIAMECQ'

The supreme achievement of John Neptune, in the minds of his tribesmen, was his encounter with the dreaded underwater monster, known to the Penobscots as the *wiwiliamecq'*; to the Passamaquoddies as the *wiwil'mecq'*. This mythological creature seems never to have been visualized by the Indians sufficiently for them to describe it. Every Indian with whom I have talked about it has had a different conception of its parts and characteristics: all they agreed upon was that it was very dreadful and dangerous. . . . It was in the guise of this dreadful underwater monster that a certain Micmac chief, inveterate enemy of our Indians, was wont to appear. The scene of the fight is always laid at Boyden's Lake, four miles from the Passamaquoddy reservation in Perry, Maine. . . .

Fannie Hardy Eckstorm,
Old John Neptune and Other Maine Indian Shamans,
1945

The old governor was a great *m'teoulin*. He had got it among the Chippewas. He said that it would come to pass that he would die before the next snow-storm. No, he did not care himself, but my husband's mother did, when she heard this, and she cried. Then he said, "Well I will try to live, or else die in a month, but it will be a hard fight." So he made him a bow, and strung it with his wife's hair, and having done this, he shot an arrow through the smoke-hole of his wigwam.

All this was at Nessaik, near Eastport. Then he said to his wife, "Take one of your leggins and put it on my head." She did so. Then he took medicine. A rainbow appeared in the sky, and a great horse-fly came out of his mouth, and then a large grasshopper. He cried to his wife, "Do not kill it!" And then came a stone spearhead.

"Now," said the governor, "this is all right so far, but the great struggle is yet to come. It is a *wiwiliamecq'* who has done this. (You know what that is: the Passamaquoddies call it *wiwil'mecq'*. It is a worm an inch long, which can make itself into a horrid monster as large as a deer, yes, and much larger. It is *m'teoulin*; yes, it is a great magician.) I am going to fight it. You must come with a small stick to hit it once, and only a mere tap." But she would not go. So he went and fought with the *wiwiliamecq'*. He killed it. It was a frightful battle. When he returned he smelt like fresh fish. Hie wife bade him go and wash himself; but let him bathe as much as he could, the smell remained for days. The pond where he fought has been muddy and foul ever since.

Marie Sakis, Penobscot, from Charles G. Leland, *The Algonquin Legends of New England*, 1884.

A SHAMAN DISCOVERED IN BIRD FORM

Once when my wife was sick, I sat up with her and soon fell asleep. While sleeping I dreamed that the ground suddenly began to heave like a wave, rising and falling round and round near where the sick one, my wife, lay. Then I saw the movement of a bird flying about under the ground and I said, "Don't hide yourself, I have seen you." The bird emerged. "I have seen you already. You were doing this while my wife was sick." As I said this fluttering he (the bird) came out and died. Then I woke up. When I awoke my wife felt better and fell asleep right away. She got completely well.

Frank G. Speck, "Texts of Some Shamanistic Tales," *Penobscot Shamanism,* 1919.

THE SHAMAN DISGUISED AS A PORCUPINE

A hunter and his partner were once away up the river trapping. They set their traps everywhere but had bad luck. When they looked after the traps they always found them sprung but couldn't find the cause. So one night they were sitting around their camp talking about their bad luck when they heard a noise outside and lo, there was a porcupine looking right in at them with a face like a man's. When he saw them staring at him the porcupine made off. Pretty soon the hunters heard another noise on the outside of their wigwam and looking up through the smoke-hole, beheld there the same porcupine peering down. Now they could see its face and it was the face of a man in their village. The older hunter took a big stick and threw it at the porcupine. It hit him in the face and he tumbled off and made away into the woods. "Now," said the hunter, "we will have good luck after this." That was a shaman. When they next visited their traps they found a good catch, and their luck continued good. When they got home they told their story and discovered that a certain man in the village had, as he claimed, met with an accident. He had his face disfigured. The hunters went up to see him and found that his face was broken just where he had been hit with the big stick.

Frank G. Speck, "Texts of Some Shamanistic Tales," *Penobscot Shamanism,* 1919.

THE SHAMAN AS OTTER

One night some hunters were camping in a wigwam near some friends. During the night an otter appeared at the doorway and one of the men in the bed at the back of the lodge opposite the door began talking in his sleep. One of the hunters awakened, seized a brand from the fire and poked the otter which ran out. A noise as of someone running away was immediately afterward heard outside. They went out and there lay the otter dead, surrounded by a kind of hoar frost, near the wind break or fence of brush which encircled the camp. The next season the same band camped at the same place and two boys of the band ran to a well to get a bucket of water. One of the boys got the pole of the well bucket stuck in his side. He staggered right over to the brush fence at the same spot where the otter had died, and a frost gathered around him. In the morning he was dead, lying in the same spot. They all thought that he was the *madeolinu* who had appeared as an otter the year before. It was an uncanny affair.

Old Joe Francis, Oldtown, from Speck, *ibid*.

A DREAMER ASSUMES THE FORM OF A BALL OF FIRE

An old man and his son went hunting. His wife and daughter-in-law did not like to stay at home so they went with him. They built their camp out of boughs and made a fire in the midst of a shelter. The father and son went out hunting and left the women at the camp alone. They were to be back in three days, but at the end of three days they did not return. The son's wife got weary and did not know what kept them so long, since it was four or five days since they had gone. That night the mother-in-law who was very fond of smoking lay down near the fire to smoke. Her daughter-in-law was lying in one corner of the camp on the boughs. The old woman told the younger that she was going to sleep and dream about where the men were, and what they were doing. When she finished smoking she lay on her back. Finally the young woman saw a ball of fire come out of her mouth. She became very frightened. She jumped up and tried to arouse the old woman, she turned her on her side and shook her. Then she believed the old woman to be dead. The ball of fire that came from the old woman's mouth went round and round the camp and around the old woman. The young woman turned her over again and when she did so the ball of fire went back into the old woman's mouth. Then she began to move about. She said that she had had a long sleep. She said, "Don't worry they will be back tomorrow. They have had good luck and are bringing lots of game. I just saw them sitting by their fire eating supper." The next day the hunters appeared with an abundance of game of all sorts.

Katie Mitchell, Oldtown, 1910, from Speck, *ibid.*

Voices 3

JIM SAPPIER

As a boy I remember Speck. He used to live in the little house. He sent a copy of *Penobscot Man* to my mother, Nataline Polchies. My father was a Malacite from Woodstock, N.B., and so was my grandfather, who was adopted into the tribe here. My father and mother are both dead now. I was born in Old Town. I went to Indian Island school to the fifth grade; sixth grade at Herbert Gray; seventh, eighth, and ninth grades at Helen Hunt and four years at Old Town High School. I entered the Air Force and I got out with an A.P.T.S.—that's a medical discharge—after one month and 19 days. Then I came back here and went to work for Eastern Pulp and Paper in Brewer.

When I was growing up I sewed shoes for my father. My brother Matthew and me used to sew a case a day in the summer, early in the morning before we went swimming or anything. We'd get up at six or seven, early so you'd get your case done, then you could play ball in the afternoon. My father taught us—hand-sewing shoes, that was a must—and cutting shoes. I learned that and how to stitch shoes, moccasins, slippers, loafers.

I was married in December, 1963, and Jimmy was born in December, 1964. In '63 I got laid off in Brewer. My mother died that year. She had been very involved in tribal politics all her life. She used to sing in the choir, and of course, since she was involved with the choir, I was an altar boy until I was in high school—nine years. But my mother had gone to nursing school in Bangor, though she never became a nurse. She was just a few months from graduating. And she had a glorious voice which she strained so she couldn't sing. Then she had goiter, too, which they didn't know how to remove in those days so after she had that operation—they practically cut her whole head off!—she had to learn to talk all over again. But she could sing—boy, could she sing!

Dad was born in Houlton, Maine, though his family came from Woodstock, N.B. He had it rough. His father died when he was just a kid, and Dad was something like the mother to the other kids because his mother went out to work. So he stayed home to take care of the family. Then finally his mother married a second time, a Frenchman, and they didn't get along, so he moved out, Dad and all the boys moved out. It was a big family, nine boys and one girl. Five in my own family, including Annette, my sister, who isn't my real sister but she lived with us all those years. . . .

After I got married, Cliff, my friend, had just got out of the service and he was doing a lot of sky-diving so I made five jumps myself. That's quite a thing. You've got to get out and grab hold of a wing strut while the plane's doing about ninety miles an hour. Once I got dragged down the runway when my chute got caught, gouged my back all up. I was working at Eastern Paper again. I worked there five years, started in the wood yard and ended up in the paper mill itself. I know the shoe industry because that was the trade that was taught us at home. I've been through the paper mills from wood yard to pulp room to paper mill—by way of the machine room, and the cutting, finishing, and shipping rooms. We made pretty good money for then, twenty-five or thirty-five dollars a day, doing piece work. I also became a paper inspector for cutting, and checking paper for oil—the grain, size, color. You name it: soft rolls, hard rolls—ripples. Then they had this big layoff in 1965. We'd go to work and work a twenty-hour week, one or two shifts a week. Then I was back hand-sewing shoes part-time. This year, 1971, is the first year in my life I haven't been drawing unemployment.

I went to Connecticut in 1966. I went to Pratt and Whitney and got a job there, but I didn't have a place to stay. So I went down to Bridgeport to stay with my Uncle Horace and Aunt Pauline for the weekend, and the following Monday I went back to Pratt and Whitney and told them I wanted to transfer to Sikorsky in the Bridgeport-Stratford area. It's ironic. I didn't know what a milling machine was or how to run a lathe. I went through a ten-week training program for machinists; then I went right out on the floor. Sikorsky runs a good shop. They run a shop where a trainee comes in, or somebody that's new, and they say, "Here's your tools, there's your machine. There's your metal and your blueprint. Go to it, Charlie!" And there you are! But being on that lathe gave me a lot of respect for the common laborer. You're working hard with these guys all day long, and believe me, they've got family problems, too.

This exam came up for a two-year training program, and I ended up in production control with this Mexican. We're the only two minorities so we hung together like brothers. Rodolfo Castillio, old wetback from Michigan! He and I chose production control. I talked him into it. He was going into ME and IE where the money is, I said, "Don't do it. Go where the action is."

The other outfits are all leaning on production control. You have to be accountable to every phase of manufacture, every phase of industrial engineering—and above all you have to be with quality control because you could spend years making one part and never getting it through quality control. We used to lock horns with the front office at least once a month. We'd tell them, "You can't be laying off this many people and expect to put out this many aircraft."

So I finished that training program and went to work in production control. Rudy did, too. Then he took a week's vacation and never came back. Come to find out he went back to Michigan and got a job in production control with Oldsmobile. So I went on full salary in August '68. While I was in training I was still working part-time in the machine shop. My wife, Bonny, was working too, in a plastic bead and key chain operation—swaging, they call it. Connecticut is a tremendous state in industry. They make everything in Connecticut, you name it.

At one time I had eleven people working under me, including two secretaries. I used to get so miserable. You come off the floor and it's hotter than hell, and I used to see my bosses, the group leaders, sitting in an office, talking and joking—paying attention to everything else but the machine shop. That irked me, because as far as I was concerned that's where the overhead was. Those two guys should have been removed. That really got me.

My wife used to come up here a lot on visits. She missed Old Town. She really missed her folks. We were having a lot of trouble with our neighbors down there, and I was really getting involved in aircraft at the plant. I had to watch who was going on strike at the railroad because if they did we wouldn't get the raw materials. Or if Johnson didn't sign this bill or did sign that one—or maybe something was going to happen in Vietnam, or Israel needed more aircraft, or Germany did, or Spain was ordering aircraft. All these countries were ordering, and you had to watch what was going on. Or if there was a war going on somewhere you accelerated your aircraft because you'd expect some general to come in and say, "Hey, we want production of these aircraft. Hire a thousand more people!" You had to be a jump ahead of everything because when the Main Office comes back and says, "What are you doing about this? Did you read the paper last night? Didn't you hear the news?" you've got to be ready.

We had this aircraft crash out here, and a general and a colonel were killed. Holy God, we grounded sixty-five aircraft throughout the entire world for three days. It was during shutdown that it happened, and overnight they called everyone back from vacation—that is, everyone except my boss: "Hang in there, Jim," he said. Hang in! Hell, I was the only one there!

So my wife wanted to come home. I got sick of it, too. You went down to Bridgeport at the time Martin Luther King was killed and you sensed something was going to happen. And it was the time of the Black Panther trials, too. I was only twelve miles from New Haven and eighteen miles from Bridgeport and you'd travel to both places anyway. I mean they didn't make me aware down there of being an Indian, but when I lived up here on the Reservation I *was* an Indian. I was Jim Sappier, and everybody knew me because they knew my parents. It was a positive thing. You met a few guys in the plant who were backward—but to find a rental down there! Well, I went to a few places at first, but after a while I'd send Bonny. Everybody thinks that I'm Puerto Rican, Italian, Spanish, Portuguese, Sicilian, Ethiopian—everything. You name it, and I was one of them—anything! So I used to send Bonny out to look at apartments. Nobody ever guessed I was an *American* Indian!

I went to this bar one night, and I only had a dollar eighty-five cents on me. There were two of us, a buddy of mine and me. And we sat down; we were only going to have one beer anyway. So we were finishing our beer and this guy comes over in this sharkskin suit. I mean he was sharp! And he says, "Hi, how are you?" and I says, "Okay." And he says, "Empty your glass." So I looked at him and emptied my glass. They were having a party over there. So he takes this bottle of C.C. and he fills up the beer glasses. He filled both our glasses. That's a whole lot of C.C.! Anyway, he thought I was Portuguese, and they were having this party and they wanted us to join them!

So my wife came back up here, and she rented this house. I stayed down there for another three months trying to straighten out the bills. Then I came up here. I didn't have anything to come back to. I had a month off. I sent out forty résumés that summer during shutdown. That was last year. Operation Mainstream was already running under Ken Thompson. They started in July, 1970, and I got through in Connecticut in September, 1970. Ken was Mainstream Director but he wanted to step down because he really wanted an Indian to run it—and I didn't know if I wanted it although I finally applied for it. I came back, and even though I was looking for a job in production control or quality control in the area, I wanted to help the tribe somehow. When they shot down housing in '68 I was back here on vacation. And when you come back here on vacation you look at the Island and you say, "What the hell, there's no change!" And then you read *The Maine Indian Newsletter* or *Akwessasne Notes* or you pick up the newspaper and you say, "The Indian is getting screwed again. Well, damn it. I can do something about this!"

I was always aware of being an Indian. I used to think that everything I do has to be better than somebody else. But even though I was away I didn't melt into the white world. I couldn't because their reasoning is simple. I mean a white is *simple*! They'll talk for hours and hours and I don't think they ever say anything—or they'll lie to you. The Mexicans I trusted. The Blacks—well, I was a little gun-shy of the Blacks. The Puerto Ricans, the same.

I don't vote, but I watch both parties and see what they're doing. Like what Nixon's doing now. I can see him dividing up OEO, trying to give it away. Labor grabbing a little; Interior's grabbing a little. I vote in tribal elections, of course, but not in national ones. We got the right to vote back in '56, and we were sitting at the supper table. I was a junior in high school, and my brother was a senior, and we were sitting down and my mother says, Mom said: "I do not want any of you kids to vote for any president, governor, senator, representative, or what have you. It's another method for them to terminate the tribe." This is what my mother told me and it still sticks with me because when you're arguing a little thing like why can't you get a liquor license on the Island to sell a little booze in the general store and you hear the attorney general say, "Well, all you need is to be a registered voter." You cannot force people to vote, it's a right which you can choose to accept or not. In other words, if they want one hundred percent voting there's something wrong. It's a sickening state when you've got a law that says if you want this you've got to be a registered voter. Well, who the hell wants to be a registered voter when you just think back a little bit: "Boy, we've been getting screwed an awful long time"?

So I applied for the job as Director of Operation Mainstream on Indian Island, and I got it and took over on October 15, 1970. Then I had problems! Ever since then I don't think I've been the same! See, I had a concept of Mainstream. I don't believe in "You give people any rope and they'll hang themselves." I say, "You give them what they want and they'll accomplish something." It's true that I don't have the qualified people in the jobs I need them in, but damn it, we can give it a whirl! I'll tackle anything!

The whole structure of Mainstream is wrong. I just went down to SBA in Bangor a few weeks ago and I said, "Who is SBA? It's a business out-fit and it's got its office under the President and it comes out to poverty areas, has them incorporate like we have with Indian Island Corporation, with sixteen out of twenty-five members of the Corporation under the poverty level, and yet there's not one penny for a feasibility study—no discretionary funds, no organizational money: not a cent!" You have a corporation that's for economic development—by white standards anything that makes money is called economic development—and you take an example: say, an Andy Aikens comes back and he's a biologist, which he is. Well, he should be our environmentalist. Along with economic develop-ment on the Island it would be ideal. You'd be going on with the old Indian concept of saving and preserving the environment—Nature—but you'd also have your economic development. Well, SBA couldn't give us any money, and it's wrong to have a corporation without any discretionary funds—plus they don't have a resource base. But they've got a program, Operation Mainstream, which is ideal at putting twenty-five or thirty people to work, including the director and the secretary. Now the Corporation is the sponsor, yet the director is supposed to be able to take care of any problem an enrollee has—placement, job referral, even personal. In order for a director to be able to sit down with his enrollee one hour a week, that's twenty-six hours. That leaves him fourteen hours a week for his own work, surveying job sites, etcetera. That's ten hours, and that leaves him theoretically four hours for staff, and then you get into why Jim Sappier is working a sixty or an eighty hour week. You get an Indian from the Reserva-tion—any Indian who is sincere to his tribe—and if he's the only person who is fully funded to do anything he'll have to do it. The Corporation and its members aren't paid. The Housing Director isn't paid; neither are the Governor and Council being paid—but Jim Sappier is.

Being on the Board of Directors of Tribe, Inc., has helped me a lot with Mainstream because I know what is going on in the different tribes. I could talk with John Stevens, Terry Polchies, Dennis Nicholas, or the Francises from Nova Scotia: they represent the Micmacs, Malacites, and

Passamaquoddies, and what they were doing I knew we could do if we could only get it going. Something had to click. I think the best thing we've done in Mainstream so far this year is the Emergency Heating Service with John Love. Thirty-five below zero, forty-two below, and those furnaces went out and it was cold! We'll get a radi-heater and throw it on a sled and drag it up to that house. The first thing you do is heat that house entirely, keep that heater going for about a half an hour—50,000 BTU's with a fan. Just blow that heat all through the house. Then after you get it heated or while it's being heated, you work on the stove or furnace. This is really ideal. Or like taking people to the doctor's or to hospital appointments—the old people just couldn't get there alone. That's Nick Sappier's job. Winterizing the homes. You should see some of these houses. A lot of them should be leveled, but the people don't have any other place to live.

Now we could have a housing program like they have Down East—people getting paid to build their own houses or renovate them. As Chairman of the Housing Authority for Indian Island I know that, but how can you do that without a resource base? Somebody has to get paid from somewhere to get the program going, and nobody down here is getting paid for a job other than their own job. I mean as Director of Mainstream I've got to worry about thirty people, and then I have to come back and do all the Corporation work referring to these thirty people and the Operation—making out the checks and having the Corporation sign them, making out invoices, Narratives, etcetera. The Narrative is the Director's job—to tell Bangor, Boston, and Washington what's been done on Indian Island. Well, I haven't had the time to sit down and write a Narrative.

I told Ken Paul, the President of the Corporation, you're not going to have economic development as long as you've got alcoholism. And you're not going to have a Mainstream unless you start fighting alcoholism. It's a big problem—and it's not the alcoholism. *Alcoholism* and *frustration* are one. Let's not call the program an alcoholism program, then; let's call it a frustration program because that's what I think it is—the pileup of years of frustration. Now we've been trying to get money from CAP for three months to have a rehabilitation program!

I'm getting tired, and it's not just physically tired. There was one time about three weeks ago I just went out and I drank and I drank and I gave my sister hell and I gave everybody else hell and I came home and I went to bed and I woke up Monday morning and I had the sickest feeling I've ever had in my life. I wanted to say I was sorry but I didn't give a damn.

I felt like somebody had gutted me right out, like somebody took a knife and just cleaned me right out. It wasn't just from the alcohol; it was my own self. I felt like I'd just gone to the limit and that was it. I was going to quit. I mean I had just had it.

I would like to see Indian unity, but I'd like to see it the way it was when I was a boy—before the bridge. People would have their little fights, but five or six men used to come down my grandfather's and they'd sit and have a beer or a cup of coffee and talk Indian. When the Priest wasn't there they'd all talk Indian! And my grandfather had open house—an open door at all times. You'd come in and somebody'd be sleeping on the couch, and I'd say, "Who's that?" and he'd say, "That's your cousin from Woodstock," or "That's another relative from New Brunswick." My grandfather was a good man. He believed in the *m'teoulin* [magic, shamanism], and he also was a good Catholic. My mother was a good Catholic, but *she* believed in the *m'teoulin*. As far as they were concerned, God was there, but they also believed in the *m'teoulin*. You can't change that. They want to change the Church, but they're going about it in the wrong way. They're changing it for the money, but they should change it for the spiritual end of it. I used to like Latin Masses. In fact I still like a good Gregorian Mass. My best Mass is the Requiem—the Dies Irae sung in Latin is beautiful. But now they've got away from that with banjo-playing and everything else—I like that, too, but I still like to have a little bit of something.

But Indian unity—we're trying! Don't rock the boat, yet. If you have control of the boat you can do anything you want with it—but don't rock it.

John Stevens' technique is, knock on the front door lightly and take the back door down!

I mention John not ony because we work together but because he's a personal friend. He's thirty-nine, been Governor Down East for thirteen, fourteen years. Then there's Terry Polchies at Tribe, and one who is coming up is Wayne Newell in Calais. He's got an M.A. in Education from Harvard and he went back to his own people. He's also directing the bilingual program for Tribe, Inc. So all of us sit down and talk and one thing you've got in common is *your* tribe as well as Tribe, Inc. And I'd like to see Tribe's language and cultural programs tied in with the Indian Academy here. Unfortunately the Governor and Council's concept is of a

Tribal Hall; mine is of an educational facility with an annex, which is your Tribal Hall. But I'd like to see the Indian Academy make it, and I would like to see Tribe, Inc., make it, too.

But there are plenty of problems. You take the thirty people I'm responsible for in Mainstream. I went out the other day and took pictures of the unemployment lines in Old Town just to prove there's no jobs. I'm supposed to get rid of the people working for me, I'm not supposed to employ them. It's my job to train them or retrain them and help them find jobs, but the companies aren't hiring anybody in Old Town or Bangor. Unemployment is very bad; they're shutting down all over—leather, shoes, woolens—yet I'm supposed to find these people jobs. They're not supposed to make a livelihood in Mainstream.

Another problem you've got on the Reservation is too many relationships: husband, wife; father, son; cousin, uncle, aunts. Interfamily relationships and conflicts, petty gripes and feuds—that keeps the people divided. Then your Old Town police department coming in here making statements like—say, a store was broken into—"Who was drunk over on the Island last night?" Or they'll come on the Island looking for two Indians because they *thought* they saw them. Something's got to be done about that.

But as far as being an Indian is concerned and feeling different from other people—I mean being conscious of being an Indian—experience is the Indian's whole bag, like growing up snaring rabbits. My brother is a good example. We were probably about ten when we got our first twenty-two—maybe even younger than that. We used to go up snaring rabbits, and this time Matt went up in the woods to get his rabbit. It was a fresh kill; he'd snared him, and this hawk was there. And Matt was walking up to it. Now Matt was young—he's going up, and the hawk's trying to get the rabbit, trying to pull it away. 'Course the hawk knew Matt was coming. So Matt walks up and takes a stick and tosses it, and the hawk jumps back. See, when an animal comes at you they try to put the old fear of God into you. That hawk glares his eyes; they look like they're turning red; the feathers stand up on his back and he spreads his wings and he jumps at you, claws out. All it is is a bluff. But when you're that young it can scare hell out of you. So Matt gets back and he brings that twenty-two up, lowers it on that hawk; then he puts his twenty-two down, lets him have the rabbit and walks off because he suddenly discovers that hawk needs the meat more than he does. It just comes to him—and he's only a kid. To experience it is something else—to tell some-body or try to teach them, you just can't do it.

I don't even know what the hell I'm doing sometimes. I can't basically sit down and tell you what I'm doing. I think sometimes I'm terminating my tribe through assimilation—truthfully I think I am, but I've sat down with my work-study kids and I've tried to deal with it, and I've sat down with a lot of other people—and I'm going to get Tribe, Inc. involved in this too!—and we've hashed out whether you can have pure economic development and pure culture. Now my answer would be "No." Not as long as the dominant society determines what *is* economic development. Then the other answer is *only* if you accept from that society what is good for your culture. You keep rattling it off like a game of chess, and you're losing because you're losing the concept when you talk biculturalism. I don't know. I would like to see an Indian be equal. Just an equal Indian, but not on *your* terms—on *his* terms. Not that the whites accept an Indian but that the Indian be made to feel there's no pressure on him to be *white*. And one way for that to happen is the white man coming to the Indian, which he *is* now. He never did that before.

For one thing the Indian won't accept anything free. Mainstream makes it on the Reservation because everyone in it is working. Not only that, you could double your money going into that if you had the funds because there's continual input into the Reservation, the input of their labor and the input of their wages. Then you go back to that gateway-city type thing where their wage money is still going over to Old Town. Well, we're cutting it down a little bit with the laundromat and superette. The tribe is small now, but as soon as better water and sewage and housing come in, I'd say seventy-five percent of the tribe will be back.

JOURNAL 5

I set off again for Old Town, last trip for a while, probably, and I wonder as I leave—always a pull to linger, when I'm about to travel anywhere (Travel? the farthest I ever go is a couple hundred miles north to Mt. Desert, or a hundred south to Connecticut—I once told someone the farthest west I've ever been is Western Massachusetts!—he thought I was crazy), a kind of magnetism making my feet stick on the doorstep—I wonder why it is such a momentous thing to travel? for me? I guess I really am an old-fashioned localist—of the psyche at any rate—and maybe just as superstitious as those ancients who scarcely ever ventured beyond their villages because the virtues of their local gods did not extend beyond the village itself or their fields and burial grounds.

This is one key to the understanding of what has been viewed as the "recalcitrance" of the Vietnamese peasants: a fierce localism because the earth upon which their homes are built is also the earth in which their ancestors' bones lie; they plant the land that is full of the dead, and over all the local gods and spirits watch. So when you forcibly relocate them, after of course having completely destroyed their homes, fields, the graves of their ancestors [remember the photo of the old woman carrying a sack of her parents' bones on her back as she entered the concentration camp in South Vietnam?], you derange them spiritually. They simply have nothing left to live for, no ground to stand on, so to speak, and the "pacification" people know this: you've got your Asian academics feeding them this vast amount of information on the culture which they then use to undermine that culture.

And I needn't press the enormous parallel between the destruction of the native cultures of America and the present ones of Southeast Asia. You can't subjugate a people until you strip them of their spiritual clothing as well as of the land in which that religious life is set, literally: I mean take a Penobscot away from the River and Katahdin, away from Glooskap's home, and he can't feel any spiritual presence. Where? in Boston? that's not his home, his

HOUSE/HOLD.

In this sense it becomes crystal clear the role the Church played in the subjugation of the American Indian and the colonization of his land by Europeans. The missionaries were the first pacification teams: the explorers claimed the land which did not belong to them; the Church claimed the souls of the people which did not belong to her. You can talk all you want about the illusory separation between Church and State (that was just the middle-class way of making sure the Church didn't hold too much nontaxable, resalable property) but it's a great partnership. What's understood is that neither party messes in the other's business, but at the same time a parallel process of deception takes place. You're sold a bill of goods under the social apparatus and God and the afterlife as either a compensation for fucking up in this life or as a salve for the guilt you feel in having to screw others in your material existence. The history of religion in the Western world is a long account of perfidy, destruction, torture, murder, and genocide, especially of dark peoples everywhere—Moors, Blacks, American Indians, Yellow people—all in the name of Salvation; and the history of Western nations is a history of the appropriation of their lands and goods under the banner of liberating them or rubbing them out to make the world safe for the white man—or his most recent excuse—Democracy!

Route 95, Mass.: leaves just beginning to turn here and there, a few maples; absolutely gorgeous rolling hills, trees, meadows, grass leveled for a highway and Nature replaced by Ferncroft Village: apartments, shopping centers, parking lots—give it a woody sounding name and you excuse the rape of the land. After all, man always improves on Nature although he tells you God=Perfection. Well, God mustn't have made those hills, then, and all those trees that stand so still just momentarily green, about to turn for the very last time in their many hundred years of life: for comes the bulldozer, you can see them all lined up like an advancing army and do trees

      Scream?   I mean literally the way they say a carrot (is it?) screams when you pull it out of the ground, do trees scream when you rip them out by their roots? Do they now? People scream when their hair gets ripped out by the roots . . .

      the Indian says
Earth is our Mother/ the grass you see is her hair/ would you sell your mother?

      and is there a white man who doesn't know that
white men and not Indians invented scalping.

      But there it is: anyone who

can scalp the hills of Danvers and Middleton, Topsfield and Boxford, New-
bury and Newburyport and call it FERNCROFT VILLAGE will sell his
mother, too, and has, as well as his children and his birthright, and not
even for a mess of pottage or a plate of lentils but for a split-level ranch
house and two mother-fucking cars—

I think it's interesting and especially fruitful to mention here the early
white man's fear of the forest in the New World and of the Red Man himself as creature of that tangled place as part of the white man's fear of the
unknown: Dark Wood of Error, etc., and of course the resonance of such
image-symbols in literature from Dante's *selva selvaggia* all the way down
to Hawthorne's dark forest of the witches' sabbath in "Young Goodman
Brown." The New World forest was wild, and no one today has any sense
from the Maine woods we do see (most growth not being any older than
the turn of the century, except the heart of the Munsungan-Allegash country where Indians have told me no white man has yet been) how dark and
dense and damp—"dank" was the word then—and eerily silent the American forest was actually. I think Audubon discovered and rendered that,
and in 1812 Tocqueville, coming to the U.S. from the forest-gardens of
France noted:

*Here man seems to enter life furtively. Everything enters into a silence so
profound, a stillness so complete that the soul feels penetrated by a sort
of religious terror . . . Immense trees retained by the surrounding branches
hang suspended in the air and fall into dust without touching the earth.*

This obtained even more graphically for the first settlers in New
England. Setting the scene for his two volumes on the Salem witchcraft
delusion of the 1690s, Rev. Charles Upham wrote (in 1867) that the Puri-
tans were the children of an age of often fanatical superstition:

*"The imagination had been expanded by credulity, until it had reached a
wild and monstrous growth . . . and New England was a most fit and
congenial theatre upon which to display its power. Cultivation had made
but a slight encroachment on the wilderness. Wide, dark, unexplored
forests covered the hills, hung over the lonely roads, and frowned upon
the scattered settlements. Persons whose lives have been passed where the
surface has long been opened, and the land generally cleared, little know
the power of a primitive wilderness upon the mind. . . .*

The forests which surrounded our ancestors were the abode of a mysterious race of men of strange demeanor and unascertained origin. The aspects they presented, the stories told of them, and everything connected with them served to awaken fear, bewilder the imagination, and aggravate the tendencies of the general condition of things to fanatical enthusiasm. It was the common belief, sanctioned not by the clergy alone but by the most learned scholars of that and the preceding ages, that the American Indians were the subjects and worshippers of the Devil and their Powwows [Upham means shamans or medicine men] *wizards. In consequence of this opinion, the entire want of confidence and sympathy to which it gave rise, and the provocations naturally incident to two races of men, of dis-similar habits, feelings and ideas, thrown into close proximity, a state of things was soon brought about which led to conflicts and wars of the most distressing and shocking character. A strongly rooted sentiment of hostility and horror became associated in the minds of the colonists with the name of the Indian."*

Charles Upham,
Salem Witchcraft, Vol. I, pp. 6–8

Given the history of Christian man in the West extirpating heresies of the Devil, crusading against the Infidel in the name of rooting out evil amongst us, whether it be burning witches in Salem, "communists" in Washington, or "the enemy" in Southeast Asia, it comes as no surprise to discover the white man in the New World attempting to civilize the Red Man and tame or cultivate his forests. If you can't convert him, you must kill or subdue him by violent means; and just as you suppress him physi-cally you must guard against what he represents to you psychologically—the embodiment, like the Black man, of all those passions, lusts, cravings, superstitions, fears, *needs* that you must subdue in yourself. For is not the Red Man our dark alter ego?

And what of the forest itself, his former abode? Perhaps our lust for the continual development and cultivation of wild places carries, along with the lust for profit, the residual, even vestigial, desire to remove the onus of the unknown, the uninhabited, the irrational (though there is nothing more rational than Nature's workings) from things and places. Hence, Ferncroft Village. And so ironically and lamentably on the very fields the farmers of Salem Village hacked out of the woods in the 17th century and which had been allowed of late to go back to Nature we now have LIBERTY TREE MALL, a shopping plaza in all its gaud of aluminum and plastic, neon lights and cheap painted cement blocks. *Liberty Tree* Mall—

but where are the trees? Ah, you can buy them at a nursery conveniently located at the edge of the mall, with plenty of parking space for all, day or night.

What the Puritan called "cultivation"—and he found religious sanction in that, too, in the providential notion of the New World as a Garden of Eden, an earthly paradise, a New Zion in the wilderness—we call "development." There's scarcely a person you talk to when you're out trying to save a marsh or keep people from destroying a beautiful meadow with a shopping center, parking lot, or drive-in who doesn't retort: "I don't see why you have to stop people from developing land—I mean, look, it's just sitting there doing nothing, you should make some use of it!" And they do, and they call it FERNCROFT VILLAGE, and another piece of earth is dead.

Outside of Augusta: a faint hue of summer (fainter than when we were returning from Gotts Island two weeks ago) lingers on the trees and grass; still some wild flowers—goldenrod and milkweed, thistle, ragged false Queen Anne's lace. But the light is different, even a scant hundred miles north. Yes, the light is suddenly bleaker.

Falls Above Bangor: stench, gulls on rocks; water so dirty it looks like soapsuds at the edges of the river; debris all over the shore and river bank, old pieces of rotting logs—death.

September 15, 1971

I'm right behind the school bus as I cross the bridge to Indian Island: stainless steel river, trees immense and still against a cloudless wash of blue sky. I scarcely noticed poor old, gray old Old Town in my haste to get here, a catch at the back of my throat as I approach the bridge or begin to drive up Center Street past the church and the first houses, maybe in anticipation of seeing what are by now so many familiar faces or just the thrill, the excitement at being able to be here again with people I feel comfortable among, people I love. It's a kind of small homecoming, though I shrink at the thought of such presumption on my part. Nevertheless I'm here again, my car will be rattling up and down Center Street and Oak Hill day and night, and I'll be walking, as I often do, around in circles, cutting through people's backyards, getting tied up in their wash, just about peeking in their windows—or feeling that I am.

The bus stops with a huge puff of black smoke out of which emerge

some teenage girls in dark pantsuits and bright purple tights, leather microskirts and brown suede-fringed boleros. Wayne's fourteen-year-old sister,
Natalie, whom I had admired dancing in the pageant in July in leather
tunic and moccasins and, because of her beautiful hair and round dark
face, had taken instantly for a Mitchell, smiles shyly at me—never speaks—
and two boys wave who because of permapressed slacks and shiny black
loafers I don't recognize immediately. In fact all the kids are dressed up,
whether it's that first day of school newness lingering or the "dress code" at
Old Town High School. ("But they don't look like Indians!")

And I mustn't
regard these people as special or apart because they are Indians. I've
got to demythologize them in my own mind, avoid both the coloration
of a romantic view of them as the descendants of the Noble Savage
or what have you and the liberal's patronizing indulgence, and sympathy,
his guilt-ridden, "I understand, oh yes I do, I know exactly what's been
done to you and I aim to make it all up to you." What I think really lies
behind the kind of "shock" I do get every time I arrive out of the white
world, the sense of finding myself among or actually seeing "different" or
"alien" people, is my inherently racist response to them as in fact *different
from me* because I as a white man am the norm, the mean, they the
divergence from it, the alien. It's very hard to dramatize; all I can say is
that it's a kind of programmed response to look at people of color as
different from *you*, not you as *different* from them: so the burden is
always upon them to adjust to you.)

Center Street has been newly paved all
the way up to Oak Hill Road. And there's a wooden shelter now on Oak
Hill, a sort of big box made of wood taken from pulled-down houses on
the Island, green trash barrel beside it, for the kids to stand in out of the
rain and wind while waiting for the school bus. (Later I heard that someone had complained, "The least they could have done was tar-paper it,
the way it is now it's an eyesore!") Of course it was erected under Mainstream and I can imagine Bengun as having worked on it.

When Mark and I were here in August we saw the Governor and
Wayne's uncle, State Rep. John Mitchell, conducting one of the state
engineers over Oak Hill Road and talking about road paving. The roads
were badly in need at least of some pothole filling. Now in the heat of
midday the tar-bound pebbles are still soft underfoot and the smell of
the tar is jarring in this quiet September afternoon of soft wind and
rustling trees, their perfume lingering in the air.

Wayne's in his car reading a letter as I drive into the lower part of his driveway and park parallel with the front of his house, with its gray sun-bleached and rain- and wind-smoothed ancient clapboards. I think he sees me as I gather up kit bag, typewriter, tape recorder, and rain gear and start up the acorn-scattered path to his back door, but he doesn't make a move. He goes right on reading the letter which I can see now on small notepaper, written in a crowded hand in black ball-point pen. He's got on a brown and white striped jersey and brown bell-bottom slacks, his hair's very long now, falling over both sides of his head and to the shoulders. He continues to read through gold, metal-rimmed spectacles and I smell the smell of a car in summer: the upholstery heated up, faint odor of gasoline and dust. Still he doesn't look up. I come up to the window. I really like this thing Wayne does; his father does it, too, and many other Indians I recall. They finish one thing completely: piece of a cross-word puzzle before starting a new thought (Norris); buttering bread before launching out on a conversation (Wayne); hammering in a nail (Bengun); lighting up another cigarette (Senabeh). They simply won't go on to another thing before attending to what's at hand. I've seen Yankees do it, too, especially in Maine, locally and on Gotts Island, where our summer house is, in Waldoboro, where we spent a summer. You go up to them and ask a question or a direction and they hear you but they go right on working and it isn't disrespect or their not having heard, it's a kind of concentration, a single attention, which enables them to finish a piece of work or complete a sentence or thought and which we urban-oriented people, our minds fragmented by continual interruptions, intrusions, like so many wedges electronically driven into our brains, a hundred an hour, can't attain, so our work, our lives, are always incomplete, unfinished. There's this sense always (I feel it constantly) of something having been forgotten: Now what was it I had to do? And you go around asking yourself all day long. You can make a list of things, but chances are you'll be interrupted during its writing, or you'll leave the list somewhere if you've been called on the phone, or you're in the bathroom trying to move your bowels and the doorbell rings or by God someone's right in your living room downstairs and you with a turd hanging out!

Wayne takes his own good time and then he looks up at me, smiles widely and says:

"Petah! Whataya say?"

I drop my bags on his back porch, as distinguished from the side porch, or steps actually, which faces directly on the yard next to his house and looks down Oak Hill to the river, and I go back to the car and bring back the two six-packs of beer I bought Wayne for a "belated birthday present."

Wayne's still in the car when I come up the path with the beer. Now, if I were any kind of reporter I'd tell you what make and model the car is (it's got a bashed-in door on the driver's side and the tires are flabby as hell—and it's sort of dull blue) but to me cars, old or new, are just so many lumps of metal. Wayne's is probably five or six years old, second-hand—just pieces of material on the landscape. I hardly notice any particularity about them; they're there and I'm here and fuck 'em—

We sit down at the kitchen table—Terri's out visiting a friend with Jason—and we crack a couple of beers.

"Hm, Schlitz," says Wayne, peering at the oversize can. We wave our cans at each other and guzzle. The kitchen's been done over completely since July—white pine wainscoting and dark wooden paneling above it, new gray linoleum on the floor. Wayne had helped his uncle who is a State Trooper and from whom he rents the house at well under a hundred dollars a month do the work. It's very well done, a really competent job of carpentry, but I haven't seen one around the Island which wasn't when you come right down to it. One thing I like, and probably haven't noted before, is that for many Indians the inside of the house counts more than the outside. You could find any number of houses that are beautifully done over inside, nice wallpapers and paneling, oak floors, well-polished or varnished, sparkling kitchens, but the outside is unpainted or peeling or there's some asphalt shingle on the outside which puts outsiders off, tourists coming through and they make with the, "They're so poor, just look at the way they live!"

Christ, Wayne's kitchen's as good as any I've seen in Gloucester. Personally, I like the raw, or gray- and black-streaked, weather-beaten, and unpainted quality of the outside of his house and his father's Cape two houses over. I tell him I'd live here in a minute.

"I know *Indians* who wouldn't," he says.

Wayne goes on to report to me he's been in touch with several people and has some job possibilities:

"I could go on the Border Patrol in New Mexico, and there's a chance to work with handicapped children in Bangor. I also saw a guy at Sylvania who's looking for a stock manager. He wants an Indian—*one* Indian—to work there. 'It has to be an Indian,' he told me—" Wayne laughs sarcastically.

"Then in the meantime there's an opening here on the Island as Special Constable, ten bucks a week and extra pay for going out on call. I'm asking the Council tonight if I can have it."

Wayne said that his brother, who travels with the Iroquois "White Roots of Peace" group, gave him a rough time when he heard Wayne was thinking of becoming a "pig," but Norris had smoothed it out in that really lovely tolerant but ironic way he has by noting wryly that Wayne's brother was a "difficult son of a gun" and Wayne shouldn't take it too hard.

"I'll have to cut my hair now," he offered glumly.

We crack another beer and I venture the remark that maybe having a job was more important for him and Terri now than *what* the job was:

"You don't have to do police work forever, you know."

"Yeah I spose you're right."

"Maybe you ought to leave the Island for a while yourselves," I say, thinking of Martin's having gone back to Connecticut.

"I don't think Terri would go. Her mother's right over there in Old Town, she can just walk there with Jason. We can drop him over there, too, any time we want to do anything—"

I wonder if I detect a restlessness in Wayne; hard to say. I could well be projecting my own growing restlessness in Gloucester, a feeling of being cooped up, penned-in, inhibited, after nine years in one town, among the same people—same faces, same ideas.

Wayne says he likes being close to his own family. If he and Terri want a bath they can always go to his father's, since they don't have a tub or shower here.

"Whether we get along with our parents or not, it's still difficult to live in any kind of constant proximity—"

"Yeah, maybe," says Wayne. He seems preoccupied.

I change the subject—or do I?

"How's Martin getting along?"

"Great! They're expecting—"

We drink our beer. It's comfortable at Wayne's kitchen table, cool breeze at the window, curtains puffed up gently with it, smell of the new wood and linoleum. Then Wayne's cousin Valerie, his Uncle Matt's daughter, comes in looking for Terri. She's somewhat shy, as are all the women here—or maybe not so much shy as customarily retiring. Valerie goes out. I commented on her brightly colored pant suit of blue and red psychedelic blotches and asked her if she made it. She said her aunt did; she couldn't sew.

"Christ, even I sew," said Wayne. "I made Terri's Indian dress and I made a shirt for myself." (I remember Wayne's wearing that shirt in a newspaper clipping of a photograph of Wayne, Martin, and Jean Thompson before the Old Town Town Council last year demanding that they pay the Indians rent for using their property.)

"You've got it on in that picture," I say.

"Yeah," Wayne chuckles, "that's when I was a radical!"

Valerie leaves, we lean back in our chairs, out comes more beer and Wayne launches out on a story about a lady "poverty-writer" who appeared apparently out of nowhere one day late in August:

"She come up the house; I still don't know who'n hell sent her to me, but in she come, looking us all over. I'd just got out of bed and she plunks herself down in my living room—she was a young woman, kind of on the heavy side—kicks her shoes off on my rug and sticks this goddamned microphone right around my neck—I'm trapped in the son of a bitch! Well, she's some kind of New Yorker, Long Island, she said, and off she goes asking me how it feels to be poor—

"Wait a minute! I tell her, slow down. First of all you're not going to get much from me. I'm already working with a friend of mine who's writing a book on the present-day life of the Penobscots, and anyway, let's get this straight—I'm not poor; I don't feel poor and I don't look poor and I object to someone coming in here and calling me poor!"

Wayne breaks into this broad smile.

"I pity the poor woman," say I.

"Oh Christ, that's nothing; I says to her, 'Well, I've told you about myself; now you tell me about yourself—what's the story of your life now?' Jesus, she didn't like that one bit. She was hemming and hawing and telling me she hadn't come here to talk about herself, and I goes, 'Well, you're poking around here asking us about our lives, we got a right to know about yours. Who are you?' Then she come out with this incredible story of all her troubles, how she's gotta do this book or this study or whatever in hell it is she's gotta do about poverty in minority groups and how she don't know anything about Indians or poor people and I tell her 'Well, you shouldn't be doing what you don't want to do.' Finally I just got up and took that goddamned microphone off from around my neck and I sent her over to Lynn Sapiel, Sammy's wife, and by Jesus, Lynn gave her an earful. Lynn's Cherokee—she's an awful big woman—and if she's in the mood for it, she'll give you hell.

" 'So you wanna know what it's like being an Indian?' " she'll shout at you and then off she goes—

"Woman told me she'd be back but she never came. I guess we scared her off!"

Around 4 Terri and Jason come in, and Terri prepares a supper for Wayne and me of minute steaks, mashed potatoes and cut green beans, which are very fresh tasting and delicious. When I ask her where they come from, Terri flashes me a Government Surplus Food tin.

"They're really good," I say, "better than name-brand beans."

"It's just Government Food," Terri says embarrassed, blushing, her white, almost transparent skin going pink.

Wayne's getting ready for the Council Meeting and I go outside to sit on the porch. It's a warm evening and the kids start kicking a football around in the yard, Wayne's little brother Carl and his cousin Burnell. Terri's feeding Jason cereal and baby food in jars. Wayne appears freshly shaved and with two more beers, and while we watch the kids Valerie arrives, smoking a long filtered cigarette, to ask Terri to play some canasta, which apparently they do every night. To make conversation I ask her what year school she's in.

"Junior," she says, "but I'm going to quit."

"Don't do that! What's the matter, don't you like school?"

"It's boring—"

"She gonna get married, for Christ sake," says Wayne.

"Finish high school," I interject.

"My boyfriend wants me to," she says.

"How old's he?"

"Twenty. He graduated already."

"What about your sister, what year is she in?"

"Oh, she likes school," says Valerie. "It's only her second year."

Rhonda comes over, heavily made up, in her "school" dress and new platform-heel shoes. She's carrying a Time-Life book on drugs. The sisters go in to Terri; they look quite a bit alike, resemble their mother, Juanita, who has just had her eleventh child: small and delicate of feature and bone, these women, with brown rather than coal-black hair; yes, bone structure like a bird's and small, fine hands and feet, thin lips, and very big eyes.

I go in to piss; the toilet's not fixed yet; you have to reach in the bowl & get the plunger yourself. I run a comb through my hair and beard, but, I think, no place to go. When I come out Tim's coming up the driveway with Jo, both are summer-dark and Tim's hair stands out a foot all over his head. My God, that Tyrolean hat still holds it down! Jo's got a loose, short empire-bodiced dress on, her body and legs plump and pleasant: she could pass for an Indian with her hair all frizzled out around her head and very black though not so coarse as most Indians' hair. She idolizes Tim, who immediately joins the football game, stands watching and at Tim's signal Jo's in the middle of the game running with the ball, her dress clinging to her body—and barefoot, too.

Wayne brings Jason's carriage out and we put him in it, prop him up to watch the game, while we take turns rocking the carriage—I tell Wayne it reminds me of when the twins would get a colic attack, both of them, at nine P.M. sharp every night and Jeane and I would put them in their carriage, heads at opposite ends, while we took turns rocking the carriage with our feet.

Wayne goes off on an errand in my car and Tim comes over to tell me he's presenting a proposal for a street academy on the Island at the Council Meeting tonight. Will I be there?

"I'm not invited."

"Go anyway," he says.

"Maybe I will."

He and Jo go off arm in arm; the kids are still playing football; then it degenerates into roughhouse—for my benefit, I think. I go back in Wayne's and jaw with Terri and Rhonda, who hands me the drug book.

"It's very interesting," she says, somewhat tentatively. Then she tells me she might go to nursing school. I nod affirmatively, but it's hard to get anything going conversationally. I end up asking questions and I know they'll be dutifully answered and that's about all we can do.

"I'll take a walk, see you later," I tell Terri.

"Where you going?" she asks. "Don't be late now!" This is a reference to my last trip when I stayed out so late talking at Ken's that Terri told Wayne she was going to "ground me." We got a lot of laughs out of that and I told Terri she was becoming quite a liberated woman which was difficult "being married to these Indians, you know—they're worse male chauvinists than the Blacks!"

And Wayne came back at me:

"You know Pete's wife joined women's liberation—that's why he come up here!"

It's suddenly quiet outside, an evening hush, deep, lovely. Ken's three kids are playing outside (the new baby, Pamela, is inside with Jean) across the street near the garden. Ken had dropped in for a minute before supper and stayed for a beer. He was on his way back from court, had on a white shirt and carried his rep tie—left over from his fraternity days at Colby no doubt (O if our erstwhile brethren could only observe what wild-eyed radicals we've become, those bankers and brokers we went to school with and from whom 15 years ago we were rather indistinguishable, all of us in gray flannels and rep ties); his red beard well-combed and barbered, he was smoking his habitual cigar, pleased he had got his case, an Indian one, dismissed. We shot the shit about Indian topics, and I thumbed the latest issue of the *Maine Indian Newsletter* with an up-to-date report on Martin's case having been continued.

Ken and Jean are living in Martin's house now so they won't have to rush their own for winter. Martin's brother Stanley is upstairs, the Thompsons all downstairs, the living room serving as a bedroom for them, too.

At 7 P.M. I start my walk. Sky darkens. Farther north here the leaves are already turning, oaks already crinkled green. I stop in front of John Mitchell's house to speak to two older men and one in his early 20s drinking beer and leaning on the hood of a late 1950s Ford Fairlane:

"You're not Wayne's uncle, are you?" I asked the oldest of the three.

"Who're you, Jesus Christ?" he asks, slurring his words.

"Of course not," I reply, getting nervous.

"What are you, college student?" the other says.

"Long time ago." I laugh not wanting to get entangled in a game of hostilities.

"Can't you see, he's a hippie," says the youngest.

"I'm too old to be a hippie," I say, discovering I'm a bit bleary-eyed, too, with all the beer I've been guzzling.

"I took you for Wayne's Uncle John." I smiled at the oldest, who had on a tee-shirt and chinos, one of those pliable cloth porkpie hats on his head.

"What are you doing here," he asks, still hostile.

"I'm a friend of Wayne's, I'm visiting him—"

"Wayne who?"

"Wayne Mitchell—"

"Who's he?"

I start off down the hill now.

"You the one writing the book?" the second one calls out.

"Yes."

"About what?" the kid asks.

"About you people," I shoot back carelessly now.

"Don't be afraid of him," the kid shouts, pointing to the oldest one; "he's just another drunk Indian!"

"So long," I say, going off.

As soon as I'm on River Road, sitting on the little bridge, where the river runs into the pond, the two older men streak past in the car, revving up the engine, and the car rattles and bangs up the hill to the school where the Council Meeting is. I figured they were headed there, but in a minute they're back again, followed by five or six other cars, people driving up and down, just keeping in motion.

I watch the surface of the river, the hydroelectric plant stark and quiet against the purple sky. It's absolutely still, and cool. It feels as though there might be a soft breeze in the air cooling everything down but there isn't; it's night coming on and I feel peaceful again and I think: Oh God, it's autumn, the ripeness of it, the smoky air already. I've hardly had my summer; winter's coming—my life's running out and I haven't done anything yet!

I get up and walk all the way down to Center Street and the big bridge, sit on a railing making notes I can hardly read in the dying light. Wayne stops in my car and asks me if I want a lift anywhere.

"Nowhere to go," I say.

Up Center Street I walk. Eva comes out of her house—tight dark-blue corduroy bell-bottoms, pretty violet knit top; she seems to have lost weight.

"You back?" she says sarcastically, disappearing around a tree.

I go up past the Governor's house and the school, all lighted up for the meeting, then I turn and double back to the cemetery. It's Wednesday prayer meeting night at the Baptist Church. I peek inside the door of the church: an elderly couple sits in attendance, hands folded in their laps. Up past the basketball court, I go. At the top of Oak Hill I bump into Jean Thompson.

"Walk me down to the meeting," she says; "come on in, too."

"Whites aren't allowed, are they?"

"Who said so?"

"They'll ask me to leave, won't they?"

"You won't know till you find out, will you?" she says in her soft low voice with its barely perceptible Maine twang so that if you met her say in Augusta you'd take her for French-Canadian, maybe educated out of Maine, which she was, and a social worker, which she is—and probably not an Indian. But here, you know she is—an Indian.

We go down Oak Hill to River Road; I remark on her red canvas safari outfit. Her hair's in a bun and she's got a couple of letter-size white sheets of paper folded in quarters the short way for note taking with a ball point. I gulp at the schoolhouse door and we go in. The room's crowded. Jean picks up two children's chairs from the other school room. She takes one completely into the meeting room for herself; I keep one outside in the corridor and sit down where I can poke my head in at the door but still be behind those sitting inside so as not to attract any attention. The meeting's been going for a while, although Jean says it probably didn't start until 7:30 "Indian time."

There are sixteen people—Council members—seated in a circle around the classroom. The Governor's at the far end of the room, near the teacher's desk. Wayne's just across the length of the desk from him. Somehow I expected the Governor to be wearing his hat that way on such an evening, warm inside more like summer, I'd come into a room and find my grandfather, his Panama tilted way back on his head.

In the middle of the circle is a microphone and near Wayne, a floor-model tape recorder with big reels turning silently. On the blackboard paper letters say SEPTEMBER DAYS in autumn colors, and in front of me in the hall, a bulletin board display: BACK TO SCHOOL ROUND-UP, showing a cartoon cowboy with his lasso around an eraser, ruler, scissors, crayons, pencil, and pad of paper. The meeting room has reading-lab booths along the back wall with individual electronic equipment in each—teaching machines?

The discussion is whether or not to repair the old Tribal Hall (near the entrance to the Island, at the edge of the river, where the new swimming pool is) or build a new one. Apparently at one time the Diocese had told them there was 30,000-odd dollars earmarked for such a project. As the talk proceeds it becomes clear that some members of the Council are partisans of the Church; others, by their curt or even acid comments, otherwise. The Governor's face reddens as the talk mounts. (Later Jean told me the taping of the meetings has inhibited the talk—"Some of the excitement's gone." But I understand that they erase the tapes after the following meeting and use them only for reference.)

Tim's just around the corner, and his mother, a large jovial woman, sits on the Council. Someone is designated to speak to Father Rokus about the money. Mrs. Chavaree speaks with some certainty about the continued availability of the funds. Someone else quips, "It's like squeezing blood out of a stone," which I find a nice pun, whether intentional or not. I almost laugh. Talk moves down the agenda to the state scholarship funds which have not been forthcoming. Mike Ranco, youngest present member of the Council, is eloquent on this.

It's 8:20 P.M. and I'm tremendously moved to be sitting here tucked away in north central Maine among Indians, autumnal evening, the familiar smell of school around me: chalk, paste, oiled floors, paper, varnish of the little desks and chairs. Outside some kids are playing guitars and singing folk songs. No one inside seems disturbed about it, or with the often rising voices of younger kids swinging on the steel fence of the school yard. Kids wander in and out of the school for a drink of water, poke heads into the Council chamber; parents get up and leave to speak to their own kids outside, return. Kids and adults are just all over the place with no special rules or hierarchy. Here children are really part of the entire life and no one is ever chasing them off or shouting at them. I've not encountered anyone who talks down to kids publicly. The kids themselves are outside day and night with no particular bed time or curfew. I like it, I admire it: this coexistence of kids and adults, the tolerance, although both are white man's words for something I really intuit as different. I think basically children are allowed, at least in some psychological sense, a rather ample autonomy, like among the Navahos, mothers not cutting their children's hair unless the child himself asks to have it cut.

The Governor announces they need a new Special Constable to replace a man who is going on the State Police. Wayne, it turns out, is the only one who presented himself. There's some discussion about procedural matters: can the Council grant this, or the Governor? Should they advertise? Somebody speaks up:

"Wayne's obviously interested, why don't we appoint him?"

Others agree, the Governor is still unsure as to whether or not it's in the Council's power since it's the Indian Agent who swears him in. Discussion is terminated and they vote Wayne in. By this time Wayne's already spoken from the floor on several matters and is running the tape recorder.

Next is damages to the basketball court, then authorizing payment to Ken Thompson for searching deeds. Routine matters, though the Council asks that Ken, who is home baby-sitting, present a formal request detailing his work.

Meanwhile Tim has handed me a copy of his proposal and I read it while some Council members come out for a drink of water and others light up:

INDIAN ACADEMY

A Proposal by Tim Love

Prophecy
"The old wise ones told me long ago why the white men were sent. Heart of All Being sent them because the white men came from a land where only white men lived and it was necessary for them to come to this place where they would learn about other races and learn to live with them, and that one day, when the Indians got the old spirit back again, they would teach the white men how to really love one another and how to love all mankind. Now because the Indians were humbled and made poor by the white man's conquest, they have been cleansed of all selfish pride. They are ready for a great awakening and they will awaken others." p. 14
Warriors of the Rainbow, *Willoya and Brown.*

Introduction
The old spirit is coming back to the Indian people of the Americas. Their services are desperately needed "to teach the white men how to really love one another and how to love all mankind." So the unity movement gains momentum, this great educational task for the mutual survival and development of all the races on this continent.
And for the first time in history, the whites are ready to listen. They are looking everywhere for solutions to their "human relations" problems. Psychotherapy, sensitivity groups, sexual orgies, primal screaming, public confession and fighting in the streets can never bring the hearts of these people back into harmony with the Heart of All Being and with the hearts of their brothers. They imagine that conflict is the way to peace and that freedom from all laws and responsibilities is paradise. These people need to learn from the Indian old and young wise ones. Those who have held to, or are rediscovering, the ancient beliefs and practices of their ancestors.
Indian peoples of the Americas have had hundreds of years of social experimentation and practice in the arts of human communication and

governance. They have much to offer the whites from this richly diverse heritage: Methods of consultation and decision-making, morality, religion, government, manhood, womanhood, spirituality, the place of man in nature, hospitality, friendship, etc.

The Indians must begin to take this knowledge and lost integrity to their white brothers and at the same time continue the spiritual, material, and educational regeneration of the Indian peoples.

The Problem

The highest dropout rate in the United States belongs to American Indian youth at the high school level.

Why does the public educational system fail the Indian Youth?

Put yourself in the place of an Indian student commuting from his reservation home to the local high school, whose majority (95%) is white, along with a curriculum that tells an Indian student so little about his heritage that he begins to wonder if he's not just a figment of someone's wild imagination. This scene is a result of gross misunderstanding by a society whose established educational system thinks it can solve the Indian's plight by churning him through the "education machine."

An example of the importance of this problem is my own home; Penobscot Indian Nation, Old Town, Maine. The atmosphere on Indian Island is very much like that of other minority areas. There is a shameful lack of pride and motivation among both the elders and young.

We need our own schools like TRIBE and Indian Academy to motivate old and young whose lives have been no more than frustration and failure. We need our own schools to teach about our long-slumbering heritage.

For many years Indian people have been told what they need, but very rarely asked. Never have they been asked to help solve some of the larger problems in American society. As a result, there is a lack of interest by the elders because they, like any other person in this land would like to be able to make their own lives. The tragedy is allowing the children to fall into exactly the same disgraceful cycle with the public educational system as the biggest obstacle.

"Let us put our minds together and see what life we will make for our children."

Sitting Bull

Proposal

We propose the creation of an autonomous, self-supporting Indian Academy for high school dropout students 16 years and older, that will be designed and controlled by Indians, and located on land of the Penobscot Nation, Indian Island, Oldtown, Maine.

Following are the main purposes of the Academy:

1. To academically prepare Indian students from various tribes of the Northeast for opportunities in higher education. Graduates of the Indian Academy would either enter colleges and universities directly, or move up to a transitional period at SASSI Preparatory School in Springfield, Mass., or Harlem Preparatory School, both of which are sponsors of this proposal.

2. To prepare students culturally and psychologically for survival as Indians in a white-dominated culture and educational system.

3. To prepare Indian students to become social problem-solvers and producers instead of imitators, consumers and dependents.

We propose that the means for the Indian Academy to achieve these objectives and become self-supporting is for the staff and students to:

1. Conduct paid seminars for corporations, schools, professional societies, etc. which teach whites the values of Indian cultures and how to practice them. This would be accomplished not by "laying down the law" but rather by explaining various Indian value systems and showing what effect they have on human relationships by comparison with the values of western culture and the quality of human relationships they tend to create.

2. Serve as paid consultants to projects and programs seeking alternative modes of social, moral and political organization.

3. Produce traditional artistic objects for religious and practical use that could be sold and the revenues plowed back into the program.

4. Establish a summer camp for urban youth, half poor and half wealthy, that would teach Indian culture and provide learning experiences in the Indian way.

We estimate that a two-year budget of $100,000 from private non-government sources will suffice as seed-money to implement the program and move it onto a self-sustaining basis.

It's 8:50 now and several people have already walked out. Tim stands up to speak and the Governor breaks in to announce he doesn't think they have a quorum any longer.

"I'm asking for your moral support," Tim says, "not your financial support. Indian Academy will be primarily for high school dropouts—"

Mike Ranco adds:

"School's just started and I've counted eight kids out on the street already. We need this program!"

Someone asks about the money.

"It's coming from out of state," Tim continues. "The people I'm working with now at SASSI Prep in Springfield are helping us find it. We've been promised a hundred thousand dollars in private funds. Once it's here it's ours—"

The Governor is still unclear as to what the Council's role in this is. Someone speaks up and says it would be nice if the Council unanimously approved the program and got behind it. They wouldn't be obligated in any way, but their support would mean a lot.

"I'm afraid we don't have a quorum any longer," the Governor says.

Someone wants to know who would teach in the school.

"Anyone who wanted to," says Tim, "everyone on the Island. Once we got going we could raise operating funds by having a summer program for city kids to come down here and learn survival techniques from Indians. Crafts, too. And they could study Indian culture."

Most people are still not clear what kind of school it would be:

"Can you get a diploma?" one asks.

"What about vocational training? We need that!"

"Will it interfere with our state funds?"

"What's the difference between this and a high school?"

It's proposed that the Governor call a special Council Meeting as soon as possible to endorse Tim's proposal. They ask Tim if he can speak to them next Tuesday.

"I have to go back to school," he says. "Someone will be here. Anyway if you're interested I'm having a meeting tomorrow night at the parish house to organize everything."

Someone calls for adjournment, there's only a few people left. I'm still sitting making notes.

On the way out Sammy Sapiel bends down to me:

"If they've got the money they ought to do it. If I had a hundred thousand dollars I wouldn't ask permission, I'd go ahead and do it!"

Gleanings/

Wayne's little brother, Carl: "When I grow up I'm going to be an archaeologist and go around digging up white people's graves."

Robert Troy Nelson, age five, to me:
—Are you Indian?
—No, I'm white.
—Then I can kill you.

September 16, 9 A.M.

I'm up in Wayne's attic sitting on the bed of box spring and mattress in the left-hand corner, a gable window at my right shoulder letting in the morning sun, old Formica-top kitchen table next to the bed with my typewriter, newspapers, my grandfather Angel Polisson's gold pocket watch I'm never without on a trip (good luck piece), *Life and Death in the American Novel*, *The Invisible Pyramid*, and *Penobscot Man*, my night reading. On the kitchen table I've turned into a desk is a gigantic 1940s-modern table lamp with a plastic bag over the lampshade, to the rear of which I've moved odd pieces of birch bark and marsh grass and a few hand tools and a jackknife. (Wayne's been making some toys—little teepees, canoes, doubtless for the shops on the Island. Many people work all winter making baskets at night by the fire, carving, putting together toys and keepsakes from ash and birch bark.) There's an army cot parallel with my bed in the right-hand corner, and above it, the other window, covered only with a screen in summer. Beneath it stands the windowpane itself, and along that wall, a couple of old baby cribs, folded up, large sheets of rolled-up birch bark, stacked window screens and Wayne's barbells: Golden Pro with extra plate-weights, gilded yellow scattered on the old piece of blistered linoleum that covers an unpainted wooden floor. A quiet room—Mark and I slept in the one opposite this, separated by the stairwell, the last time I was here. That was Wayne's grandmother's and was furnished as a sleeping room with Franklin stove. Wayne says many nights in winter he'll come up next door, light himself a fire and sit either at the desk or in an armchair reading, "Sometimes just putting my thoughts down on paper—"

The room I'm in, although more a storage area, is comfortable, lived in. I could stay here indefinitely, though it's probably very cold in winter.

I sit in bed, back against the wall, pad of yellow paper in my lap with no urge to get up and get moving. One thing that has grown on me during my visits to Indian Island is this unhurried quality of people's lives. I find I come wanting to do so many things, see so many people, go out and find them, but after even a day I slow down (I'm fully dressed even now) and just let my mind play over what I've seen and heard. Wayne, Terri, and Jason are still asleep downstairs; the Island is incredibly quiet and I luxuriate in this peace and sudden lack of anxiety I feel, the subsiding pressure from within me to "work" and everything in the environment saying "take it easy," or really saying nothing, just being.

noon

The place, again—

On River Road, at the river's edge. I slide down a hard-packed clay embankment, looks like a bear slide, stop, on my toes at the very edge of the river on a protruding boulder. The water has a high polish, grass at the edge points up like yellow-tipped needles. It feels like summer, hot and still, but the green really wants to leave the trees, *is* already, and the light isn't the same: it's gone softer, mellower. Above on the roadway leaves have collected, a few maples, some scattered willows. The sun is hot when you stay under it, but like the sun in Venice in late September it doesn't burn or tan you.

Today is the stillest, the cleanest I've ever seen the Penobscot. I can smell it, that brackish smell fresh water has. I put my hands in it, they are yellow under its surface. Children's voices float over from the school yard. I'm entirely isolated at this point, can see across the river to a few ill-kept houses in Milford, some farm equipment. Then the town: a church or two, a school, a few newer houses but desolate-looking, some trailers.

This is the side of the Island that faces Old Town center. Overlooking the side that faces north and up the river, above Old Town's Fourth Street, is a development of pink and white split-levels and ranches that look in their odd and sterile neatness more impoverished than any shack on the Island.

But I keep coming back to the place itself, which I know Mark's photographs will capture. It is so beautiful in and of itself, so intimate a part of the people's lives. So much of just this mile or so long island has been preserved, and it's a miracle, really. You can't go anywhere in Old Town where there isn't some blight on the landscape: that atrocious airport that scarcely anything bigger than a biplane can land on. And yet the residents have to listen to the roar of engines all day long and the Indians actually have to feel the damned things pass over, see them, and see the airport too, where at the rear of the Island it obtrudes as gashed earth while the Island is lush and green, forested, willows trailing in the silver water, the whole like a giant green canoe filled with grasses and herbs floating ever so softly upriver to Passadumkeag, Mattawamkeag—the secret dark interior of brooding Maine.

I've seen the Island nearly winter-bare in early May, and in its early spring greens at the end of May. I've been here in full summer in late July and early August, and now in early autumn I feel the sense of a turning in the year and in people's lives, a hint of how it must be to experience the death and rebirth and how, when it was so vital, so organic in actuality and myth and ritual, it was so deeply intimate, probably still is in the people's lives. That instinct must still live, else why does the Island itself retain its primordial freshness while Old Town decays in brick and concrete, covered over in bright-death plastic and cheap metal?

3 P.M.

An inordinately warm, still, even muggy day. It couldn't be anything but Indian summer. While I write I'm looking out Wayne's attic window, down on Oak Hill Road where Center Street comes up to join it and where Oak Hill dips down on the right to form a bridge between the river itself and the pond whose edges are laced with grass and lily pads.

I stopped by Mainstream to chat with Ellen Lolar and Vickie White. We sat in a single room into which Jim Sappier and desk, Ken Thompson and desk, Vickie and desk, Ellen and her folding chair, mimeograph machine and copy-maker, files and coffee equipment are crowded. The interior walls are just insulation-packs, windows all out for summer. It's really just a shack with Mainstream painted in dripped white letters on the door, quite makeshift and nice with a pleasant atmosphere inside of hopefulness: picture postcards of Indians and Indian places, sent obviously by friends and relatives ("We're all relatives"—Jean) on vacation trips; some Polaroids of Indians in native dress at the pageant and posters listing activities and achievements: house repairs, etc.

Ellen keeps the books; Vickie's the secretary to the project and its director, Jim Sappier. Ken writes proposals, drafts letters, and does all the legal work. Mainstream comes under the Department of Labor and was set up by the Penobscot Indian Corporation, which in turn was chartered by the State of Maine, March 4, 1970, as a nonprofit corporation for "charitable, educational, literary, and benevolent purposes."

The women explained that the employment situation is "really desperate." The main source of work for Indians has been the shoe shops. Penobscot Shoe has already closed one shop and Old Town Shoe is laying off workers. Most men between 55 and 65 were finding themselves without work, and since they can't get Social Security until they're 65, ten years of their work-life were lopped off.

Present funding from the Labor Department allows for 700 hours of work a week, and "trainees," as they're called, are hired on the basis of available time and work, putting in a basic 35 hours of work a week. Women are paid $1.80 and men $1.85 an hour. (I wonder why men are worth a nickel more?) Forty percent of the work force must be at least 55 years old and no one under 22 is hired (Youth Corps normally takes care of them). Trainees also have to be under the poverty level. Fifteen percent absenteeism is allowed. (As of September, 1971, there are 30 full-time employees in Mainstream.)

In the first year of its life Indian Island Mainstream ran a 24-hour emergency heating service, which finally had to be cut back to seven hours a day because of lack of funds. People could have repairs made on the spot to correct heating failures, and this was of tremendous help, especially last winter when temperatures were predominantly below zero from December to February 5, and sometimes as low as 35° below zero!

Mainstream runs a blood bank, a free ash-wood program so that the aged can have this material for basketry. They sponsor adult education classes which are compulsory for their trainees as well as discussion groups and counseling for everyone. They arrange free transportation for the elderly to hospitals and medical appointments as well as such home services as cleaning, snow removal, laundry, and even bathing, presumably for the infirm. In the course of the year 52 Island homes had been worked on. They are repaired and winterized or have had their interiors finished, including carpentry, electricity, heating. Frozen pipes were thawed and new heating was installed in several homes. A burned-out home was entirely rebuilt, foundations on several homes reinforced, new chimneys erected, floor posts replaced. One of the most useful projects is the tool-lending program under which anyone can borrow tools which would be beyond his means to purchase, such as small or portable power tools.

Someone who has not seen this work with his own eyes, or who cannot picture a morning on the Island like this morning, men walking to job sites with tools, Bengun with some planks on his shoulder, Norris caulking the storm windows of the convent, Eva's house in the last stages of its rebuilding, people continually in and out of the office, could shrug all this off as "making work," a kind of miniature WPA. I have the conservatives in mind, as I write, most of whom are rich or at least affluent (I've never known a poor conservative!) and have never experienced the poverty that exists here.

But elderly people have been saved from freezing to death and the health of young children has been strengthened by their ability to live in a tight house in a cold winter. Granted, the state supplies fuel oil—$85,000 worth last winter—but if your stove won't heat properly, or you need a new one the oil's no good to you.

The alternative to something like these valuable Mainstream projects (before the advent of the Penobscot Indian Corporation, which can lend money to people like Tim's father, who set up his laundromat this summer on Center Street, and which now saves people the drive to town, or the new Island Housing Authority which will be helping to erect much-needed dwellings on the Island) was for many a rather dismal unemployment. People who have worked all their lives and who feel still young and able do not like to sit home in front of the TV all day while others go off to work each morning. They sit and watch their homes decay around them for lack of money for repairs; they feel their own lives degenerating, too.

(Several people I've talked with have told me about using the $18.00-a-week food allotment for beer or whiskey. Sometimes it is more immediately therapeutic to get stinking drunk and forget the bills hanging over your head, the general hopelessness of your situation, a marriage degenerated into endless labor for bread, children doing poorly in school or dropping out—teen-agers on drugs. It can become a lifelong habit, an escape. Everyone talks about it openly here: alcohol and the Indian, but alcoholism is not the problem, it's a symptom of the problem, like dope in the total culture. Our leaders and millions of cops, school principals, teachers, and administrators—even physicians—still think that narcosis-as-illness is the disease. What's diseased is the culture, the society: and narcosis is one of its eruptions. It's like the immense shortsightedness of a book like *Crisis in the Classroom*. The real crisis is in the culture, the failure of the schools a symptom of it—the failure of all institutions to respond to the basic needs of the people, and the sense you get ultimately that rather than serving us, we are, all of us, in the employ of the government, our lives pissed away paying for weapons that destroy people with whom we have no quarrel.

5 P.M.

Rode to Elton with Wayne driving my car to see Indian Agent Ellis at his home re when Wayne was going to get sworn in as Special Constable. Ellis hadn't arrived and we took a turn around his farm, a huge cow barn full of cows, several cars around, naturally à la Maine farm, and a logging truck and equipment. Wayne said Ellis must be logging his property. We drove up a side road, unpaved and so bumpy we had to creep along it, to find ourselves in the middle of nothing but forest—nighthawks diving, rabbits scuttling under bushes. Wayne showed me a logging road into the woods and there were piles of stripped trees here and there. Again, that evening quiet. I remarked to Wayne how incredible it was to find this really thick woods and only a few miles north of Bangor!

"There's a lot of wilderness left in Maine," Wayne said, "a hell of a lot and I'd like to see it kept that way."

"The only way to do that," I said, "is to keep it out of the hands of politicians who can't wait to give it away to developers and industrialists."

I went on to tell Wayne about a documentary I'd seen recently on "First Tuesday" about the Zuni and how they were "developing" their lands for their own benefit—which development consisted of the blessings of apartments, motels, and tourists' accommodations. The commentator lamented the passing of Zuni culture, focusing mostly on sad old people— 95-year-old sheepshearer who would be a "relic of the past" when the Zuni quit raising livestock—and then flipping over to the young dancing to rock music, dressed like "any American teen-ager." (Point: well, folks, when the kids are rocking and rolling there's no chance for the old culture to reassert itself.) What they didn't suggest was the real and valuable connection with the old Indian culture implicit in that aspect of youth culture the kids were participating in: community, dancing—a mythology of themselves as "a people" in the sense of sharing a manner of dressing, a music, a language, their own ethics, a life-style.

On the ride back to Old Town (Ellis never did show up) Wayne turned off the road above Milford where the river forks around a narrow island into a stream which you can cross over a metal footbridge to get to the little island itself, strewn with pine needles, making a kind of picnic ground where Wayne said the local kids go parking. We climbed way out onto a fairly large dam over the main branch of the river and you couldn't hear yourself talk with the roar. The rush of amber-colored water—at least it was free of the "suds" which indicate serious pollution at this point— was thrilling. Wayne climbed down to the river, stood right over the roaring water calmly smoking, but I remained up on the dam content to marvel at the water's power and imagine how it must have been during the logging season. (This was the last year logs will come down the Penobscot.) A river is an altogether different phenomenon than the sea which I know so well in Gloucester and Frenchman's Bay.

I met Wayne's cousin Burnell on my way to Tim's meeting. He was hanging around the school yard—and off the fence, of course. He came with me to the parish house door. No one had arrived yet, so I walked with him back up again. I asked him how he liked school. He said, "I hate it."

We stopped in front of the Governor's wife's store and he asked me to "lend" him four cents.

7:30 P.M.

Parish hall. Tim's meeting—an extremely comfortable and brightly lighted place, polished wooden floors, painted wall-board walls, composition-board ceilings, indirect fluorescent lighting. There's a smaller room in front with a bookcase full of novels and religious books. Some tables. This meeting room has a kitchen area with stainless steel sink, a new stove, and a club-size coffee maker. You could have any kind of meeting, dance, or party here. It's by far the newest, most elegant structure I've seen on the Island. Black and white posters on the wall:

YOU'VE THOUGHT ABOUT THE PEACE CORPS
NOW
THINK ABOUT THE PRIESTHOOD

and

SERVICE IS THE NAME OF THE GAME,
THINK ABOUT THE PRIESTHOOD

A crucifix, of course, but someone has chalked under it, "Think Indian."

Tim and Jo are here now. I come in with Ken and Jean after meeting them on the way down. Earleen Paul, who works with Mike Ranco in the tutoring program and is a senior at U. of Maine—short, solid girl with fair skin and octagonal-shaped glasses, dungarees—is here along with her sister Kathy—white, torn-off dungaree shorts, long hair—and Stanley Neptune, Martin's brother. He has the same glossy black hair as Martin and wears a short beard and mustache. There are a couple of older men; Nick Ranco is one and they are representing the Corporation and Housing Authority. Norris was invited but couldn't make it; neither could his brother John who hadn't returned from Augusta yet. Also Andy Aikens and his wife Cynthia. He's a biologist, Vandyke beard, sharp eyes; she, a teacher. Both have M.A.s and came up from New Mexico. They would like to stay here permanently and "help out."

Tim gives the background again. I'm impressed by the quiet yet authoritative way he handles things. I had no sense when he took me around the Island in May that Tim had this other side. He teaches American Indian culture in Springfield as well as going to school there himself and he and Jo have made a life there for themselves. And he brings back this lovely idea for the Island.

He wants to set up a board of directors. The money really will be available. They do need certified teachers, and of course several just happen to be right here in the room, although ultimately everyone on the Island, especially the adults, are potential teachers.

Jean says:

"You send a kid away to school to be colored white and tied up in knots, he'll come back here and tie us in knots, too."

Jim Sappier, who is also on the board of Tribe, Inc., asks about affiliating:

"They might be able to put some money into Indian Academy."

Tim thinks it's a good idea and says it's too bad that Mike Ranco, who is now at Bar Harbor for a Tribe meeting, couldn't be here tonight. Mike, he says, is really interested in the idea of a summer camp stressing survival techniques and Indian culture to provide funds for an ongoing school.

I tell them about Cape Ann Cooperative School, which we are starting in Gloucester, essentially the same kind of thing, a free school, for kids 4 to 10 in which they control what they learn, when they learn it, and how. We now have a director and a full-time assistant. They teach and help locate people in the community who can give instruction in carpentry, potting, painting, dance, drama, etc. Parents will either teach or contribute three hours a week of work time. I tell them we incorporated as a nonprofit educational corporation so that we would be eligible to receive funds from federal and state government for experimental pilot programs in educational innovation, also private grants.

Ken adds that he figured they would do likewise and offers to prepare the papers. They discuss who will undertake what.

I recall sitting in meetings all last winter in Gloucester: peace groups, local politics, ecology-action, co-op school, sometimes two meetings or more a week. I come up here and go to two meetings in two nights. But this is the way things get done: no glamour, no flash, just a hell of a lot of hours thrashing things out, and, as always, a few people—the same few—doing all the work, carrying the load, realizing these small projects which slowly but surely make inroads into the established system.

Here everyone is patient, they smoke and quip and Kathy goes out for cans of Coke. The meeting has a seasoned quality. Old pros here, no hotheads, no counterproductive arguments or harsh words, just good talk and hard work.

Decided: to incorporate; to seek facilities for opening not later than next year; to draw up a list of all resources and resource people on the Island; to explain to people just what Indian Academy is all about; to try to involve everyone here in it; to make it work.

9 P.M.

Ken, Jean, Kathy, Stanley, Tim, Jo, and I go up to Ken and Jean's kitchen to drink coffee and eat cookies (all four kids asleep in the living room next to us) while Ken pulls out the typewriter and he and Kathy set to work typing letters to all the proposed members of the new board of directors inviting them to another organizational meeting next Sunday evening. They also write to the State House for incorporation forms. We listen to a record of Micmac and Malacite songs in the light of a single lamp on top of the refrigerator (the electricity comes in from Ken's trailer as Martin had paid a deposit for electrical service but hadn't had it put in yet—he used oil lamps); Stanley's dog sleeps under the kitchen table; Jean helps Jo sew up her bell-bottoms while Tim tells Jo he'll take her into Old Town tomorrow for a new pair of shoes. Later Ken and I talk Indian books and he tells me he reviewed *The New Indians* for one of the national Indian papers last year and that he didn't care too much for it, said it didn't jibe with what he and Jean had observed on their trips or heard from some of the people they met. He said he objected to its tone more than anything else; he felt some of it was overdramatized, that the language often strained for effect. I told him I thought it should be read along with Vine Deloria's *Custer Died for Your Sins*, and although I agreed with everything Deloria wrote, I felt I had to close my mind—or maybe my conscience—to him while I wrote this book, but that I'd never do another one: that was the Indians' work from now on.

And yet I sit thinking: these are Indians, except for Jo and Ken and me—but Jo and Ken are almost Indians, they live an Indian life with their Indian mates. And what is an Indian life? What do Indians do nowadays? I can only describe what these Indians do. They work very hard every day to help make a better, more authentic, more honest life for themselves and their people. They don't wear native dress, but they *own* native dress and they know when to wear it. They spend a lot of time at meetings, meetings which they themselves call and which, often, they alone attend. They write a lot of letters and talk to a lot of people; they publish a fine newsletter, these Indians in Maine do. They live simply in simple houses; they grow their own food organically and they raise a few animals for food, too. Their pleasures are few: Ken has his cigars, a tin of kippers now and then, beer; when they travel they usually visit other Indians. And Indians come to them—and not a few whites, like myself, whom they receive if they are not busy and whom they send away if they are busy. Yes, these are Indians: Ken and Jean in the living room and kitchen of an old gray house. The kitchen is to eat and live in, it's an office and a reception room and a party room. There is a battered portable record player on the floor of the kitchen, some law books are stuck around on shelves, as is the mimeograph machine which prints the *Maine Indian Newsletter,* a box of Pampers, some pencils and cooking pots, all equally of use. I think to myself, there is more validity in these people and their lives than in many an academic salon I've sat in discussing Hegel's *Phenomenology of Mind.*

September 17, 1971

Long talk with Wayne about Indians and politics, the first time we dealt with the subject at any length. I reproduce some of it from memory:

Peter: I've found it very difficult to pin Indians down as to their politics.

Wayne: It's hard to.

Peter: I have a sort of feeling that if it got right down to the nitty-gritty you could get most people around here to admit they oppose the war in Southeast Asia as bad politics, or as an evil in itself. I even think some would have no trouble in linking up our government's destruction of a Yellow people and their way of life in Vietnam with the white destruction of American Indian culture. But nobody talks even on those obvious levels. It's very difficult to get people even to talk about Democratic party politics. Not too many people vote, do they?

Wayne: They don't involve themselves—

Peter: I found that almost everyone I've talked to in one way or another—consciously or unconsciously—has turned his back on white society.

Wayne: I've been asked to register for the national and state voting but I'm not because I just don't believe in the system.

Peter: You don't and I talked to Jim Sappier last night. Jim doesn't vote.

Wayne: My father doesn't.

Peter: Your father *told* me he doesn't.

Wayne: Why involve yourself in something that's slowly but surely destroying itself, when you can be a part of something that is living, is trying to thrive—has a very low, low opinion from other people but yet you look around? The Indian may be poor, he may not have very much of material things, but he has one thing and that is his closeness with nature. There aren't too many whites that have that because they've grown accustomed to material things and don't give a damn about Nature and what Nature's purpose is. And that's the main reason why you'll find the Indian won't involve himself in a self-destructive type of situation.

Like I said he has his way of thinking and his prophecies are coming true now. The Hopi predicted that the white man would pollute the whole world, the air and the water, and it's all happened, it's all *in being* right now.

We feel a kinship with all the other Indian people in America because an Indian thinks his way and all Indians think that way pretty much. There may be tribal differences, but essentially there's an Indian way. Now if you were an Indian and you went to an Indian Reserve out west and you told them you were a Penobscot Indian from Indian Island, Old Town, Maine, you would be welcomed. But if you were white and from Old Town and went to Los Angeles, California, and told them that you were a white person from Old Town, Maine, they'd say, "Big god-damned deal!"

Among Indians there's just a certain feeling there that's deeper than any white person can ever hope to fathom. It's endless affection and consideration for each person's welfare.

Peter: So you feel there's a people here in America that you do feel a kinship with, an identity with?

Wayne: Right. I have respect for them.

Peter: And you can sit here in your house on the Island and you know that there's *people* somewhere?

Wayne: And it's not people who are trying to gain political power or material goods. It's just people, earthy people—human beings. Nature's people because they have that respect for the one thing that should be respected in this world—that's Nature. Fuck politics!

Friday, September 17, 1 P.M.

The Indian Island School is located on the corner of Center Street and River Road. Surrounded by a steel-wire fence, it faces the Governor's house. On its right flank and across Center Street is the Baptist Church with its new combined parish hall and youth center just off to one side of it (though connected). To the rear of the school lies the new cemetery with its headstones, some imposing, some simple, and a scattering of small white crosses with the names of the dead hand-painted on them.

The school is built in two sections, old and new. There is a combined 5th- and 6th-grade class in the old section, which also houses the 2nd, 3rd, and 4th grades in a more "open" plan as well as a new library which is also public. The new section contains the first grade and kindergarten rooms upstairs and a combined cafeteria and gymnasium downstairs: a big, well-illuminated room about 50 feet by 50 feet, with flexible wooden floor, marked off for basketball and tennis, gray plastic tumbling mats up against the cinder-block walls, two rows of long tables with benches, suitable for use as dining or classroom tables. Sister Mary Conrad of Bangor teaches first grade; Sister Doreen LaBree of Lewiston, the middle grades; and Sister Celestine of Houlton, who is also Principal, the older children.

The school day begins at 7:45 with a free breakfast for everyone. Josie, the cook, beloved of all the pupils, serves eggs, bacon, toast, and cereal to the children who, according to Sister Celestine, would often come to school in the morning having had "little or no breakfast."

"It's not because of poverty," she added. "It's disorganization. Some families have a hard time getting organized in the morning."

Classes start at 8:30. At 11:30 the younger children have lunch, and the older ones have it at 11:45. There is a recess or playtime, and the second session begins at 12:30. School is over at 2:45. According to Sister Celestine children can remain on the Island from kindergarten through the 6th grade. They can attend public or private schools from 7th grade to 12th with their tuition paid by the State. Those who qualify for higher education are also eligible for State scholarships in the form of tuition payments or abatements. Last year fifteen Indians graduated from Old Town High School. A couple have gone on to other schools.

At present there are 41 children in the school with the three Sisters of Mercy teaching.

Sister Celestine explained that the Sisters are the oldest order in Maine. They have previously had missions in the Bahamas, "but we consider the Indians our mission now."

The Indian Island School is a public school and comes under the jurisdiction of the State Board of Education and the Commissioner of Education. The Sisters of Mercy teach, according to Sister Celestine, at the request of the inhabitants.

"They said they would feel better if we taught here, too. But we have had lay teachers. Mike Ranco taught science here for two years, and Senabeh was hired by the State last year to teach Penobscot language and culture but very few people came."

"Fortunately," Sister said, "we tape-recorded all his classes so that the children can listen to them. You should have seen Senabeh all dressed up in a suit with a white shirt and a tie. He looked so distinguished—he's such a handsome man!"

Sister Celestine continued:

"We're trying to help them bring back their culture. They're so geared to the earth. When hunting season comes or when it's spring we lose them! It's really wonderful! But they have an identity problem—"

Next door Sister Doreen was conducting a reading lesson:

"The way to find ideas. You must pay attention to your five senses," she read from the textbook. "What are they? . . . One way to use those senses is to think of things like a birthday party or a day at the beach—"

"Now tell me one thing you think of."
Children's answers:
—Presents?
—Cake?
—Games?
—Balloons?
—Noise-makers?
"I'm surprised no one mentioned ice cream!"
Children laughed, added:
—Cupcakes.
—Soda.
—Kool-Aid.
"Be sure to think of your five senses. Use them to find ideas. Now let's think of another *familiar* situation. What about the school yard at recess?
—Kids.
—Playing a game.
—Beanbags.
"Think of things that you taste, that you smell and hear. See, we have loads and loads of ideas now—we got them from our five senses—
"We want to share them with others so we write a story about them.
"We have all these ideas, for example a school yard at recess. Now write me a sentence using one idea—"
—Eat chips.
—"You have to *tell* me something about it."
—I like to eat chips in the school yard.
"Be sure to think of your five senses. Use them to find ideas.
"Put your pencils down now."

I continue chatting with Sister Celestine in the new library. With the help of Claudine Bunting of the Veazie School Library they got the first one thousand books catalogued last summer, and they are now finishing the second thousand. Some titles spotted at random: *The Confessions of Nat Turner; The Last Angry Man; Drums Along the Mohawk; Speak, Memory; Squantum, Friend of the White Man; Vietnam Diary; The Uses of the Past; Dog Years; The Agony and the Ecstasy; The Rise of American Civilization; By Love Possessed; Doctor Zhivago; Penobscot Man; The Patriot Chief; Ishi; Custer Died for Your Sins; Our Brother's Keeper; The*

New Indians; Bury My Heart at Wounded Knee (this last, continually out
and in great demand; they have several copies).

On the wall above us is Mike Ranco's enormous relief map of the
Island, green for the land, blue for the water. We sit at one of the ample
worktables in comfortable plastic body-form chairs, surrounded by the
books, a thick blue carpet on the floor, the smell of paper and paste, and
a lovely tranquility.

I tell Sister I could sit here for hours; libraries are among my favorite
places. I've practically lived in them, haunted them in European cities for
their warmth, and I did not mean necessarily the fire of ideas. (You could
stay warm in cold northern England in a public library. I did one late
Saturday evening ten years ago, incredibly homesick for America, among
little old ladies with shopping bags and men in workman's caps, turning
the pages of magazines and newspapers while I roamed the shelves looking for something from America—from New England—something to allay
the terrible nostalgia, the sharp sense of separation from home intensified
by the bleak icy January winds—Lancashire under a dusting of snow, Black-
pool as deserted as Revere Beach in winter—and finally I lighted upon
Walden, opened it at random:

The first sparrow of spring! The year beginning with younger hopes than
ever. The faint silvery warbling . . . what at such time are histories,
chronologies, traditions, and all written revelations? The brooks sing
carols. . . .

Christmas was over. England was frozen, London blanketed in fog. I returned to Italy, resolving to be home in Gloucester for spring, and I was.

"Stay as long as you want," says Sister Celestine, getting back to her
classes. I make notes, thumb the pages of books. Two kids come in to
browse; Sister Doreen looks out of her classroom after them. They smile
shyly at me. I close my notebook, get up and go out.

Warm September afternoon, memories of myself at their age at the
Hovey School in Gloucester, itching to get out, hands on the clock creep-
ing as though nearly frozen, to 3—3:30—then up, line up, jackets on,
and the mad dash for home, my bedroom, and The Wizard of Oz, which
I first read in spring of my first-grade year and my son read in one afternoon before he entered school this year in a beautiful reprint of the first
edition published by my dear friend Peter Smith of Gloucester.

September 17, Friday

I saw Wayne sworn in as Special Constable at the Indian Agent's office. On the wall is a December, 1942, Boston *Globe* rotogravure spread, antiqued by the sun, of how the Penobscots are just as patriotic as everyone else, in fact even more so—they fought on the Colonial side in the American Revolution! There are several photos showing Chief Poolaw, Air Raid Warden, with his assistants, and Princess Watawaso presiding over peace-canning, basket making: group shot of old people in tribal dress raising Old Glory. The photos show no bridge, of course; and the ferry to the Island, two cents—a long, thin boat, looks almost like a batteau, full of people coming across ("We suffered before that bridge"—Peter Neptune.) I find it odd to see these photos of Indians from when I was five years old. The photos seem older because they reinforce all the old stereotypes. I suspect that Poolaw, who married a Penoscot woman, but who is himself a Kiowa from Oklahoma and goes there each winter, came here and filled the niche of unofficial symbol—Uncle Tom-tom. He was a stereotype whites could deal with; when you needed a picture of an Indian "in costume" you could find him in his wooden teepee, like the Indians you used to see years ago attached in the summer to souvenir shops and tourist attractions in Maine and New Hampshire. (I remember a Young Thunder Cloud in North Conway who said he'd been to Gloucester to speak—at a parochial school, of course.) Poolaw no longer wears native dress nor performs "authentic Indian dances" outside that teepee; he sells factory-made moccasins and plastic Indians from Hong Kong. In fact he doesn't even tend shop; he has a girl for that and he comes in to smile and nod, dressed in an expensive maroon sport shirt and gray summer slacks; wearing horn rims and with his hair neatly trimmed he is quite indistinguishable from the white businessmen on vacation who come to his shop for some Indian "atmosphere." He is at the entrance to the Island. Beyond him, where few people ventured formerly without remarking the "poverty" is where the Indians live—and where the new consciousness resides.

The Indian Agent, Raymond Ellis, is a rotund, pleasant man who was talking with a local builder who wanted to hire some help. Bengun's name came up, and he, Wayne, and Ellis began to chat about getting some heat into certain houses before winter.

Ellis winked at Wayne:
"You young fellers don't need any heat!"

Builder:
"Yeah, Wayne, what do you need with a furnace up there?"

Wayne:
"Oh, I got my own heat, don't you worry!"

Builder:
"So do I, kid, I'm only 39!"

All of us stood up while Wayne was sworn in. Wayne held a burning cigarette in his left hand (was dressed in yellow sport shirt, herringbone slacks, leather boots with a strap); Ellis, pulling at the side of his pants did the swearing in from memory: "Do you swear to uphold the Constitution of the United States and fulfill the duties of your office etc. . . . so help you God. . . ."

"This could be the beginning of a career in law enforcement for you, Wayne, I'm glad you're showing interest," said Ellis.

When we got home Terri said:

"Now we'll know who our friends are."

Donna Francis was there with her two children. She had called in a food order to Ellis and had asked Wayne to pick it up for her. I had to remind him to do it. I think he was nervous.

Later Rhonda came in to say that Burnell had got expelled from school today and her younger brother Mark had had his head knocked together with another kid's—twice—by their teacher.

Wayne appeared in the Constable's uniform they'd dug up for him. With his long hair and metal glasses he looked as though he'd found it in a secondhand store and was parading around for the camp of it rather than getting ready to make his first "rounds." Actually he only has to wear the badge where it can be seen, the jacket if he feels like it.

"I suppose I'll have to cut my hair," he says, going out.

I go to dinner at Ken and Jean's to eat incredible homemade pea soup, gorgeous fried yellow summer squash, and fresh pickerel from the river. A real feast with homemade bread, too. Tim and Jo are there, Kathy and Stanley. Wayne pops in later. We drink beer and talk; Ken and Jean tell stories about their trip. I listen, take no notes, mental or actual. I don't even ask questions. I'm sick of being a human recorder, an asker of questions, a data-freak. All I want to do is continue sitting here comfortably as I am, listening to good people talk about their lives, enter myself into the talk rather than holding back, listening objectively. I begin to get angry that I'm writing this book: why don't I leave these people alone? Why can't I just come and enjoy their company? Then Ken hands me another beer, Jean says "We got to clean up this soup"; I accept both, I eat and drink.

Later at Wayne's, Terri's playing canasta with Rhonda and she tells me this harrowing story of a couple in Howland who recently got a neighborhood girl to baby-sit and when they went out she was just sitting there alone listening to records. They said she seemed fine. About midnight they called her to tell her they'd be a little late, and she replied, "That's okay, everything's fine. I've got the turkey in the oven." They thought it sounded strange so they rushed home to find their infant in the oven. They rushed the baby to the hospital but it died of severe burns two days later. The girl had apparently been taking some "drug." Terri thought it might be LSD.

September 18, Saturday

Evening. Violet sky after rain all day. The tops of the trees—red, gold, orange from the sunset. It looks like October already in this light—

Walked downstreet to the bridge. Saw Burnell and asked him how he got expelled. He said the Principal had called him into the office after he played a trick on a kid which entailed Burnell's closing a desk top on the kid's head. Just something silly: "Listen to that noise inside the desk." Kid puts his head inside, bang. So the Principal gives Burnell a big lecture, and B. says "Shut up." Principal hits the ceiling: "Shut up? I'll tell you who's gonna shut up, you take this note right home to your father!" Burnell didn't, he showed it instead to another teacher who was apparently sympathetic about the whole business but the Principal found out B. didn't take the note home, got upset and sent B. home, too. I asked B. what he thought about the whole thing.

"I don't care anyway. I hate school. It's boring."

Then he told me about a friend of his brother Mark's who had his head slammed on the radiator by a teacher. The parents sued. There was another teacher so deaf she couldn't hear what the students were saying, so she was constantly after them for what she took to be "mischief-making."

"They beat kids all the time in Old Town," Burnell said. He rode off on his bike.

"Twelve, thirteen years old," I mused, "and it's begun already—the big *turn-off*."

I walk to the middle of the bridge. Nightfall. The kid who made the crack about "another drunk Indian" in front of John Mitchell's the other night's here with a friend. They've both got Army surplus field jackets on; they lean against the railing smoking. I go up, lean on railing myself a couple of yards away, put my notebook in my workshirt pocket, my mechanical pencil in outside denim jacket pocket, say "Hi."

"You get all your information?" the kid asks sarcastically.

"No," I smile.

"What are you looking for, anyway?" he asks, belligerent.

"I'm interested in how people live," I say.

"Go and see Papa Ellis," he flings at me.

"That's one side of the story," I answer.

"That's the only side," he says, leaving.

Last tinge of violet on the river. The water's gone dark blue now, dogs barking, scud of dark-blue cloud. I'm going upstreet, back to Wayne's.

Up in Wayne's attic. Fifteen years ago I sat in Brunswick, Maine, on just such a Saturday evening—alone, listening to Stan Kenton's "Cuban Fire" and writing poetry about the "sad trumpeting of fall." Had anyone suggested that some years hence I should be sitting in the attic of one of the oldest houses on the top of a great hill, overlooking the Penobscot River and an Indian Reservation in Old Town, Maine, I'd have been incredulous, perhaps astounded. It wasn't in the cards. "What have I got to do with Indians?" I might have answered. I thought I had more to do with the novels of Gide and Sartre, the poetry of Ezra Pound, the music of Alban Berg. I vaguely knew there were Indians in Maine but any image I might have had then of them or their lives would have been more like a clearing in the pines, a couple of teepees, perhaps a wooden hunting camp. You never saw an Indian at Bowdoin College, and when I visited a friend in Orono I seem to recall his telling me that Indians lived near there. My head was in Europe—I would rush to Italy when I graduated, and did. But I was already reading Henry Miller's *Tropics* by the time I graduated in 1959; I was into the America of Jack Kerouac and Allen Ginsberg, much to the dismay of my ivy-educated Christian-humanist English instructors who spent their days explicating what to me already had become the predictable intricacies of Yeats and T. S. Eliot. D. H. Lawrence had blown my mind—would you believe, I wrote a senior thesis on myth and *The Plumed Serpent*?—and in it I talked about Indians! This took me back to Gloucester, more accurately Elliott Rogers' farm in Annisquam where Elliott, who went all the way back to 1623 and the first planters of the town and is now dead, would do what Thoreau did with the young children of Concord: you'd be walking along, perhaps on the edges of his tilled land and Elliott would muse, "Now let's see. . . . Hm. . . ." He'd bend down, turn over a few clods of earth and uncover an Algonquin arrowhead for you to take home. I still have them. So the seeds had already been sown—

> *And this one walked from one*
>   *end of the field*
> *(the old field, Comiskey Park,*
>   *The Indians*
> *Di Mag) to the other, to where*
> *the Atlantic is, looking*
> *for local gods. And finding*
> *(solamente)*
> *himself*

Charles Olson,
Letter to Fielding Dawson,
The Black Mountain Book, 1970.

Wayne's downstairs in the kitchen with his Uncle Matt who's cutting Wayne's hair. Terri's playing cards with Rhonda. Valerie stopped by for a hand of canasta before her boyfriend picked her up. I asked her how many nights she went out and she said, "Every night."

On the way upstreet I cut over to Senabeh's shack just at sundown but the place was dark. He had wash outside and his campfire was out, no utensils around, his door closed. I noticed the entire shack had been newly tar-papered. I also remarked his garden out back which I hadn't seen when Mark and I visited. I had noticed Senabeh across the street from the Mainstream office a couple of days ago, either working or talking to the men who were working on Eva Ranco's house, passing the lumber in through the window. I waved but he didn't see me. His face was somnolent and he was concentrating, it seemed, on his cigarette almost obscured in those exquisite fingers, his hair a little longer at the back of his neck, not as white as I thought I remembered it to have been, much grayer. I figured tonight he might have gone hunting for a few days.

The teen-age kids, with younger ones tagging along, were congregating at the bridge, getting in and out of cars, driving each other across the bridge or upstreet then downstreet.

At five Terri had roasted a chicken with delicious stuffing and we had mashed potatoes and corn. She said she'd make Jello later "for a snack."

Later I went downstairs to see Wayne's hair. Half of it was cut, not really that much off—it would have passed for long hair in the early days of the Beatles.

Wayne's poking around looking for his old horn-rims. He said his new glasses with the gold frames don't look right with shorter hair.

"They don't make it with the badge he wears," Matt said.

Border Patrol, State Police, Sylvania stock room, handicapped children, psychiatric hospitals?—I wonder where Wayne will go now. I want to try to persuade him to get back into psychiatric work, maybe go to school someplace in Indian Studies if not social science. He would probably make a great therapist, an exceptional teacher. I can see Wayne catching the imagination of students with his talk about the Indian way and the white way, the sacredness of every living thing. But I am thinking white myself when I begin to place Wayne in the category of jobs and positions. The white world dominates culturally as well as economically, and the sad thing is Wayne wants somehow to "work with people" but all that's open to him locally is, as Raymond Ellis put it, "law enforcement."

Around 11 P.M. Terri called me down for Jello. She was sitting at the kitchen table in blue jeans and a blue and white striped jersey, smoking. I asked her if she would mind having to move if Wayne got that Border Patrol job.

"He probably won't," she said. "I think they give it to their own State Police first, don't they?" Then she said, "Oh I don't know if I could leave here. I'd miss my parents!"

I asked her if she'd ever left Old Town.

"No, I've never been away," she said.

When Wayne came back in at 12 it was really chilly so he put on the big Duo-therm oil burner that heats the living room and two bedrooms downstairs. There's an oil burner in the kitchen stove to heat the kitchen.

"They're both going all winter long," he said.

September 19, Sunday

Chilly morning. Bright sun. The smell of oil from everyone's stove on the air. Damn cold last night. I put the window up in Wayne's attic and used two blankets, too. I talked with Mike Ranco at his grandmother's house— cozy, small house with Indian wall hangings, two old women gabbing pleasantly in the kitchen while Mike and I talked in the living room. Afterwards I went over to Norris's to take a look at a Wesleyan honors thesis in anthropology a friend of Wayne's had done and which Norris has been reading. I found Norris next door in an apparently empty house he also owns and in which Norris has set up a study with shelves of books on Indian anthropology, culture, history, archaeology, sheaves of papers, folders. Norris got out the thesis, Greg Buesing's *Notes on Wabanaki History to 1800*, offered in June of 1970 toward a B.A. with honors. He said there wasn't much in it that I would find useful, as he understood my work, but that it seemed to him a thorough job, mostly about the Passamaquoddies. (Wayne later told me Buesing and a friend had recently got themselves committed to a mental hospital in Aroostook County so that they could report on—and share in—what they had heard was mistreatment of the patients there. He said he would keep me posted on it, and in any event, he thought whatever came of the experience would be "explosive.")

Norris and I went out to his car where I put the Xerox copy down on the hood and flipped the pages. Looks very good and I wish I could borrow it and read it, but I think, my God I've got my work already cut out for me, I'd better stay away from the historical questions for now—maybe later.

"I guess it's not particularly what I'm after," I tell Norris.

"I could have saved you the trouble," he answers, his eyes twinkling. Experience, I think, and not age has gently, often intricately, etched itself over his face, but his eyes are alert, bright, youthful. His speech is of a man ageless.

"I guess so, Norris. See you later."

"Good luck. Come back. Take care of yourself."

I bring my bags down from the attic. Sitting in the kitchen at the breakfast table is a white girl, quite blond, with a fine profile and soft smile. I'd seen her earlier walking on Oak Hill with several of Wayne's little cousins. She's from Portland, goes to U. of Maine in Orono, and was in the tutoring program last year when she met all the Mitchells. The children are mad about her.

Wayne and Terri are up early, Jason's gurgling and chortling in his highchair. I say good-bye. Wayne walks me out to the car.

"Drive carefully," he says, waving me off.

I've already said good-bye to Ken and Jean. I'll stop downstreet for Tim and Jo, who will ride with me to Route 495 in Massachusetts on their way back to Springfield.

EPILOGUE

I have now returned from Maine, and think I have had a quite profitable journey, chiefly from associating with an intelligent Indian. Having returned I flatter myself that the world appears in some respects a little larger, and not as usual smaller and shallower for having extended my range. I have made a short excursion into the new world which the Indian dwells in or is. He begins where we leave off. . . . The Indian who can find his way so wonderfully in the woods possesses so much intelligence which the white man does not,—and it increases my own capacity as well as faith to observe it. I rejoice to find that intelligence flows in other channels than I knew. . . .

Thoreau to H. G. Otis Blake
August 18, 1857

Winter is in and over us here in Gloucester, and I sit in my book-lined study that smells of the wood from the bookcases and of the old paper from 19th-century volumes of Emerson and Thoreau, my old town histories, mildew of the pages. The room is embued with my sweat, the sweat of almost four years of work in fits and starts on stories, novels, essays, letters to editors of newspapers. The drawers are filled with pages of words, and the place smells of me and whatever labor or toil I've exacted from myself here.

So did Wayne's attic after a while, and the room at the Anchorage Motel in Old Town, our bedroom on Gotts Island, and the little reading rooms in the libraries of all the places I've lived in or visited. I suspect I've left quite an olfactory spore behind me, however ephemeral.

And winter is in and over us, as it is on Indian Island. Nights are 35° below zero if this winter is anything like the last and a lot of people will be cold down there: even in mid-September they were starting to button-up all over. I miss my friends on Indian Island. By my last visit I could start at the bridge and begin to walk up Center Street, past church and rectory, past shops and houses, past the Lovarama. Robby Troy Francis would tag along after me, and Burnell would sweep in beside me on his bike; Eva would nod and sometimes smile; Stanley Neptune and Kathy Paul would flash by in the open silver-gray Ford with Connecticut plates, the dog Tracy in the back seat. I'd say hi to Sammy and Jim, Bengun and Leo; Vickie and Ellen would wave at me from Mainstream, while Ken and Jim would be bent over their latest proposal or report.

People I knew would wave or say hello and the people I didn't would nod. Almost everyone would acknowledge me, as they don't fleeting tourists and out-of-staters who stray onto the Island, one of whom I was when I drove onto the Island myself on that first gray afternoon of May 7, 1971, trees still stripped and bare in places as spring does come late in the north.

It made me so happy, that walk, gave me the feeling—or was it an illusion?—of belonging if only briefly to someone else's world. Like the day I talked with Sister Celestine and she seemed a bit stiff and nervous at first and I was sweating and I hoped she noticed it because I didn't want her to think I was putting *her* through the third degree. We began to relax and talk finally and I was very much at home in the school library—the place in the world I'm most at home in—and I was thinking of how I'd just like to sit there all afternoon long and write my book there (and I did, a few pages in my notebook). Then Sister and I got going on the people and she told me how much she loved Senabeh and Mike Ranco and how much she thought of Sipsis and Jim and about what she saw as the Penobscots' "problem of identity," and we quipped about "Indian time" and how the people were attached to the land and the seasons and got that faraway look in the eye, that restlessness in the bones in autumn—ah *Kimskasoldin!*—during hunting season and how wonderful it would be if you could use all this instinct in teaching.

That was mid-September and already the leaves were turning; we had had our first decidedly chilly night. Wayne put the heat on and Terri with eight-month-old Jason sitting bolt upright in her lap and I and Wayne ate Terri's homemade peanut butter cookies (which Terri made after I told her my wife baked for me every Saturday night and its being Saturday night made me homesick!) and flicked back and forth between "Championship" wrestling and Frankenstein's (Maine *is* spacey) country and western talent extravaganza on TV. The leaves were turning and the next morning I left for Gloucester taking with me as far as Route 495 in Massachusetts Timmy Love, one of the first

Penobscots I had met in May, and his girl Jo. When I met Timmy he was a dropout (a push-out, really) from Old Town High; and when I came back in September he had returned to the Island with the proposal for establishing a free school or street academy for dropouts right on the Island, teaching everything from the native languages and culture to auto mechanics. So in one sense my taking Tim and Jo away with me—he was the Indian I talked to most on my first trip: he'd taken me painstakingly over every inch of the island, telling me who lived in every house, and the name of each street and place—brought one part of my experience full circle. Surely a circle of no large circumference topologically, though I have learned to respect all circles, indeed to begin to think in circles as Indians do (and live in) and as Black Elk says the white man has no respect for.

Now winter has the Island in his grip, the old Ice God has loosed his cold breath on Panawapskik and Orson Isle on the margins of the river and in the earth of Oak Hill burial ground, where in their ocher beds the ashes of the first people of the New World, the Red Paint Indians, ancestors of Martin and Tim, Eva and Earleen, lie in cold dust.

Yes, winter, and I wonder if Bengun and Senabeh have enough to eat and a tight roof and where Bengun is living now. I wonder who has dropped out of school and who has been pushed out. I wonder who will go to Southeast Asia and die there and who will go and come back and live again on the Island, or who will leave and never go back again.

Finally, as I bring to a close these scarcely complete and surely imperfect pages, I regret all the things I have left out, all the people I might have spoken with had I been perhaps more persistent, bolder; the lives I might have made clear for the reader, the homes I might have described, the stories I might have retold I keep saying to myself, "If I could only begin all over again, have the year allotted me once more. I could put so many more things in these pages."

But I'm through, I'm abandoning the book; the pages will be off soon to Boston; the photographs are already in production. You might think I would beg the reader's indulgence, announce a companion volume— _Glooskap's Children Revisited; Further Conversations with Senabeh_. No, I shan't write again about my friends whose friendship and patience, whose understanding and hospitality I have probably abused no end in these pages. All the things I could have done I won't do, but I hope they won't remain undone. I hope the next book you read about my friends will be written by one, or several, of them. I hope the younger people will persuade their grandparents, their parents, and their aunts and uncles to tell all those stories which need to be told directly to Indians and not to white men if only because the world has such need of them. I wish Norris would write or tell his life story: I hope Suzy Dana will live a little longer and do more than simply utter a vocabulary, even though that vocabulary's loss will be a nation's loss. I hope that Tim will come back and be a teacher, and that the virtue of Senabeh's medicine and his living presence on the Island will not be lost. I hope Mike gets that degree, even though he and I both know he really doesn't need it. I hope Wayne and Terri, Martin and Kathy can overcome the difficulties of an honorable but regrettable poverty, and the deeper ones of inevitable marital crisis (as I have not been able to): bringing up children, somehow, to live in a sick and demented culture, in a world on the brink of destruction. I hope the babies born during the tragedy of Vietnam will grow up to be Indians first because they will be better Americans for it. I hope, finally, and with all my heart that someone on the Island, some one of Glooskap's children, will find a way of mastering all that knowledge and wisdom buried for thousands of years which all men need to know again if they are to survive, and which for centuries they have tried to beat out of Indians only to destroy that wisdom and scatter the bones which house all that great spirit.

They tell the story that just as he came mysteriously out of the East and the rising sun one day and made their world, the trees and flowers and the animals and all his children, Glooskap did, he left melting into the sunset in the west—but not before promising to come back and help his children in their time of greatest need. He said he would help them throw off their burdens, drive their oppressors from their lands, and make them happy and prosperous again. Glooskap, according to some people meant "Liar," and he also had white skin. Yet, according to others, Glooskap, or *Klose-kur-beh*, also means "The Man from Nothing," simply, he who came out of the void. He did vanish into the west but he left behind the Penobscot people, his own children who had children of their own. So Glooskap remains in those children, and in them he has sown the seeds of their own liberation, for it is just possible that far from being "overwhelmed" by those we have oppressed, we will be liberated by them as they liberate themselves.

Yet Indians, at least those I have met or read about, are not optimists. No one who has suffered so deeply and so interminably at the hands of other men can ever be an optimist, at least with respect to his own situation. Some years ago an old Passamaquoddy woman told Mrs. W. Wallace Brown of Calais how she had heard it would all turn out:

Me hear how some say world all burn some day, water all boil all fire; some good ones be taken up in good heavens, but me dunno,—me just hear that. Only hear so. World all gone. Dunno how quick—mebbe long time; all be dead then, maybe, guess it will be long time.

Gloucester, February 2, 1972